THE SECRET SCIENCE AT WORK

BOOKS BY

MAX FREEDOM LONG

The Secret Science Behind Miracles
The Secret Science At Work
The Huna Code in Religions
Growing Into Light
Self-Suggestion
Psychometric Analysis
What Jesus Taught in Secret

THE SECRET SCIENCE AT WORK

The Huna Method As a Way of Life

MAX FREEDOM LONG

 DeVorss *Publications*

ISBN: 0-87516-046-8
Twenty-fifth Printing, 2001

DeVorss & Company, Publisher
P.O. Box 550
Marina del Rey, CA 90294-0550

For more information,
please visit our website: **www.devorss.com**

Printed in The United States of America

To the HRAs

with my thanks and *aloha*

CONTENTS

		PAGE
	FOREWORD	ix
CHAPTER		
I	REDISCOVERING THE LOST SCIENCE .	1
II	GETTING ACQUAINTED WITH THE LOW SELF	14
III	DEVELOPING THE LATENT ABILITIES OF THE LOW SELF	33
IV	AKA THOUGHT-FORMS, AURAS, AND THEIR MEASUREMENT. THE "AURAMETER"	49
V	TELEPATHIC CONTACT BETWEEN PERSONS	61
VI	MANA AND THE SURCHARGE OF MANA	72
VII	THE HIGH SELF	84
VIII	MAKING THE PRAYER OF THOUGHT-FORM CLUSTERS	97
IX	CONTACTING THE HIGH SELF AND PRESENTING THE PRAYER . . .	115
X	SUMMARY OF THE HUNA PRAYER METHOD	127
XI	HEALING BY LAYING ON OF HANDS .	137
XII	THE TELEPATHIC MUTUAL HEALING GROUP	150

CHAPTER		PAGE
XIII	CONTACTS MADE THROUGH SIGNATURES, ALSO SIGNATURE AURAS AND MEASUREMENTS	169
XIV	MORE FINDINGS OF THE HRA . .	182
XV	THE PROBLEM OF THE UNANSWERED PRAYERS	194
XVI	THE PROBLEM OF THE BLOCKED PATH	209
XVII	ARE FIXATIONS BROUGHT OVER FROM FORMER LIVES? ARE THERE UNSUSPECTED SPIRIT OBSESSIONS? . .	222
XVIII	THE VARIOUS DEGREES OF FIXATION AND OBSESSIONAL INFLUENCE, WITH A SELF-TEST CHART	239
XIX	CLEARING THE SLIGHTLY BLOCKED PATH	248
XX	NEW LIGHT ON THE TEACHINGS OF JESUS	265
XXI	THE SECRET MEANING BEHIND THE BAPTISMAL RITE	277
XXII	THE SECRET MEANING BEHIND THE FOOT-WASHING RITE	291
XXIII	THE SECRET MEANING BEHIND THE COMMUNION RITE	301
XXIV	THE SECRET MEANING BEHIND THE CRUCIFIXION	315
XXV	CONCLUSION	330

FOREWORD

My first book, *Recovering the Ancient Magic*, which reported on the psycho-religious beliefs of the ancient Polynesians and endeavored to explain the magic used by the native priests of Hawaii (the *kahunas*) was published in London in 1936. It came out in a small edition of less than a thousand copies and was distributed mainly in the British Commonwealth before the outbreak of World War II. During the war the plates and remainder of the book edition were destroyed by enemy bombing. Though so few of the books had been sold, it had been placed in libraries, and over a thousand readers wrote to me concerning the discovery of the ancient system. A lively and valuable correspondence ensued, and much additional material from related fields was sent to me.

In 1948 a revised and greatly expanded book on the same subject was published in America under the title, *The Secret Science Behind Miracles*. This was a book which I had hoped would put readers on their own feet, so to speak, in trying out the old methods if they wished. However, hundreds of letters soon poured in asking about self-help, or just asking for help.

It was clear that some method must be devised to handle this unexpected flow of questions, and also there seemed here to be a promise of help for further research and practical tests. So with the help of some of the letter-writers I organized a loosely knit group with members scattered from Australia to England, all through North America and even in the troubled parts of the European continent. This group took up with me the further studies of the old system and, especially, the task of determining whether or not we had learned enough about the theory and practices to be able to perform miracles ourselves. Our interest was centered mainly on miracles of bodily healing, but included the healing or correcting of circumstances, social tangles, financial failure, and mental derangements. All of these things had been successfully accomplished by the *kahunas*.

The word *kahuna* is an ancient term and is in use today. It is pronounced "kah-hoo'-nah" and means "keeper of the secret." The word for their secret lore was never found. The code of secrecy had been so strong and so well kept that it may never have been given a name. Or, if it had, it may have been too sacred to mention, like the name of God in some cults. The name we used, for this reason, was *Huna* (pronounced "hoo'-nah"), which means "secret." So it came about that in our search for a name for our new organization, since our project was research into this and related systems, and into psychology and psychic science, we decided upon "Huna Research Associates"—HRA for short.

As such, we began work which was carried on through the medium of letters. A little later I co-ordinated the information for the use of all by issuing a mimeographed bi-monthly of eight pages, the HRA "Bulletin." In the HRA were some of the best students of the materials of this field to be found. There were also those who had little understanding of what was being tried out, but who needed healing for body, mind, purse or circumstance, and for that reason joined in the work as best they could. Some were gifted with psychic abilities or natural healing powers. There were several who just "went along" out of curiosity, doing little themselves but watching eagerly to see what the others accomplished or discovered. Many carried on experiments with vigor and enthusiasm. Occasionally people dropped out, and always others were coming in. Every six months I cleared the list of those who had not sent in the requested reports, which were the measure of our progress. Thus the group has maintained an average of a little over three hundred members.

At this time of writing, five years after the organization of HRA, the work of uncovering and testing Huna has progressed to the point where a further report is in order. We have accomplished much, and we have learned much that we did not know at the beginning. In this report I shall endeavor to give the reader the latest findings of the HRA and of myself, as well as instructions in the methods we have found best for the practical use of Huna. While the reading of *The Secret Science Behind Miracles* is an excellent preparation for the approach to the use of Huna, enough basic information will be incorporated in this book to give a working picture of the system of beliefs and practices upon which experimental work has been based.

No attempt has been made to present information in

the exact order in which it was obtained over the five year period. Working instructions are first given for the basic action involved in making the Huna-type prayer. Following that is given information covering work to be done along other healing lines, either with or without the use of prayer methods.

Interspersed with the instructions will be found explanations of the sources of conclusions, of symbols, words and word-roots familiar to Huna, but which are also found in other religions, mainly Christianity. These will tend to show that the meanings ascribed to Huna are well founded. This is essential in order to establish sufficient confidence and belief in the system to make it acceptable, for unless one is convinced that the instructions are based on valid data, no benefit from our findings and experience can be had. That the same truth pervades all psycho-religious systems is apparent. The basic elements of Huna are a part of the ancient wisdom found in some proportions in all religions. Huna is compatible with other systems. It interferes with none of them, but makes possible a greater understanding of the old truths.

The purpose of this work has never been to start a "cult." It has been, and continues to be, that of helping people to help themselves and each other through the use of Huna methods. The research has by no means been completed. Concepts advanced at this time are open to change when new information is brought to light which justifies such change.

The goal of the work is not only the healing of body and mind, or social and economic tangles, but a restoration of the lost knowledge of a way of life such as was taught not only by the *kahunas*, but by Jesus, and by many great initiates of the past under an ancient code of secrecy. With the breaking of this code the "True Light" can be given to the world, to be known and used by all who have "eyes to see and ears to hear."

CHAPTER I

REDISCOVERING THE LOST SCIENCE

The field of this study was Hawaii, geographically the most isolated part of Polynesia. It was a virgin field because, in spite of startling evidence of the powers of the kahunas (the priests and magic-workers of olden times), anthropologists had tossed their works and beliefs into the discard as "superstition." The Christian missionaries, arriving in 1820, disapproved of miracles performed by natives, and bent every effort toward eradicating kahuna beliefs.

The Hawaiian Islands had been isolated from the rest of the known world for centuries until Captain Cook discovered them in 1778. The inhabitants were primitives, but primitives of high intelligence. The historian, Toynbee, describes them as having an "arrested civilization." They had come across the vast Pacific from some other lands, as their legends tell, sailing their outrigger canoes, guided by a knowledge of the stars. Just where their original home was has never been proven. Some authorities believe that it was in the Near East, and that they migrated thence by way of India.

I am inclined to agree with this view. Wherever they came from, they brought with them in the form of legends, accounts paralleling those of the Garden of Eden, the Flood, Jonah and the Whale and other Old Testament stories. The fact that there was no story concerning Jesus would indicate that the migrations were begun before the time of Jesus.

Toynbee thinks that the civilization was "arrested" because the travelers found a spot ideal in climate and providing food easy to grow and to garner, so that there was no "challenge" to improve their condition further. I am convinced that the kahunas amongst them deliberately sought an isolated spot so that they might preserve from contamination their secret knowledge. They must have seen this knowledge distorted, forgotten, buried in autocratic dogmas before they left their homeland. In Hawaii they were able to continue the use of their knowledge for the tribal good, and it was centuries later that the dreaded contamination set in.

It is true that the Polynesians did not invent mechanical arts as a mark of developing civilization, such as spinning, weaving, pottery making and basketry. They made paper cloth by beating together wet strips of bark, while containers were made of shells or gourds (calabashes). Simple nets were made of twisted fiber strings to form bags in which to carry their calabash containers, or to be used in fishing. Strings were used to snare birds and animals. Knives and axes were made of shell or stone. Fire was known and used. Houses were made of thatch over wooden frames.

But this indicated no lack of intelligence or ability. Their basic or race talent lay, not in mechanics, but in a peculiar ability to arrive at an understanding of human consciousness, its nature and divisions, and the forces through which the elements of consciousness work. This knowledge, used by the kahunas of the tribe for the performance of miracles, they preserved and kept

2

secret. And with the advent of modern days the Hawaiians changed in a single generation from people of an arrested civilization to a people accepting and making use of all the amenities of modern civilization.

When I came to know that there was a "sacred language" hidden in their ordinary every day language, I thought that it must have been constructed in that way when the language itself was invented, back in that dim and misty past before they had migrated from their homeland. This idea was given some basis in fact when, after the publication of my first book in England, W. Reginald Stewart of Brighton, England, wrote to me. He told me that when a young man, a foreign correspondent, he had heard of a tribe of Berbers living in the Atlas Mountains, in Africa across from Spain, who possessed a great knowledge of "magic," and whose tribal traditions indicated a migration westward from Egypt.

Mr. Stewart sought out the tribe. It was a small one, and in it there remained but one individual who knew and could use the ancient system. This was a woman, and her title was *quahini*, which was not a Berber word, but, as it was learned much later, a variation of the Hawaiian *kahuna wahine*, meaning "woman kahuna." After some difficulty, Stewart succeeded in getting himself adopted by this woman as a blood son, with much ceremony and ritual. Only as a blood son was he eligible to receive the training he desired in the knowledge and use of the lore which made the performance of miracles possible.

Together with the daughter of the woman kahuna he began his training, being taught first the general theory

3

of the ancient system of psychology and associated religion. Demonstrations of different kinds were made to illustrate points. The instruction, it was explained by the teacher, could be given only in what she called "the sacred language." This was not the Berber dialect which the tribe used. Stewart had great trouble getting the meanings of words translated into the Berber and French, the latter language familiar to him and the teacher, but he made slow and steady progress in understanding and gradually accumulated a word list covering most of the important words in the "sacred language." His training was halted when the theory had been but partly covered. During a clash between two tribes which were not related to the one with which he had identified himself, a stray bullet struck the teacher and killed her.

When, a great many years later, in his retirement, Mr. Stewart ran across my report, he found that it described in part what he had learned in North Africa. Comparing his yellowed notes and his word list, he saw to his surprise that the "sacred language" was unquestionably a dialect of the Polynesian of today, the same language of which I had given word examples in my book. A long correspondence ensued between us until his death during World War II, and helped to substantiate my findings and further my research.

The most convincing proof that the ancient knowledge was originally well known and used in the Near East, was uncovered in the fourth year of the Huna Research Associates' work. We found that in many parts of the Old Testament, from Genesis on, there were Huna teachings mentioned and accounts given of the

4

miracles performed by initiates who used the same knowledge, but who were not of the Polynesian tribes who were even then beginning their long migration to new homes in the Pacific—or, in the one case, going west to settle in the Atlas Mountains.

In every instance, the veiled references were hidden under the typical Huna symbols, of which much will be said later on. These formed what may be called a "secret code," for want of a better term, and made it possible at this late date, because of the rediscovery of Huna, to understand what was meant by the initiate kahuna who wrote the account of the Garden of Eden, or who gave the report of the miracles performed by Moses and Aaron in Egypt and, later, in the days spent by the Children of Israel in the wilderness. Farther along in the Old Testament we find initiates into Huna speaking, and are able to decode the prophesies of Isaiah and Jeremiah to get back plain and simple Huna.

In the New Testament is to be found the same code, and the same use of symbols to conceal the Huna knowledge. Jesus, the Great Initiate, strove to spread the same basic beliefs in the same symbols, and to initiate his disciples. He performed typical miracles after the manner of the kahunas, and observed the ancient cult of secrecy with care. He gave the disciples the Huna, or mystery, teachings concerning the "Kingdom of Heaven," so that they, too, could perform miracles and understand the hidden truths.

Before going farther, I should like to recount the way in which I began my long research into the ancient knowledge of Huna.

When I first went to Hawaii, about thirty-five years

ago, I was fortunate in making a friend of a distinguished and elderly scientist, Dr. William Tufts Brigham, long curator of the Bishop Museum in Honolulu. For forty years before our meeting he had been observing and recording the performance of miracles by the kahunas. He could attest to their many miracles of healing, and had taken part himself, under their protection, in fire-walking over red-hot lava. He had accumulated evidence on weather control by the native priests, and many other minor miracles.

But what he had been unable to discover was *how* the kahunas performed the miracles. They were his friends, they liked and trusted him, but they did not divulge their secret. Always, he noted, they used prayer and chants and rituals as part of their work. These they were willing to have him hear and observe. But how did these work miracles? He assured me that there could be no magical power in the *ti* leaves used in fire-walking rites, nor in the ritual calabash held in the hands when winds and weather were being controlled.

Obviously the power came through prayer to some Unseen Force or Intelligence with which the kahunas knew how to make contact. Not just once in a lifetime, but often and consistently did they work their miracles through prayer. My own interest in the ability of some human beings to overcome the ordinary "laws" of the physical world was of long standing. I had spent years in the study of various religions wherein miracles are reported as possible through the help of a Superior Being. I had pursued clues through psychic science, and especially had I tried to find some explanation in the study of psychology.

So Dr. Brigham, knowing that the end of his life was approaching, and having found a young man with a consuming interest and desire to dig deeper into the mystery, made ready to lay his robe on my shoulders. He trained me in the proper approach, and gave me all the information he had gathered over the long period.

At his suggestion I checked his accounts with both natives and white people, verifying the facts and adding to the material. Always I asked *how* the kahunas had performed the miracles. No one knew, and with the natives the whole subject seemed to be taboo. Unfortunately, the younger generation of Hawaiians had been more interested in modern things than in the ancient lore, and had not taken the training needed to learn to bring about miraculous results. And now there was no one to give the training, for death had taken the old kahunas whom Dr. Brigham had known years before— not one of the really expert ones was left. I was able to find only two or three who knew even parts of the lore, and from these I could get only the smallest hints of what really lay behind their prayers or ritual observances to make them effective. Finally I came to acknowledge the fact that the kahunas were irrevocably pledged to secrecy. After the death of Dr. Brigham I carried on for sixteen years alone, trying to break this code of secrecy. I found many new and authentic stories of the miracles, but always the secret eluded me. Giving up in 1931, I left Hawaii. I was still convinced that miracles of many kinds were possible, if one only knew how to perform that inner act which could make the prayer or ritual effective.

In 1934, long after I had given up hope of ever solving the problem, I awakened one night with an idea. The idea, followed by much painstaking effort, provided a clue to the mystery.

To make a long story shorter, let me tell what I found rather than the exact and slow steps by which I found it. Starting with the idea that the kahunas must have had words in the native language with which to tell budding kahunas how to perform miracles, I began to study any and all words in the Hawaiian dictionary which might have named something that had to do with man's mental and spiritual nature.

Almost immediately I began to find such words. To my surprise, they named in unmistakable terms the "parts of mind," as we call them in modern psychology. They named and described the subconscious and the conscious. Further, they named the superconscious, which religion alone had recognized as the spiritual part of man. They had words for three kinds of vital force and even for the "complex," as discovered by psychoanalysts. In the matter of morals, they had a dozen words to our one to describe the fine shades of difference between such things as the "sin of hurting another," and the complex, which to them was also a "sin." It was gradually revealed that the kahunas had, in truth, a profound understanding of the way the human mind works, and that was the beginning of breaking the code. I proceeded eagerly with the study of words.

The Polynesian language is a very simple one. To make the longer descriptive words, small words or roots are merely added together. (A word is a verb or a noun according to its use, the passive voice is indicated by a short suffix, tense is shown by adding another word to

8

the sentence to show time and direction.) It was in the translation of the root words that the startling disclosures began to appear.

Let us take, for example, the word for the subconscious, *unihipili*. I was attracted to it only because it had for one of its three outward meanings, "a spirit," the other two being "a grasshopper" and "leg and arm bones." This is a long word and is made up of several short root words, each of which has several meanings of its own. None of these roots or their meanings describe either the grasshopper or the leg and arm bones. Several seem to have nothing to do with a spirit, but describe the subconscious so well that anyone who is at all familiar with the modern findings concerning the nature of it will be struck at once by the fact that the subconscious must be the thing described—that this kind of "spirit" *must be* the subconscious.

The roots describe it as a "spirit" which does things which the conscious-mind-self (or spirit) knows nothing about. It is secretive, and it works silently and carefully. It may refuse to do things it should do, and may be stopped by fear of punishment. (Root *nihi.*) It is a spirit which adheres closely to another spirit, in this case the conscious-mind-self, and it acts as a servant to it, accepts orders from it, but is often stubborn and refuses to obey. (Root *pili.*) It is a separate and independent spirit or self (root *u*) just as the conscious-mind-self and superconscious self are separate and independent spirits. This subconscious spirit is, usually, closely tied to the conscious-mind-self. It is a spirit which manufactures and handles vital force. It lives in the physical body and with this it covers itself as well as

9

the conscious-mind-self, or *uhane,* "the spirit which talks." It hides things (such as the complex). It is a spirit which is weakened if its supply of vital force is stolen from it by obsessing spirits.

This will suffice to show the method used in finding the hidden meanings in words. It also discloses the fact that the kahunas knew what we call the three "parts of mind" as *three separate entities or selves.* It is important to remember this as we go along.

Rather than use the Hawaiian terms for the three selves, we of the HRA found it easier to call them the low self, the middle self and the High Self.

By the same kind of slow and patient effort, I uncovered the kahuna belief that the three selves dwell in three invisible or "shadowy" bodies, one for each self. Roughly named in modern terms they are the "etheric doubles" of the three selves. However, here we have retained the Hawaiian term, *aka* bodies.

Mana is another word we have retained. This is the vital force, the life force, and on it depends all of the activities of the three selves. Created automatically by the low self from food eaten and air breathed, it is used by the other selves—but is stepped up in vibratory rate, as it were, as it passes from one self to the next.

The three selves, each in its own *aka* body, and each using its share of *mana,* are connected with each other by cords made of the same *aka* substance of which the *aka* bodies are made.

All of these things will be explained and expanded later to give them meaning and perspective, but it is enough at the moment to mention them, show that they were presented under a "trinity" pattern, and go on to tell of the symbols found in the language.

The kahunas did not conceal the secret lore only in words and roots. They also used symbols. For instance, instead of always using the word mana for the vital force, I discovered that they often substituted the word for "water," *wai*. Finding it consistently used in many compound words or phrases where mana was evidently under discussion, I came to see that "water" was the symbol for mana. Where it was the vital force generated by the low self from foods and air consumed, the symbol of plain water was used. Water raised to overflow, as from a fountain, was the symbol of the vital force being accumulated in a surcharge by the low self. The vital force of the High Self, originally taken from the low self by way of the connecting aka cord, was symbolized by clouds and mist which are made up of fine droplets of water. These, when falling in the form of fine rain, symbolized the return of the vital force which had been transformed to carry the blessing of the High Self as it fell on the middle and low selves to help and to heal.

The tree and vine were also used as symbols, the roots being the low self, the trunk and branches the middle self, and the leaves the High Self. The sap circulating through roots, branches and leaves represented the mana.

Our concern is to learn to understand our three selves, and how they can be made to work harmoniously together. Only then can man be completely integrated, as he was surely meant to be. We think we know our middle or conscious self very well, but we can find out many surprising things about our mental habits which have a disturbing effect on this integration. Few people are very much aware of their low or subconscious self, its capabilities and its limitations. It is necessary to *seek* to know and understand it, so that we may train it to work co-operatively with the conscious and superconscious parts of mind. As for the High Self, which has no limitations except as imposed by the low and middle selves through failing to do their part, we will find practical proof of its powers, once we have learned to make and sustain working contact with it.

The first and continuing interest of a large number of the Huna Research Associates was in learning how to make an effective prayer. They urgently needed help beyond their known resources, help in solving the many problems which confront us all. They accepted the fact that only by making an earnest effort to understand the three selves in their invisible bodies, and the mana which can be made more powerful and effective, and then by putting the information into practice, could a proper test of the way offered by the kahunas be made.

We found that there is often a need to unlearn other ideas which have been dogmatic rather than well proven and tested. (To do this, and at the same time change old habits of thought to the new, as practice is begun toward making effective prayers, may take some rereading and reviewing of this report.)

Many who had read my last book sought healing of the body by means of some kahuna, in spite of the fact that I had stated that there are no practicing kahunas now left in Hawaii, and that I myself am not a kahuna.

They were aware, as we all are, that there are traditions down the years of the healing by "laying on of hands." It is true that there have been a very few especially gifted people who have had power to heal in this way, even though they have never heard of Huna or the many things which enter into the subconscious or superconscious activities that are automatically set in motion as healing is undertaken. The same may be said for those fortunate people who are likewise gifted in the matter of prayer, and who can voice a prayer and have it answered with a high enough score of success to be beyond and above the "chance" average. We have had a few such people in the HRA work, most of them because they have been eager to learn what lies behind what they do, and so to improve their score of results.

Common sense dictates that we avail ourselves of all effective and powerful aids of modern medical science in the matter of healing. Some grades of kahunas used what they knew of remedies, such as herbs, and also used *lomi-lomi* (manipulation) in curing the sick. But it sometimes happens today that medical science gives up a case as lost—only to find that it has been "miraculously" cured by methods other than scientific.

The real point of the whole matter is that one can and should learn to work with his own vast and untouched powers, to the end that he attains health and keeps it. Further, if he so desires, it is possible in many cases, I believe, for him to develop himself into a kahuna, and so become a healer of others.

CHAPTER II

GETTING ACQUAINTED WITH
THE LOW SELF

We begin, then, just as we did in the HRA, to try to discover all that we can about our low self. In using this term, it must be emphasized that it does not mean that the subconscious is "low" in an ignoble or degraded sense. It means simply that it is the lowest of the three selves in the scale of growth or evolution.

The concept of unconscious mental activity was first explored in modern times by Sigmund Freud. To him and his followers we owe much, but he precipitated a real war. Even today, a few embattled and embittered psychologists are still holding out against his findings. To do so, they have been forced to fall back into Behaviorism, and question the very nature of consciousness as something apart from the chemical processes of the body. Fortunately, the great majority of psychologists have accepted the subconscious (our low self) as a fact, and as a most valuable discovery. For this reason we need not pause to belabor the question as to whether or not the kahunas were right in believing in a low self. Nor need we go to great lengths to explain, as I did in *The Secret Science Behind Miracles*, the reasons for deciding that the low self is a separate entity and not a part of the middle self.

The kahunas evidently considered the low self something that must be understood at all costs. Their word for it, *unihipili*, used in Chapter 1 as an example of deriving the secret words from the small root words, contains still more meanings than were set forth there. They had an alternate word, *uhinipili*, meaning the low self, which repeated some of the roots but contained others, providing additional meanings. Also there are "cross reference" words and symbols.

The total of all these tells us the following things about the low self:

(1) It is a separate and conscious spirit or entity, just as are the middle self and the High Self. It is a lesser god in the making.

(2) It is the servant of the other selves and is attached to the middle self as a younger brother, and cleaves to it as if they were two parts of a thing which has been glued together.

(3) The low self has control of all the various processes of the physical body, and of everything but the voluntary muscles. In its aka body it can slide into and out of the physical body. It is in the body as a pencil in a case. It impregnates every cell and tissue of the body and brain, and its aka body is a mold of every cell or tissue or fluid.

(4) It, and it alone, is the seat of the emotions. It is the one who sheds tears. If one disbelieves this, let him try to shed tears of grief all by himself as a middle self, and see how impossible it is. The tears will not flow until the emotion of grief has been aroused in the low self, in this case by the middle self, with a special effort to think of sad things and cause the low self to recall them and live them over. Even this may not be

enough to bring tears. On the other hand, one may unexpectedly read, see or hear something which touches the emotions, and the low self reacts of its own accord and embarrasses us by a sudden shedding of tears.

Love, hate and fear all come from the low self as emotions, and they may be so strong that they sweep away the will of the middle self and force it to join in the feeling of the emotion, or in reacting to it. The understanding of this is important because we are often carried away by the emotions of the low self, and in this way are overpowered by it and led astray. The major job of the middle self is to learn to control the low self and prevent it from running off with the man.

(5) The low self manufactures all the vital force, or mana, for the use of the three selves. Normally, it shares the mana with the middle self, who can then use it as "will." (*Mana-mana:* divided, or shared, mana.) In making a prayer, the low self contacts the High Self by means of the aka cord, which it activates, and along which it sends a supply of mana to be used by the High Self in answering our prayers.

(6) The low self receives all sensory impressions through the organs of the five senses, and presents them to the middle self for explanation. (The middle self is the reasoning self which knows what to make of the evidence presented, and orders action if need be.)

(7) The low self does the work of recording every impression and every thought. It may be said to make a tiny mold of the aka substance of its shadowy body, something after the manner in which we record sound on a phonograph record, or words by writing them down on paper. All sounds, sights, thoughts or words, come

16

in "time trains" or units which contain many single impressions joined together. The kahunas symbolized these as clusters of small round things such as grapes or berries. Ordinarily, these microscopic clusters of invisible substance are carried in that part of the aka body of the low self which impregnates or identifies itself with the brain. But at the time of death, the low self in its aka body leaves the body and brain, as a pencil is pulled from a sheath, and in doing so takes with it the memories.

(8) The low self responds swiftly to the command of the middle self in recalling often-used memories, so that the impression given when we talk or write is that we of the middle self have all memories right in hand for use at all times. This is the ideal or normal condition in which the co-operation of the two selves is nearly perfect. When the High Self can be included as a unit or full partner in acts which involve its help, all is well. If, on the other hand, the low self, for various reasons, is out of hand and the three selves cannot work smoothly together, trouble is sure to follow.

(9) The low self is the one which can be influenced or controlled by mesmeric and hypnotic suggestion. It also plays a major part in implanting the thought-forms of ideas to be suggested to another, in the aka body of the one willing to accept suggestion.

(10) The low self has complete control of any use of the low mana, or basic vital force, and of any use of the aka substance of its shadowy body.

(11) The low self may hold unrationalized ideas in its aka body as memory clusters—ideas which the middle self was not in condition to rationalize when formed.

17

These can seldom be recalled by the middle self, which is unaware that they are there and so cannot ask for them to be sent up. As the low self reacts to these "fix-ations" or "complexes" so strongly that the middle self cannot control it, trouble comes from that direction.

There are other things which are known of the low self and its proclivities, and these will be stressed as we come to them. But there is a point that needs to be brought up here and emphasized strongly. Modern psychologists, of whom Jung is a good example, have written repeatedly of how dismal and savage and wicked the low self or subconscious is. They tell of their ex-periences in psychoanalyzing people and of the shock and horror experienced by their patients upon having the subconscious dredged and its complexes and irra-tional urges and memories brought to light.

Huna offers much to correct this one-sided and mis-taken attitude. If we agree with the kahunas that there is growth or evolution in the world, wherever there is any form or level of consciousness expressing itself in life, we must agree that the low self, like the middle self and High Self, has come up by an evolutionary process from lower levels. The low self form of men-tation is very limited. The middle self has evolved to the place where its reasoning power is vastly superior, and the still more highly evolved mentation of the High Self, because it transcends both memory and reason, is almost beyond our comprehension in its nature.

By comparing the power of the more evolved ani-mals, as for instance, the domesticated horse, cat or dog, we see that the low self is not greatly superior to them in evolutionary progress. Like them, it observes and remembers and uses elementary reason. Like them, it feels emotions of love, grief, anger and fear. In short, it is also an animal self—the human animal part of man, resident in a body just as are all animals, but with the advantage of having with it as a guest in the body (or as a companion after death when only the aka bodies are inhabited) the middle self—the reasoner and wiser guide.

From this point of view, the shuddering away from the dredging of the low self by some schools of analysis is the wrong attitude entirely. The animal low self still has many purely animal instincts and urges. We understand a savage when he does things that would revolt a civilized man. We understand a dog or cat when it pounces on a rat and kills it with savagery and satisfaction. If the primitive urges (or possibly race memories, as Jung supposes them to be) are discovered latent in the low self, or even slightly active, when we dredge deeply, that is no reason for condemning the low self in disgust.

The task of the middle self is to teach and guide the low self—to bring it along in its evolutionary growth as rapidly as may be, and to help it to be less animal and more human. (Just as the High Self offers guidance and instruction, if we will accept it, to us who are middle selves, so that we may grow toward the next level of consciousness with its superior mentation.)

The worst and commonest mistake made by the middle self is to get down on all fours, so to speak, and share all the low self animal savagery and emotional conditions. This is all too often done, especially when the low self is badly out of hand because filled with

19

complexes. But it is, most emphatically, not the normal thing to do. There is no sadder spectacle than that of a middle self forgetting its position as teacher and its dignity as director and ruler of the low self—forgetting to the degree that the hates, fierce and savage angers, and abysmal fears of the low self are not only shared but encouraged. One does not wallow with the low self, even if it is badly darkened within. One pulls it out of the mud, washes it clean and teaches it how to act like a man. Our task as middle selves is *primarily* that of learning to work consciously and properly with both the low self and the High Self. Everything that is said in the following pages is aimed at explaining how this is to be done.

Never forget that the normal low self is dear and bright and loving, that it is endlessly faithful and willing and eager. If it is not, then it is part of our task to learn why, just as we would work to learn why a sick child is cross and stubborn, and to correct matters.

Getting acquainted with the low self can be a delightful occupation, as many HRAs discovered early in our work. We discussed the ways and means of getting acquainted in early Bulletins, and fell into the habit of speaking of the low self as "George." This came, of course, from the saying, "Let George do it," which is so well suited to the low self, since it does at least nine-tenths of the work of the physical man. However, like an "old dog," it can be taught "new tricks" only by the persistent effort of the middle self.

Many of us took to addressing our low selves as "George" or as "Georgette," only to discover that the low self has very definite ideas of who and what it is and what it prefers in the way of a name. But let me start more or less at the beginning and tell the story—it is greatly worth while because it will give the methods which you, the reader, may wish to test in your turn, and put to good use.

First, one must believe that there is a low self, that it is really there to contact. Second, one sits down in a quiet place and invites the low self to make itself known. One may speak to it aloud, and one should then wait patiently and watch to see what impressions come into the mind center which the two selves share. George may send you a thought of his own accord, or he may wait, not sure of what you want or are planning to do, and watch for some mental command which will instruct him as to his part in the new activity.

It often pays to hold a long one-sided conversation with George on the first sitting. Tell him you have decided that the pair of you should get better acquainted, and should have fun learning to play games together. This may seem childish—but the low self is something like a very precocious child. It can be whimsical, clever, obliging, willful, stubborn or eager—according to its particular nature. No two are alike, any more than any two middle selves, and there is no knowing what one's individual low self is like until one takes time to get acquainted.

As a rule, nothing much happens at once. But, with a little explanation, one of the new games can be begun soon. The low self almost always likes games, and it likes the same games you do (otherwise you wouldn't like them). Suggest aloud to George that you will tell him what things are to be found in the memory trove,

21

and he is to see how fast he can find them and bring them up to be enjoyed. A man can go back to a favorite childhood toy such as a red wagon, and a woman to a favorite doll. Or there may be other loved objects or perhaps games that were played. Select one, or invite George to bring to mind the memory of the one he liked best. I did that, myself, in making my early tests.

I suggested that we go back and try to remember the gift we liked best when our third Christmas came around. I was obediently given the memory picture of a toy mule that bobbed its head. I considered it interestedly and found that it still brought a little touch of pleasure, after all the years, but while I waited, other memories, long forgotten, flooded my mind. There I was again, so small that I sat on a stool and used a kitchen chair for a desk while I carefully drew a picture. My sister, a bit older than myself, was suddenly there beside me directing my efforts. A warm emotional glow crept in, and an almost breathless concentration as the drawing absorbed the little boy who, mysteriously, seemed again to be a little part of me. It was a strange sensation, a delightful one, and I did my best to show my appreciation and share the pleasant emotions and memory with my low self.

It soon developed into a most gratifying experience. I had almost nothing at all to do but stand by and cheer and share and observe out of the corner of my eye, so to speak, just what George would bring up. The old room which had been misty was found little by little, a corner here, a bit of furniture there, but even though George tried and I waited, we could not find all of it.

Then, with a rush, George began bringing his treasures to me, dusty with the passage of years and dim in parts, but alive and glowing with the emotions of pleasure or contentment which they brought back to be shared and relived. There was the summer, all without warning, and we were wading in the little brook outside the kitchen door. In the brook was the little turtle which we loved and admired, and, best of all, there came my mother's call from her kitchen, and with it returned such a fragrance of fresh hot doughnuts just off the stove that it fairly made my mouth water. I asked George, after a pause in which we enjoyed the dough-nut fragrance and ate one to the last crumb, spicy and hot, whether he could find anything else we had ever shared which was as good.

That brought up a vivid picture of a still smaller boy, and together we stepped into it and took over. We were seated on a pile of books on a high chair at my grandmother's table, and the surroundings were very new and strange and wonderful to me. I looked out of a window on the sill of which red geraniums were in bloom. There was a red and white checked cloth on the table, and in my two hands I held with great care a glass goblet with round knobs on its sides and a long stem. The taste of the rich milk reproduced itself vividly. I saw my grandfather's bearded face and the twinkle in his eyes.

A day later, we communed together again, and for many days thereafter. We explored our mutual likes and dislikes, taking turns at deciding what we liked best and remembering it. We covered the things we did, the things we learned to make, the things we learned or did or failed to do at school—even the things we liked least to do.

Step by step, we got acquainted. I found that my George was only slightly interested in certain things that I thought were most interesting. For instance, I thought it would be enjoyable to recall the look of the schoolroom in Wyoming where I had passed my eighth grade days, and to remember the way my teacher looked. George, however, took no joy in that year. Try as I would, I could not get him to find for us the slightest thing concerned with that school year. I still do not know where the room was or who the teacher may have been, though the grades before that all came back in fair detail, and also the grades on through high school, normal school and into college. As soon as I can get around to it, I shall go into the matter of that blind spot in our mutual memories and see what George has buried there—it may be something very important. He may be hiding a choice fixation which focuses on that grade or, more probably, on that teacher, whoever she may have been.

My experience has not been unusual. Letters from HRAs rolled in telling of blind spots in their memories, and of odd little ways they had found to be part of their low self activities.

It is surprising how rapidly one becomes aware, in a strange inward way, of the personality and "thereness" of one's low self. A spirit of comradeship develops and a new awareness that was never there before. And, as one comes more and more to the full realization that George is the one who must set all emotions going to repeat themselves to match memories, one becomes progressively more able to detach oneself from those emotions and to look on them with keen interest while letting them vibrate and buzz and churn—no longer getting caught in their stream to be carried away.

It is a very rewarding thing to become increasingly able to stand off and be the serene judge when events agitate George. Moreover, if one stands apart and is not swept away in the emotional flood, one can give George a hand and pull him out of it quickly. The damaging worry streams that repeat themselves, often when there should be sleep and rest, are the hardest to learn to avoid as they come unexpectedly into flood. But with practice they can be side-stepped just as they start by providing George with a constructive line of thought as a substitute.

As a matter of fact, most of us have found that it is not George alone who needs to be trained—it is also the middle self. And often the realization has been rather a shock when we have been brought face to face with the fact that we have been sitting idly by most of our lives while we have let George run the show in any hit-or-miss way he might choose.

Once a fair start has been made in the direction of becoming acquainted with the low self, the next stage of training can be undertaken. Up to this point we have had to be content with a mixture of the responses which George has given without our help, and those which have been called up partly or completely by our suggestions to him. What is needed now is a way to put George entirely on his own.

The use of the pendulum has served this purpose.

For our requirements it is necessary only to find some small object which will serve as a weight when swung from about three inches of thread or cord, preferably silk. The bob, as the weight is called, may be a large glass bead, a round button, a small crystal such as is used on chandeliers, or any small object which can be strung on the thread. I have seen a finger ring used, also a cross on a fine chain.

Hold the pendulum by the thread about three inches from the bob, and ask George to use the involuntary muscles to make the pendulum swing as he wishes. Because the involuntary muscles are the ones used, we have in this method a way of setting the low self free to make up its own mind about what its answer to a question will be, and then to make it known to the middle self by certain swings of the pendulum.

A set of rules of the game (called by the water dowsers a "convention") must be decided upon by the middle self and carefully explained to the low self, so that George will know how to respond correctly. These rules vary among dowsers and other operators of the pendulum. My personal convention is that a swing crosswise to the body means "yes," one back and forth from the body, "no." A swing diagonal to the body indicates "in doubt." A clockwise circling swing means "good," and a counterclockwise swing "bad."

A right-handed person will hold the pendulum with the first two fingers and thumb of the right hand, the reverse for those who are left-handed.

George will often understand better if a sheet of paper is taken and six-inch lines are drawn on it and marked to correspond with the "yes" and "no" swing directions, the diagonal and the circling—the circling directions being indicated by arrows for "good" and "bad." Numbers can be expressed by the number of swings given in answer to a question. The pendulum is held so that it clears the paper. The elbow is kept from resting on the table in the preliminary trials, as this gives George more freedom with the arm. Later on he will be able to swing the pendulum while you make yourself more comfortable by supporting your arm with the elbow on the table. Great care must be taken not to swing the pendulum with the voluntary muscles.

When ready, tell George to watch while you demonstrate how the game is to be played. Hold the pendulum over the paper, and say, "This is what you do to say 'yes,' and this to say 'no,' " and so on. Swing the pendulum yourself with the voluntary muscles which are under your control, and show how it goes. George learns quickly, and unless he has a hindering reason, will join in the game at once.

Now stop swinging the pendulum yourself, but hold it suspended ready to swing, and say to George, "Now you try. Give me the swing for 'yes.' " Give him time, and if he cannot do it, demonstrate again, or several times, or perhaps rest until later and do it all over. You might also tell George that he is really a very important fellow, and that it is therefore important that you two learn to converse in this way so he can give his views on things that come up.

Only a few of the HRAs failed to get George to cooperate with the pendulum. On the contrary, some of the Georges were like playful kittens and had a fine time playing with the pendulum, swinging it in circles and lines with no semblance of the proper movements for a conversation. In several instances, it was found that the object used in making the pendulum was disliked by the low self, and that by experimenting with several trinkets or small objects one could be found which won the approval of the low self and was promptly set swinging. (Often a heavier pendulum will work better.)

The identifying feature of this first test is that when the pendulum is swung by the low self alone, there is little or no sensation felt by the middle self—that is, no feeling that the middle self is in any measure swinging the pendulum. This is, in part, because the motion of the hand which starts the pendulum and keeps it swinging (under the control of the low self) can be so slight as to be undetectable. The slightest impulse will build up the swing, and the automatic resistance of the hand to the momentum and gravity pull of the swinging bob will act as an amplifier, so that the more the swing is resisted, the wider the swing will become.

It is seldom possible to know much about the personality of the low self until the pendulum comes into use and allows it to act on its own. One low self may be a very sedate and sober entity, another playful or wayward and hard to hold to any task. Remember that the variation is similar to that which may be observed in children. It is, indeed, much like getting acquainted with a child. Confidence is to be won, things of common interest to be found, and a bond of warm and confiding trust and friendship built up. Some low selves will respond to scolding, others will sulk and refuse to obey. Many have to be coaxed, but usually the best way to get co-operation is through praise and love and quick forgiveness for failure to obey or co-operate.

At this stage, and until one is sure that he has become well acquainted with his low self and its inclinations, we have found that it is well to go slowly, act circumspectly —and above all, avoid letting the feeling of impatience with the low self, or with the entire training project, get the upper hand. Let yourself just once throw the pendulum aside and cry out in anger, "The thing won't work, or else my low self is a complete numbskull!" and thereafter the low self may never respond or take kindly to the exercise (or, as it is best to call it, "the pendulum game.")

Reward is something used in training animals. It is also of use in training the low self. The reward may be praise each time the order is properly obeyed, and a few have even used a tidbit as a reward, the low self enjoying the nibble of something it likes. (Of course the middle self also enjoys the nibble, the two working in the body as such a close unit.)

As soon as the low self has learned how to use the pendulum and responds accurately when you ask for the swing in a specified direction, simple conversations can be commenced. You ask the questions and George answers with the pendulum. The questions must concern things which you are sure the low self knows well and understands. Of course you will both know the answers at first, and this enables you to check on the accuracy of them, and judge the progress made.

Soon the questioning can be shaped to ask George's opinion on simple matters, or to ask him to guess. If you are not sure what time it is, make a guess—as, say, fifteen minutes after the hour. Then let him make his guess, by giving the right number of swings to count out the minutes. Or you may suggest guesses for George, such as twelve minutes, and he can swing "no" until you hit upon the number he chooses. Check the clock then, and praise him if he is right—don't blame him if he is wrong. George is a good hand at telling time, as those people know who never need an alarm clock, and usually responds well to this exercise, so it is an excellent one with which to begin a practice session.

Some Georges like to count and are expert at it. One HRA borrowed his wife's button box, and would place a handful of buttons on the table, smooth them out, and both he and George would take their turns estimating the number of buttons in the spread. His George soon proved twice as fast and twice as accurate as he was at the game, and was warmly praised.

If George makes no response to a question after a proper pause to give him a chance to answer, it will provide the opportunity to get still better acquainted by asking a series of questions aimed at getting his reasons for not liking that particular question, or finding out why he did not answer it. He may, just at that time, have wearied of the game. If so, he will usually admit it when asked in a friendly manner. If wearied, George should be excused for that sitting, and the regular activities of the day resumed. George is often very stubborn, sometimes moody, and sometimes impatient. Unless you happen to have him in better control than most, do not try to force him at times when he does not wish to play. (Also you may have touched on a complex of some kind that has caused George to close the session, or to get the jitters, or to react in some physical way that will be easily noticed in the bodily sensations or reactions.)

Unlike the game of recalling memories and living them again with their full emotional content, the pendulum game tends to cut the two selves apart so that emotions are shared less or not at all. It is well, however, to watch for any feeling of emotion which George may share with you, and if none comes when questions are asked about people or things which you think should arouse low self emotions such as love, fear or hate, be sure to ask questions as to what George's private reactions may be. "Do you like Mr. Black?" you may ask, and watch carefully the answer. It may be of importance, because the low self of Mr. Black is very apt to feel toward you and your low self very much as your low self does to his, which would cause the middle self of Mr. Black to feel the same way. If George has an unreasoning dislike for Mr. Black, he can often be talked out of it. It is worth trying, and the reward may be a helpful friend instead of a potential enemy.

Above all, avoid as a pestilence the temptation to ask George to predict future events, or to get in touch with the spirits of the departed and give messages from them through the pendulum. Such operations are dangerous as well as useless at the primary stage of training, and, if indulged in at any stage of the work, come only in what may be called postgraduate work. This cannot be stressed too strongly.

George is usually very obliging. He often wishes very much to favor you when you ask him a question

31

concerning the future, or perhaps someone at a distance. Reluctant to disappoint you, he will try to oblige by inventing the answer, and in almost every case will give you the answer he thinks you expect, whether it be because of fear or hope. This effort to accommodate not only gives you false information upon which you may act unwisely, but has resulted many times in getting poor George or Georgette branded a most unreliable low self, and a liar of the first water.

Moreover, once so disgraced and made ashamed, the low self may refuse entirely to continue the training, and to learn to do his part expertly in making the Huna type of prayer—the prayer which can be made successfully *only* when ALL THREE SELVES are doing their allotted parts from the beginning of the prayer to the providing of the materialized answer.

CHAPTER III

DEVELOPING THE LATENT ABILITIES
OF THE LOW SELF

The low self has three little-understood abilities which are entirely lacking in the middle self, but which are of the greatest importance when it comes to making an effective prayer.

These abilities are part of the heritage of the low self, just as are its basic instincts, its ability to remember, and its ability to use the five senses. Many people, quite without knowing it, cause their low selves to use the abilities we are about to consider, and because of this, make prayers which are answered. Unfortunately, the majority of those who pray have low selves who do not use these abilities, and these get scant results, if any.

These three abilities or native faculties of the low self may be described as follows:

(1) The ability to sense radiations from things, objects and substances when these radiations are of such a nature that they are not registered by the usual organs of sense which give us sight, sound, smell and tactile or temperature sensations. (We shall take up this latent ability later.)

(2) The ability to fasten to a person or thing with which contact has once been made, an invisible thread of the aka or ectoplasmic substance of the shadowy body of the low self. The root word in the Huna name of the

low self, *pili*, has for one of its meanings that of "sticky." A crude illustration of the idea may be found in what happens when one touches something such as sticky fly paper, then when withdrawing the finger, draws out a thin thread of the sticky balsam—this thread making a connection between finger and fly paper. Contact may be made with things or objects or people by touching them, by seeing them (along the line of vision) or hearing them. Once such a contact has been made and an invisible aka thread has been established to connect one with something, this thread is more or less permanent, and is attached to the aka body at the region of the solar plexus. After the thread has been established, the low self has, for one of its latent abilities, the faculty of reaching out a projection (we call it a "finger") of its aka body substance, to follow the connecting thread and enable it to find and make full contact again with the person, object or thing at the other end of the thread. Each time a thread is thus followed and fresh contact made with something, the thread is made stronger, more permanent and easier to follow.

(3) The third latent ability is one in which the established aka threads are used in two different ways:

(a) The aka finger, once protruded and projected to follow the established thread, can carry with it a portion of the aka duplications of the organs of sense. (When we die and live in the aka body, all the organs of sense are duplicated in aka substance, and we see, hear, smell, etc., just as when in the physical body. In "astral projection," soon to be mentioned, the entire aka body is projected to a distance, and there it uses the senses, just

34

as if the body itself had been projected, gathering the sensory impressions of what it experiences.)

The projected aka finger, although it is but a tiny part of the entire aka body, can use all of the five senses to get impressions of the thing with which contact is made, and these sensory impressions can be sent back along the connecting (or thickened or activated finger-thread) and presented to the middle self. These are delivered not exactly as the usual sensory impressions are presented by the low self through the use of the physical eyes or ears, but in the form of an impression which is more like the *memory* of such impressions. For example, when impressions of an object are sent back, they will seem more like an imagining than a reality—more like any one of a hundred mental pictures which we can conjure up on the spur of the moment. This will be made clearer as we proceed.

(b) The second use of this third latent ability is that of reversing the flow of impressions along the connecting aka finger or cord which has been put to work. Not only can impressions be gathered and sent back along the cord to the middle self, but impressions can be sent the other way. These impressions have to be changed from the actual light, actual sound or actual smell of something, to memories of it—to THOUGHT-FORMS of it. These are tiny impressions stamped on microscopic bits of the aka substance, and several such bits may be joined together into a cluster to convey the several impressions needed to tell what is being thought about. This sending of thought-form clusters (instead of the actual sensations or the actual things sensed) is called TELEPATHY.

The need to train the low self to use these three latent but natural abilities, is paramount in prayer because ALL PRAYER IS TELEPATHIC. And what we are working toward in this discussion is the understanding of the means of making prayers that get results.

The Bible tells us that "God is a Spirit." In this the kahunas concur, adding that the High Self of man is also a spirit. Only the low and middle selves live in the dense physical bodies, with physical ears and eyes. The High Self, to whom all prayer is first directed, even if intended for Ultimate God, *has no physical ears. It hears no physical sounds.* No matter how loudly and earnestly we speak to it in words, it has no way to hear us. Our one and only way to get our prayers to it is through the telepathic sending of thought-form clusters of the ideas embodying the things for which we pray.

Therefore, because only the low self can make the contact with the High Self by extending an aka finger to follow the established aka thread to the High Self— and, furthermore, because only the low self can make our prayer ideas or words into thought-forms and send them along the activated aka cord—it follows that unless we train the low self to understand the use of this latent ability, and then to use it when we wish to send out a prayer, NOTHING WILL BE ACCOMPLISHED.

This is one of the greatest secrets in Huna, and it explains what has always been the trouble when prayers are apparently unheard. (Witness the constant cries of the Psalmists, pleading to be heard.) *If we wish to make sure that our prayers reach the High Self, and do*

*not die on our lips as "empty words," we must put te-
lepathy to use.*

God created man in His own image. Men, like God,
have their creative ability, even if it be infinitesimal in
comparison. God created by the use of the "Word"—
by first deciding what was to be created, then by visualizing it and causing it to take form. Man must decide
what he wishes to create before he begins to pray.
Prayer is simply asking the High Self to take its proper
part in creating the desired conditions for which we
pray, and to use its superior mental and creative abilities
to help bring about desired states or conditions.

Huna divulges to us the fact that ALL THREE
SELVES OF THE MAN have their parts to play in
the creative operation of prayer. If any one of the
selves does not do its part, the operation is useless.
And, if the low self is not taught to send the prayer
telepathically, after first reaching out to activate the aka
cord to the High Self, nothing happens. The tragedy
of the twenty centuries that have elapsed since Jesus
lived and taught, is that this part of the secret was lost
—that men failed to retain the knowledge of what
prayer was, and how to use it.

The fact that there are aka threads, and that they may
be followed by a projection of the aka finger, and activated and put to use by the low self, seemed mere fantastic theory to many of the HRAs at first. But when
the information was put to use, and, after the practice
period needed to train the low self to use its latent abilities began to show results, the matter appeared very
simple. One must know the theory in order to train the

37

low self in the best and most rapid way, but once the training is accomplished the low self *automatically* responds and begins to play its part whenever a prayer is to be made.

Most people are familiar with the use of telepathy in their own lives, at least to a slight extent. Thoughts pass between man and wife, or between friend and friend, very frequently. One of the HRAs, when he understood what telepathy was, very quickly learned to call his dog by this means, no matter how far into the fields the dog had wandered.

In our HRA work, then, our first step toward learning to make the effective type of prayer was to teach the low self to project an aka finger, and next, in combination with that action, to project it far enough to follow an aka thread to its end and make contact with what lay there.

"Astral travel" has been a popular subject among writers on psychic subjects, and the reader may be acquainted with the book, *Projection of the Astral Body,* by Carrington and Muldoon, in which it is well demonstrated that the entire aka body of the low self can be projected to a distance, connection with the physical body being maintained only by a cord of aka substance. However, as the reader may also know, and from experience, this is a feat not too easy to perform.

What is far easier and, in truth, all that is necessary at any time, is the projection of a very small part of the aka body. Even the most untalented low self will usually show little hesitation about projecting an aka finger an inch or so from the body, even on first trials, and later on it will become both willing and able to reach out in this way as far as necessary. In his book, *Thoughts Through Space,* Harold Sherman has given a glowing account of his telepathic contact with Sir Hubert Wilkins, the arctic explorer, if the reader wishes to verify the fact that distance makes little difference in projection and telepathic sendings.

One of the easiest training devices is to be found in what we call in the HRA the Box Experiments. To try this, get from the drug store a set of six pill boxes, the size or shape or color makes no difference as long as the boxes are in every way identical. Once the boxes are procured, select six small objects of any kind so long as they are different. They may be buttons, keys, spools —anything that is handy. Into each box put one object. Close the boxes and place them on a table. Now close the eyes and stir the boxes around to shuffle or mix them, so that it is impossible to say which box contains which trinket.

The low self is then asked to project an aka finger through the cardboard (aka fingers go easily through porous substances) to discover what trinket is in each box. Or, one can tell George in a simple explanation, that he has already fastened an aka thread to each trinket by the simple process of handling and boxing them and that he can follow the aka threads into the box with his projected aka finger and find them easily. Once found, he is to sense the trinkets in any way he wishes, and send back to you along the aka cord to the body and the middle self the impression of what is touched.

George may take some careful instructing at this point. It has sometimes proved helpful to take a pencil and make a rough drawing of the hand being held over

39

a box at a distance of an inch, and of an aka finger projected from the physical finger and into the box to touch a trinket. Dotted lines do well enough to indicate the outline of the projected finger and the object hidden in the box. George will, quite naturally, have to understand well what is wanted and be made to feel that it is important. His first impulse will be to reach out, grasp the box, open it, look inside, and in this regular and entirely physical way find out what is in each box.

This natural response and action must, of course, be restrained, and George must be given the reasons why he is to use the projection method. He may be told simply and directly that when he learns this first part of the work, he can then use telepathy—and that, once that is learned, he may be able to help make prayers and get many desirable things through the help of the High Self.

Fortunately there is already, for every one of us, a strong aka cord of connection established between the High Self, the low self and the middle self. This is established at the time of birth or earlier, and needs but to be activated and put to use. The middle self, while connected with the other two selves by aka cords, does not have the ability to use the telepathic mechanism. These are in the province of the low self. (If it were not this way, our prayers would always be answered if it were right that they should be.)

My own set of pill boxes with which I originally trained my George contained an old car key, a small magnet, a wooden spool, a small tan-colored pottery elephant, a pair of green plastic dice with white spots, and a razor blade scraper in a red plastic cover.

I provided paper and pencil to keep track of my "guessing" scores, and anything beyond one successful identification of an object out of six tries, was set down as above "chance." I held the first finger of my right hand just above a box, waited for George to find out what was inside and give me the mental impression of it, then wrote down the impression and went on to the next box. When all six boxes had been handled in this way, they were opened and a check made with my list to see what score of success I had attained.

My experience was very similar to the experience of the many HRAs who made training tests at later periods. At first the score is very low. Then, with daily practice periods of from fifteen to thirty minutes (never working when there is a feeling of impatience or weariness felt in connection with the effort) the score begins gradually to improve. Some low selves learn much faster than others, and some make surprising scores almost on the first trial. The usual thing is for the score to improve over a period of a few months to the point at which six out of six correct indentifications are often made. But on off days, or when George is not interested, the scores may run far below chance, seeming to indicate willful refusal on the part of George to cooperate. It may be only that George, who is a creature of habit, is agitated because some task usually done at this hour is being neglected. At any rate, it is time to stop practice for the time being.

The finger may be held at a greater distance from the box as practice goes on, and eventually the contact may be made simply by the natural aka projection that accompanies the act of looking at the boxes from as far away as they can be clearly seen. In one of the early HRA groups which met each week to carry on such training tests, different members frequently acted as shuffler and score keeper, presiding over the set of boxes which were laid out on the carpet at one end of a large room. The others took turns sitting at the opposite end of the room and trying, by visual contact alone, to identify the objects in the boxes. It was not at all unusual for a perfect score to be made.

One of the things which we learned to watch for was the tendency of the low self to give to the middle self a symbol instead of the direct thought impression of the trinket in a box. I was once working with a borrowed thimble in one of the boxes when instead of giving me the impression of the thimble, my George preferred to give me a mental picture of a needle threaded with white thread ready to use in sewing. At first this symbol substitute puzzled me, but soon I learned to pause to consider such symbols, and to deduce from their nature what trinket was being indicated. Instead of the impression of the car key, I often got a whole car of some indefinite kind which seemed to be composite of all the various makes of cars ever known intimately.

A slightly simpler method of identifying the objects in the boxes involves the use of the pendulum. In this method the pendulum is held over each box in turn and one says, "Is this the spool?" or "Is this the key?" going through the list of objects. (Here be sure you have established your own convention for a "yes" or "no" or "doubtful" type of swing, so that the answer can be given.) This method has one decided advantage in that it provides a clear indication by way of the pendulum whether George believes a certain thing is in a certain box or not. In the other method the imagination often enters into the work, and one may imagine that George is presenting an impression when he is not.

Whatever method is used, the basic training is much the same, and once the low self learns to understand and to respond to the request to make contact with a person or thing—or, when the time is ripe, with the High Self —this part of the training can be called a success. Further practice may include telepathic exchange between two people, pictures being the easiest to send and receive.

Dr. Rhine, of Duke University, has made Extra Sensory Perception (ESP) acceptable to all but the most conservative. The tests made by his students have included cards rather than boxes, a special card deck being used in which simple figures replaced the ordinary face printings of the standard decks. In the HRA groups we used these ESP cards often, and found that the same increase in scores was recorded as with the boxes.

The theory offered by Dr. Rhine to explain the ability of the experimenter to identify the turned-down cards has never been too satisfactory. In Huna terms we would say that the low self projects an aka finger, pushing with ease through the cards, and senses with the finger what symbol is printed on the lower side of one card, or of a number of cards, down through the deck. In Dr. Rhine's effort to explain what is done, he suggests that the subconscious of the experimenter does a far more difficult and complicated thing—that it penetrates the future, clairvoyantly, and is able to report back to the conscious mind what cards *will* be turned up, and in what order, when the cards are removed one by one from the deck at a slightly later time. The kahunas believed that only the High Self is able to see accurately into the future, and that when such seeing is demonstrated, it is because the High Self has looked into the future and given the information thus obtained to the low self, which passes the information on to the middle self.

Another explanation offered at times to cover the ESP results when the cards are used, is that everything constantly radiates a form of energy peculiar to its composition, shape, bulk, density, etc., and that the subconscious self has among its latent abilities that of sensing radiations of this nature although they are too slight to be registered by the physical senses.

There is no doubt that the low self has such an ability, and that it can be trained to use it by a majority of people, given sufficient time.

Radium is a prime example of a substance that radiates force as it gradually expends itself and changes to another less active substance. Carbon, while radiating in a much slower and milder manner, has the same properties. The radiations of carbon from burnt wood brought to light in archeological diggings can be measured by sensitive instruments and the age of the carbon accurately ascertained to determine the time when the fire was lighted by some ancient people.

Water dowsing depends on the radiations from water flowing under the ground, and the low self—usually with the aid of some simple instrument like a forked twig, or even a pendulum—can sense and report the presence of the water. A good dowser can determine through the instrument the amount of water available, its depth, and whether it is hot or cold, pure or impure. Several of the HRAs have demonstrated this water dowsing ability, and one of them is a very well known and busy professional whose work is to find water and determine where wells should be drilled.

The explanation of the ESP powers, however, in terms of these radiations, is far from satisfactory. For example, let us say that an ESP deck lies before one on a carpet, and on the cards are a number of different symbols, all printed on paper with the same kind of ink. The only thing to make them different would be the shape and size of the printed symbols, and these—in order to furnish the low self with a means of identifying them and distinguishing one from another—would have to send off radiations which were distinct and separate. (Otherwise there would be a mingling of radiations and no "radiation pattern" for the low self to pick up and recognize.)

This difficulty would be still greater in the case of such a trinket as the razor blade scraper which I used, and which had the steel blade enclosed in a red plastic cover. As is agreed in scientific circles, radiations moving outward from any center tend to move in all directions if not hindered. They would not come in "beam" form from the scraper in its brown cardboard box, and travel—as in our HRA group tests—straight from the scraper across the room to the experimenter at the other side. Moreover, in the case of the scraper, the radiations from the steel would be intermingled with those of the plastic, the cardboard of the box, the brown paper of the box cover and the pigment in the white ink

45

printing on the cover. Add to these radiating substances the carpet, the floor, and the other boxes in the set, and there would result such an intermingling of radiations that the low self would hardly be able to sort them out unless it had a tuning device similar to that used in radios, but hundreds of times more complicated and selective.

Dr. Rhine's more recent experiments, in which the "will" is used to influence the position in which dice fall, gives further credence to the aka finger theory, and the experiments in psychical research circles with "telekinesis" is even more evidential. In the latter, many objects have been moved or lifted by psychics, and this without physical contact with them. The explanation offered for this is that "ectoplasmic rods" (or threads) are projected from the hands or body of the sensitive or psychic, and that these fasten themselves momentarily to the distant objects in some way and exert actual physical force to move them. (This force will be discussed at some length later on.) This explanation is entirely in line with the theories afforded us by the kahunas—and again, it may be seen, the matter of radiation may be ruled out as responsible for the psychokinetic effect.

The ability of the low self to extend a protrusion of his aka body is of extreme importance to the study of Huna and to anyone wishing to put the ancient system to practical use. For this reason we need proofs of the fact of projection to give full confidence. There are many on record for which there is no space here, and I will mention the following piece of evidence because it is of recent date and should be fairly easy to check.

The March, 1952 issue of *Stag* magazine contains an

article written by John Zischang about an interesting case which has been reported to me from several other quarters. It concerns an Italian, Achille D'Angelo, now in middle age, who makes occasional visits to this country.

In his youth, when walking twenty paces behind a beautiful girl in Naples, he felt an overpowering urge to reach out and touch her, and his hand involuntarily made the motion of a caress. The girl reacted as if actually feeling the hand, cried out and turned to see who had touched her. Seeing no one closer than twenty paces away, she fainted—supposedly from the fright of the supranormal experience. D'Angelo, having discovered the power in this way, vowed to use it only for good, and set about experimenting with it. It proved useful in healing, and he became well known.

His power was tested in New York under psychical research conditions, and in full light he demonstrated his ability to project an invisible hand and make its touch clearly felt by subjects who sat quietly with closed eyes. The writer of the article mentioned relates that he was startled on one occasion by having a finger jab him sharply in the back of the neck, and learned later that he had felt this when D'Angelo had jabbed at a woman of the local Society of Psychical Research as part of the demonstration. D'Angelo explained that he had learned early in the course of his experiments that he could not control the projected part of himself—in the tangible form of a hand—and be sure what person or part of a person it might touch.

Neither the investigators or Mr. D'Angelo himself were able to give an explanation of what happened

47

when he visualized touching a person, and made touching motions at a distance.

The fact that touches could be made at a distance in this way, proves the projection of the aka finger conclusively. But, in addition, the lack of ability to dictate the place on the person which should be touched, proves that the middle self of D'Angelo was *not* the self doing the actual work—it was the low self, and the low self is characterized by its reluctance to accept control when it wants to have its own way. (Which takes us right back to the need for training.)

Before going on to discuss the fine points of telepathy as it is used in prayer, we need to pause to consider in detail the nature of the thought-form, which must be properly understood in order that prayer structures can be correctly built in advance for the later telepathic projection to the High Self.

CHAPTER IV

AKA THOUGHT-FORMS, AURAS, AND THEIR MEASUREMENT. THE "AURAMETER"

When the kahunas and their people passed through India, they left there a certain amount of their lore. Or perhaps the people of India developed the same lore in part for themselves. In either case, the idea of the THOUGHT-FORM, and that "a thought is a thing," came to the western world during the latter part of the last century by way of Theosophy, which is based largely on a certain part of the beliefs held in India and Tibet.

The concept of the thought-form has been greatly changed from its Huna original. Western writers have speculated, and in India much contamination has been added to a once simple idea. One is now told in all seriousness that he can concentrate deeply and create by means of thought an invisible creature of mind which can be animated with life and sent to help or hinder others. The dread words "black magic" are whispered in this connection, and it is related that evil men and women have created evil creatures of thought, and that these have been allowed to roam uncontrolled around the invisible world and cause endless trouble. They are said to be similar to the "astral shell," but to lack a conscious entity or "self" to animate and direct them. In some way, this astral shell is supposed to remain suffi-

49

ciently alive to roam the world after the manner of the thought-form creature, and cause trouble in a similar way.

Huna brings us back to the original concept of the aka body of the low self, and the thought-forms. A thought-form is an impression molded in the invisible matter of the aka body of the low self. A number of related impressions make up a cluster of thought-forms, and such clusters record and contain the memories of complete events. No thought-form *creatures* can be created by thinking. A thought-form memory of a whole series of events cannot become the invisible body of a spirit, self or unit of consciousness.

We have already discussed the Huna belief that places the memories in storage in the aka body of the low self, rather than in the physical brain tissues. But recent medical discoveries have demonstrated that the aka of the brain, during life and consciousness, interblends with corresponding parts of the physical brain. Openings cut in the skull to bare the outer layer of the brain in the region above and behind the ears, can be touched with a needle carrying a mild electric current, and, without injury to the patient, can cause him to remember and even live over in vivid detail events of his past life. No evidence has been found of cellular change in the brain tissues to indicate that memories are impressed there, but it cannot be denied that the right stimulation will cause memories to be recalled. There is something there in storage that is both material and real, even if invisible and intangible.

In various groups engaged in the study of psychic science during the past hundred years, much has been done experimentally to try to photograph thought-forms, or to cause them to impress themselves on photographic films when the films were brought into contact with the head or hands of one concentrating on the thought of some object such as a cube or globe. Some results have been obtained and recorded in reports, articles or books, but the images on the film have been none too definite.

Recently our HRA research turned up an excellent physical method of proving the verity of thought-forms and the aka body or "aura," as postulated by Huna. It was found that these things could be measured by the use of an instrument of an almost unknown type, which had been developed by a professional water dowser of Elsinore, California—Mr. Verne L. Cameron.

This instrument is called the "Aurameter." Its inventor, some years ago, began dowsing for water with a forked willow twig. He was working over a known underground stream, but for some time was able to get no response whatever. Then, as he relates in his book, *The Aurameter,** "I finally developed the 'feel' of the switch and a kind of consciousness of throwing into it what I call an auric charge. The switch then began to react very powerfully, and my long years of experience as a dowser had their beginning."

In his search for a better instrument than the willow fork, he invented and tested a number of devices, finally settling on two which were simple, light, compact, very serviceable, and unique in this field. Neither of these instruments made a bit of sense in terms of modern science. Repeatedly he demonstrated them to scientists

* A mimeographed book sponsored in 1952 by *Borderland Sciences Research Associates,* 3524 Adams Ave., San Diego 16, Calif.

in the hope that they would be understood, or at least accepted, if for no other reason than that they worked. At least they worked for persons sufficiently psychic to learn to operate them.

The first instrument of the pair is something like a large jackknife with a ball weight on the end of a thin round blade. The handle of the knife is held in the hand with the blade closed and the ball up, in such a way that the blade, which is balanced so that it will barely stay up, can fall to the open position when the pull upon it from underground is slightly increased.

As everyone knows, gravity is supposed not to change appreciably as one walks along a level road. But *something* was found by Cameron to increase if, when walking along a level road, he happened to pass over a strong underground flow of water, for as he came above it the delicately balanced blade and ball were pulled down as if by additional gravity, the blade falling always to the open position.

One of the peculiarities of the instrument was not discovered until some time after it had been put to use. This was the fact that there was a delay of from 20 to 30 seconds between the time at which the operator took the instrument in hand to begin making tests of any of the kinds mentioned, and the time when the pull developed sufficiently to overbalance the weighted blade and make it fall. This "time lag" was also "unscientific," but it was there just the same.

The second instrument, the Aurameter, is built on a different principle. In it the weighted blade is fastened to the knife-like handle with a pivot-bearing to allow it to move freely from side to side when the blade is held horizontally above the ground. (Or, to clarify, one might say that this knife remains open all the time, but that the blade is free to swing back and forth horizontally, just as a pendulum swings from a vertical support.) The instrument must be held so that its ball is slightly tipped upward, in order that the tip should be balanced—otherwise it will be pulled by gravity and caused to flop off to one side or the other.

In many respects the Aurameter resembles a pendulum, although the latter is suspended from a cord or thread and swings away from a vertical line instead of on the horizontal. However, the main difference is that while the two instruments just described seem to react to the presence of water as if gravity had been made to pull harder, the pendulum does not. The pendulum has to rely on the low self of the operator to sense the presence of water, and to cause the pendulum to swing according to a prearranged code, or convention, to indicate the water.

The willow or hazel twig, or even a fork of whalebone or a fork of bent wire, in the hands of a good dowser, however, will be pulled downward as an underground flow of water is approached, and often with such power that if the green wood fork is gripped very tightly to try to prevent it from dipping, the bark will be twisted from the wood where it is gripped in the dowser's hand.

Many tentative explanations have been given for this strange force which acts like gravity but which seems to have little or nothing to do with it. Of all the explanations, the best and simplest seems to be furnished by the ancient Huna system. In terms of Huna we may say that the low self, once it has learned the convention to be used between itself and the middle self to indicate the finding of water, will proceed (a) to find the water under the ground by means of the sensitivity toward radiations natural to itself, and (b) to cause the dip of the forked twig or the fall of the weighted blade, or the horizontal swing of the Aurameter ball.

It may be explained that combined aka substance and mana, or vital force, flows into the instrument which is used, and there—under the direction of the mind of the low self—exhibits its uncanny characteristic of acting as living, intelligent substance and force. It acts by actually pulling or weighting down the ball of the blade, or the tip of the forked twig. The time lag, which is noted in the reaction of all these instruments, seems needed to allow the low self to cause the aka substance and mana to flow, or project from the hand, into the instrument to make it ready to respond to the direction of the low self. (It is interesting in the above connection to note that Mr. Cameron spoke of "throwing into it what I call an auric charge.")

The underground flow of water is located by Mr. Cameron by crossing ground, back and forth, while carrying the first instrument. The fall of the ball-tipped blade may indicate the presence of water, or, if there is no water underground, it does not fall. But if it does, the second instrument, the Aurameter, is then taken in hand and Cameron backs off and again approaches the same spot. The Aurameter blade, which cannot fall, swings strongly *away* when an approach is made to a point above an underground flow of water, as if avoiding a rising aura chimney sent up by the water.

This aura from water may be large or small, according to the size of the underground water stream or body. In many cases the water is coming up from deep in the earth at the spot, and so gives a circular aura chimney. If the water is hot, the aura is usually oval in shape. Also, the radiation comes up in the form of a wedge, roughly speaking. If the water is far down, the end of the wedge at the surface of the ground will be broader than if the water is close to the surface. Because of this, the depth of a well needed to tap the water will be determined by a test to find the width of the wedge. These shapes are determined by feeling all around them with the Aurameter, which reacts *away* from the wall of the radiations.

There is much more to this work than can be explained here, and water dowsing by trained individuals of the proper psychic gift is an established and respected practice in many other countries, though less well known here. The Canadian and Australian governments have professional dowsers constantly at work locating water. In World War II the success of the African Campaign to rout the Germans under Gen. Rommel hinged on whether or not the official dowsers of the British army were able to find water to supply the troops on the march. One famous instance was that of the successful location of a fine flow of pure water in a valley where all former wells had been scant in flow and their water so filled with minerals as to be unfit for use.

When, as a reader of *The Secret Science Behind Miracles*, Verne Cameron first called on me, he brought his instruments and a study of them was begun which was reported later in many HRA Bulletins. Cameron proved to be a treasure trove of information, for in addition to experimenting with his instruments in the measurement of the aura of flowing water, he had measured the human aura, as well as the auras of objects, plants and animals. Naturally, the HRAs were extremely interested when he joined their numbers and demonstrated with ease the discoveries he had made a few years earlier.

The human aka body or aura or "etheric double" had been studied by Dr. Kilner some years before this, and through a colored screen he and his friends had been able to see it as it extended beyond the physical body, sometimes extending much, sometimes little, and often protruding at the center of the body to go out to meet and touch the protruding aka body of someone greatly loved who was coming near. Mr. Cameron had found with the Aurameter that the outline of the aka body could be measured with accuracy, even if not seen.

The aka or body aura was like that of underground flows of water inasmuch as it seemed to possess a force charge that would push away the head of the Aurameter when it was moved to the outer edge of it. By keeping the instrument moving along, up or down or sidewise, at just the point where the push on the Aurameter tip could be felt, the outline could be traced. Normally, the aka protrudes only a few inches from the body except at the shoulder blades and over the genitals, at which points the aura extends farther. Spots in the body which were not normal, as defective organs or teeth, were found to have the aka over those parts swollen and made to protrude unusually far. Joints, as in the spine, which needed adjustment showed aura bumps over them which disappeared when the adjustment had been successfully made.

Incidentally, Mr. Cameron made tests with his Aurameter in San Diego, California, which convincingly showed that the spirits of the dead survive and live in their aka bodies (the combined middle and low aka bodies—that of the low self being far more dense, even if still invisible).

Mr. Mark Probert of San Diego, a well-known medium, has a number of spirits who come to speak through him when he is in a trance condition. On this occasion, he went into the customary trance and a spirit spoke through his lips, carrying on a lively conversation and showing much interest in the Aurameter which was being tested. He readily agreed to stand beside the medium while Mr. Cameron tried to locate his aka body and trace its outline. He found it at once, and outlined it with as much ease as if it had belonged to a living man.

The spirit then suggested a test. He said that he would hide in the room, and that if he could be found with the Aurameter when Mr. Cameron and the others could have no idea of where he was hiding, the test would be evidential indeed. He was given a moment to hide, and the search was on. The Aurameter was used to feel here and there, up to the ceiling and along the walls, and back and forth across the room. In a few minutes, at the floor level just below the edge of the large table which stood in the center of the room, the Aurameter head was pushed back. It had come into contact with the aka body of the spirit. In a matter of seconds he was outlined, sitting crosslegged on the floor, his face toward the medium, his back toward Mr. Cameron. The spirit, speaking again through the medium, verified his position, and explained, "I thought you would expect me to be standing in front of the boy and facing you, so I sat down, to fool you, and turned to face him."

In this experiment something very new and important had been added to the annals of psychical research, and Huna had been given one more proof of its correctness.

And now we come to Mr. Cameron's discovery that a mental image or thought-form of an object could be made, and that the Aurameter would subsequently react to it as it does to the human aura. Most convincing tests were carried out in which Mr. Cameron would go out of the room while others agreed upon what object was to be visualized to make a thought-form of a certain shape at a certain place. Cubes, globes, vases of varying shapes—all sorts of things—were visualized and were promptly found by Mr. Cameron when he returned to the room and began to feel at the designated place to locate the shape with the Aurameter tip.

One peculiar thing was often noted: that the visualized form often seemed to have grown or contracted very much, when found. This, however, was in accord with the beliefs of the kahunas, who knew that the aka body could be made large so that it protruded greatly, or so small that it retreated inside the body completely. Thought-forms proved to have the same quality. They could be made microscopic in size to be stored in the thought-form clusters of memories, or could be expanded to the size of the things which they represented.

One of the most convincing tests of the Aurameter was made when a member of a group which was visualizing a circle standing on edge on a table, busied himself to visualize a square on the same spot, without telling the others. Mr. Cameron came in, began his testing, and paused. He tried again more carefully, then ran around the thought-form with the Aurameter slowly, following with great care each curve and angle. "This seems to be a circle with a square of smaller size superimposed upon it," he observed. "The corners of the square stick out beyond the circle a little bit at four places." It was only then that the gentleman who had added the square explained what he had done.

Having considered the latest proofs of the ancient belief that "a thought is a thing," we can round out our mental picture of how the low self, using its five senses, and guided by the middle self, observes what is happening and makes invisible and microscopic thought-form records to serve as memories of events.

The middle self plays its part in this work by deciding what each event means and what its relation to other events may be—or, as it is termed, "rationalizing" it. The memory cluster of thought-forms, once it has been given its rational meaning and significance by the middle self, is stored by the low self in the aka body. (When the middle self, for some reason, does *not* rationalize it before this storing away, trouble follows, as we have said.)

What we think or imagine is also recorded in the same way in memories and, as time passes, we accumulate a vast store of memories which are represented by thought-form clusters. In so far as our mental lives are concerned, we are "what we think," and if the think-ing is imperfect, or there are memories made by the low self without the proper rationalization touch of the middle self, they can cause much harm to mind and body—a very important matter which will be discussed farther on.

For the moment, however, our attention needs to be focused on the part the thought-form clusters play in telepathy, and upon the best ways of teaching the low self to use telepathy.

CHAPTER V

TELEPATHIC CONTACT BETWEEN PERSONS

When two friends, or two members of a family, understand how the low self works, they may profitably begin the practice of sending telepathic messages to each other.

We know, from the box and cards experiments, how the low self projects an aka finger along an aka thread to obtain information. We know that when we wish to send a message, it goes along the aka thread in thought-forms, the reality of which seems to be sufficiently proved.

One more thing needs to be introduced at this point, and that is the part that mana, the vital force, plays in telepathy. We have seen that mana flows from the low self of the operator into the Aurameter to cause it to react. Likewise, the mana flows along the aka cord between two people who are in telepathic communication.

The invisible aka threads or cords may be likened roughly to telegraph wires over which messages can be sent. They carry mana much as wires carry electricity. Just as the telegraph wires carry symbol messages to the receiving end, the aka threads can and do carry—on the flow of mana running through them—clusters of microscopic thought-forms. When received by a low self at the far end of the thread, these thought-forms bring mental impressions which convey the message. The recipient's low self then presents them to the middle self as impressions which are similar to memories when they are presented—things that just "rise in the mind."

We still do not know what form of force mana may be. It certainly is not electricity of the electromagnetic type, and it acts more like direct current of the type generated through chemical action. However, it is characterized by the fact that it seems to be a *living* force when aka body or aka cord substance serves as a storage place for it, or as a conducting wire or rod or cord. It has another characteristic in that it seems to find in the aka substance a *perfect* conductor. Ordinary direct current electricity cannot be sent far over a wire before it weakens to the point of nothingness. All long power lines carry alternating currents of high voltage.

In telepathy we have proof that the aka thread is a perfect or living substitute for a wire, and that the mana flows as easily over a connecting thread half way around the world as across a room. The popular theory that telepathic sending is similar to the sending of high frequency radio waves through the air, as in a broadcast, has been proven a fallacy. The radio waves fade and weaken inversely as the square of the distance traveled, and with a power plant as small as the human low self, a broadcast of this type would hardly be able to reach farther than a few feet.

In beginning the practice of telepathy with another, it is well, at the start, to be together. Later the two may try sending messages at a distance from each other. One person sends the thought-forms, the other is the recipient—these roles being reversed during the practice period. The aka threads are already well-established between friends. (Strangers establish them by the exchange of glances, or, better still, by shaking hands.)

The middle self of the recipient has the greater task at the outset. It is none too easy to make our middle selves receptive and mentally quiet so that the low self can present the telepathic impressions it has picked up. This is because, in the course of our daily work of living, George is standing by constantly to be ready to take orders and to carry them out. From the time he lets go of his dreams in the morning and his man awakens, he must be ready to catch the slightest command—the command to glance at the clock to see whether it is early or late, to look about to locate some article of apparel, to obey the order to pick up a watch with care and fasten it on the wrist without dropping it.

If there are moments when the man is entirely idle, and when the middle self is not asking help in recalling memories to be used in thinking of this or that, George may indulge in a little daydreaming. He may bring up memories of his own accord and present them to the middle self. Most low selves are endlessly helpful and anxious to see that the work of the man is properly done. In a quiet moment of rest, the low self will make haste to remember all the things which should be done. It may take the opportunity to remind the middle self that it should phone the garage about the battery, or water the new bed of seeds in the back yard.

If we are worried, George will try to help by recalling for us the memories of the conditions which we are

63

worrying about and trying to correct. In fact, he is so industrious in this matter, when strongly impressed with the necessity of adjusting worrisome circumstances, that he may keep one awake half the night with the constant presentation of the worry materials and with emotions to match them.

Because of this habit of keeping alert to obey the orders of the middle self, George may be said not to "know what to do with himself," if he is released from duty and told that he is to be on his own for a time. So he must be told carefully to take over and perform tasks that he alone can perform. He must be told that the middle self is not able to direct him, as it would be if a nail were to be driven at an exact place in a wall. We might say that George is given the hammer and nail and told to go out, find a wall, mark a good place on it to hang a picture, and to drive the nail—then to report just what he has done.

You have already explained to George that there are aka threads well established between you and your friend, and that these are now to be activated, or put into use, so that thought-forms may be sent back and forth along them to convey the messages. You tell George that your friend is about to send a message, and that he is to receive it, then present it to you just as he would a memory. After that, keep hands off George, mentally, and stop offering suggestions and advice.

The friend signals that the sending is starting. You relax your habitual grip on George while you relax the body. You do nothing that will need the attention or help of George. You try to clear thoughts from your

64

mind so that it will be empty and ready for the message to be pushed into the focus of consciousness.

You wait a moment. No impression comes. If you are like most of us, your impulse will be to jerk George back and start telling him afresh what he is to do, urging him to give the message to you, or telling him that you sense no message. This unfortunate action would be comparable to calling a dog back after sending him to search for a ball lost in a weed patch (having made sure, of course, that the dog first knew what was wanted of him). If, before the dog had got well started on his search, we called him back to see if he had anything in his mouth, or if we kept calling him back to give him his orders all over again, the ball would be found only after a long delay, if at all.

Carrying the analogy further, suppose we had trouble with the dog because there were rabbits in the patch, or he had a bone buried there, and he decided that chasing the rabbits or digging up his bone for examination might be more important. Or, the dog might not be just sure which of several old balls in the patch he was to find and bring back. He might even get the idea that an old shoe or glove would do better. Just so, George may have difficulty understanding what is wanted. Instead of waiting for the thought-form message to come to him from the sender's George, along the connecting aka cord, he may rush to the other George and begin doing mind reading—may begin examining the memories stored in the aka body of the other George, and begin sending back to the middle self a fine collection of shoes and gloves and old balls—but not the right ball.

Then, too, since George is a most obliging fellow and strives to please, if he cannot get a message for his middle self he will sometimes do his best to manufacture a substitute. He will guess endlessly, if you will let him, and keep giving you impressions which belong to the old memories and which are imaginings, pure and simple.

The low self must be kept at the work of finding the ball, and only the ball, but must be given its freedom while it makes its search. To keep it on the job and prevent it racing away after rabbits, the telepathic practice often goes best at first if George is given something to do that is real and not imaginary—such as holding a pencil over paper and drawing a picture of the thing which the telepathic sender is gazing at and sending. The act of drawing tends to impress George that the work is vital and necessary, and to keep him attending to it and trying to pick up the impression through the projected thought-forms.

The inexperienced telepathic sender, on the other hand, may send poorly, so making the receiving something that demands more waiting and more patience. For beginners, it is a good idea for both to provide themselves with paper and pencil, so that the one who tries to send can draw carefully and slowly, while holding the command over his George to send a picture of what is being drawn, to his friend, the other George across the room (or, later, across the city or state).

A simple symbol or outline drawing of a form or tree may be used. Pictures have proven easiest to send and to receive. Colors are easier to use than sounds or tones, and smells or tastes are easier to transmit than physical sensations of hardness, softness or warmth and cold.

To send the message, "John, stop at the store on the way home and get a pound of butter," is difficult if the words and sounds of the words are to be sent. But the mental picture of a store and a package of butter is fairly simple. It is not at all uncommon to find husbands getting telepathic messages of this nature from their wives with certainty and precision. One HRA reported that he usually got the message to bring certain things home with him when waiting, in a momentarily relaxed state in his car, for a traffic signal to change.

If, when the telepathic practice is undertaken, the low selves seem to take a long time to do what is expected of them, a preliminary practice may be tried in which one sits down with paper and pencil and invites George to present an idea for a picture, or the mental picture of some event. Ordinarily, we prompt the low self to guide it in giving us the needed and wanted memories with which to do our thinking, or with which to carry on a train of thought in speaking or writing. All normal memories being tied together by aka threads so that they are not lost or isolated events, but woven into the fabric of time and place, the memory of a childhood event will be tied to other memories of the same period and places. If, for instance, I think of my childhood and wish to recall the name of an old playmate, I give George the hint of what is wanted by dwelling on something that happened in connection with the playmate. George starts pulling up memories at a great rate, following the connecting aka threads from one memory to another of those tied into the same time-place group. Sooner or later he finds the name of the playmate and presents it.

The invitation to George to go on his own for a time,

decide what to recall, and to recall it without prompting —then to present it to the common center of consciousness, will almost always get results. A few daily practice sessions with this exercise will teach the middle self to keep hands off and let the low self do what is required of it. It will teach the calm, quiet attitude of attention and expectation which is necessary on the part of the middle self, and it will teach George to be more sure of himself, more confident that he is doing the right thing.

If one lacks a partner with whom telepathic experiments can be carried on for a few minutes daily, there is another and slightly more difficult exercise which furnishes excellent training. This is exercise in what is called "psychometry."

To try this, it is necessary to borrow from a friend some objects owned and used by a third person, known to the friend but not to the experimenter. Articles such as a ring, a penknife or fountain pen, or other trinkets which have been worn or used habitually, are excellent for this purpose because the owner will have attached strong aka threads to the objects. Hold each in turn between the hands for a time, after instructing George to put out an aka finger, feel along the aka cord connected to the object, and bring back an impression of the owner. After sufficient practice at instructing George, then relaxing and waiting for him to act, he will begin to present to the focus of the middle self consciousness his impressions of the person at the other end of the aka cord attached to the object. These impressions can be remembered or written down, and a later check for accuracy may be made with the friend who has made the loan of the articles.

In psychometry tests in one HRA group, a box was passed around to collect objects to be used in the tests. The objects were then distributed, the persons receiving them not knowing to whom they belonged. The woman who happened to be holding my watch, reported that she sensed the owner of the watch as an elderly gentleman with a white beard and a very kindly personality. When I claimed the watch, there was much amusement over the apparent mistake, but I at once explained what had happened. The original owner of the watch had been accurately sensed and described. He had carried it for several years before his death, and I had only recently received it as a gift from his daughter.

Since this incident touches on the fact that the aka threads may lead to persons who have left this life, it may be well to point out that this very fact is one of the many strong evidences of human survival of personality. The aka body retains the memories, after physical death, just as in life. And these memories, as well as the general appearance of the person as outlined in the surviving aka body, make possible the bringing back of information sufficient to identify the individual, as in the case of the former owner of my watch.

Failing to get impressions by means of psychometry from George, one may fall back once more on the pendulum, as several of the HRAs were forced to do. With the pendulum in hand, and using the convention that has been set up for "yes" and "no," George can be instructed to follow established aka threads to a friend, find him and indicate by a "yes" through the pendulum that contact has been made. That accomplished, questions can be asked and answered to tell where the friend is, how he is, what he is doing, and whether he is with others or alone. A record of the answers may be kept, the time of the day noted, and a check for accuracy made as opportunity offers. One HRA had a young relative whose business took him all over the city. By this method he was able to trace the young man's movements accurately. In time he took to holding the pendulum in one hand and pointing to different sections of the city on a map, while George stood by to give a "yes" swing when the right place was indicated.

All of these exercises in training the low self to develop its native telepathic ability are valuable, because they make familiar the method of directing the low self to follow the aka threads to some person or thing outside oneself. The same method is used when we wish to contact and send a message to our own High Self.

From what we now know, it is evident that the region of the solar plexus—in the aka body, not the physical— is the one at which the connecting threads are fastened. From this point they may run in any direction, and evidence accumulates to indicate that there are, during all our years, very strong aka cords which run from the solar plexus region upward along the spine and out through the top of the head. This cord is the natural link of connection between the low self and the High Self.

And what activates this cord? It is the mana, the vital force. We have spoken of mana in connection with the work of the dowsers, and in the use of the

Aurameter. We have just explained how it carries the thought-form clusters along the aka threads in telepathy. Of infinitely greater importance is the fact that mana carries the thought-forms along the strong aka cord connecting the low self to the High Self. It is the force which makes possible the correct and effective making of a prayer, as well as the answer to prayer.

CHAPTER VI

MANA AND THE SURCHARGE OF MANA

The totem pole of the North American natives, embodying as it does a set of ancient concepts which now are vastly and sadly muddled, gives us one of the finest symbols for the three selves of man, and for the mana or life force they use.

In the totem pole there is a central column made up of one figure set directly above another. Very often the two lower figures are standing on an animal, and are partly joined as if one sat on the shoulders of the other, his legs clasped with the arms of the lower figure. This pair would be a fine symbol of the relation between the low and middle selves, closely united, but one a little higher than the other in the climb away from the animal world (symbolized by the animal at the bottom). Still higher up, and seldom so closely united, comes a figure which often has spreading wings, and which is ideal as a representation of the Guardian Angel or High Self, whose symbol is a bird. In Christianity it was the dove which came from heaven to alight on the newly baptized Jesus.

The central trunk out of which the images are carved can stand for the basic mana, as taken from the food we eat—be it of the vegetable or the animal world—and the air we breathe. This mana is taken from the food and air by the low self and is stored in its aka body, but it is shared with the middle self and the High Self. It might be guessed that if there are more figures carved on the totem pole above that which we select to represent the High Self, these may represent an ever-ascending scale of Higher Beings who also must be furnished with mana if they are to have enough of the gross and heavy force of the physical world to work in its materials and make needed changes.

The mana, when used as the life force of the middle self is changed in some subtle way. We do not know just how. The kahunas of old symbolized this as a *dividing* of the basic mana into two kinds, and called it, in the divided state, *mana mana*—indicating by doubling the word the fact that it was doubled in its power so that it could be used by the middle self to command and control the low self. This is the force we know vaguely in modern psychology as the "will." It is also the force which should at all times be strong enough to make the low self obey every order, but which, as it is easy to see, is seldom used in its full strength—resulting in the low self getting out of hand frequently with most of us.

It is so much easier to "let George do it" than to decide for ourselves what is the best thing to be done and then hold George with a firm grip of "will" and make him do it. Most of us have experienced the failure to keep up a diet, or to stop smoking, or to give up any bad habit. In some cases, George behaves like a frightened horse which takes the bit in its teeth and runs away. Once he gets to running, there is little to be done but let him go while the driver hangs on and hopes for the best. Once George, with his genius for forming habits, learns to do a certain thing in a certain way, he does his very powerful best to prevent the middle self from breaking him of the habit.

It is not generally known that we can use certain exercises (about to be described) to accumulate a surcharge —an extra large and powerful charge—of vital force at any time we need it, providing we are in fair health and are not starved. We can use these surcharges of mana in several very valuable ways, particularly in healing ourselves and others, and in making a prayer that will have real working power.

The kahunas believed that by an action of mind a man adds to the amount of mana he has already created from food and air consumed, by quickening the extraction process. This theory is supported by our physiologists, who have found that when we digest our food it is not all used at once, but is changed to glycogen, or blood sugar, and oxidized with oxygen from the air we breathe to give us such amounts of force and strength as we may need for the work we happen to do. If this is true, and there seems no reason to question the findings, the low self, who attends to all such matters, can at any time begin to take in more air and cause more blood sugar to be burned to create more of that strange chemically-manufactured force we call mana.

The low self learns to do this, in most cases, with very little trouble. Given a natural talent for this work and sufficient practice, he becomes expert, and, as some of the HRAs saw demonstrated in 1950, can project the great surcharge at a relaxed individual and knock him unconscious to the floor—not that any good HRA would be party to such activities. (This demonstration was

74

made by a traveling mesmerist in Hollywood, California, and not as a part of the HRA testing.)

The most interesting thing about mana is that it seems alive and seems to have a form of intelligence of its own. This is not really so. It can act only when it charges and vitalizes aka substance, as in an aka finger when it is projected, and the consciousness is invariably that of the low self who is dictating the projection and also the things it is to do. (The exception is when a disembodied spirit seizes control and draws the surcharge of mana into its own low self aka body and uses it there.)

The accumulation of a surcharge of vital force is accomplished just as is the swinging of the pendulum, or the identification of objects hidden in cardboard boxes —simply by explaining to George just what he is to do, and then asking him to try to do it. To help him, after we have explained that we want him to burn more food in the blood stream and make a great deal more vital force to add to that stored already in his aka body, we can use the voluntary muscles and start breathing more deeply. This will furnish the air to be used, as well as suggest what we want done.

Another thing we can do is to perform a few setting-up exercises while we wait for George to begin working. This always starts the low self to manufacturing more mana, otherwise we would use up what we have in a few moments and begin to feel faint. Every athlete knows that he can go only so far and so fast on his "first wind"—which is the charge of mana he happens to have in the body and aka body at the start—but that in a short time he gets a fresh supply of strength—his "second wind"—and can then keep going steadily and at top speed.

Or, instead of exercising, we can assume the mental attitude of one getting set to run a race. We hold the picture in mind of getting ready to run, we breathe more rapidly and tense up the muscles a little. George seldom fails to get the idea then, and will begin creating the desired mana.

I told in *The Secret Science Behind Miracles* of the practical methods taught by Baron Eugene Fersen for creating a surcharge of life force in the body. He toured this country some years ago, giving lectures and presiding over classes. His term for mana was "Universal Life Force," and he had some idea that there were three grades of it. However, he did not know of the three selves of the kahuna belief, nor of their three manas.

The basic difference between the Fersen theory and the kahuna theory as we see it, hinges on the matter of where the surcharge of life force comes from. Baron Fersen believed in part with the religionists of some schools in India, that there is a Universal Life Force which is everywhere, much like a great ocean of force spread through the universe, and which is drawn upon by all living things for a share of its life-giving power. The kahunas left nothing behind them, when they disappeared from the face of the earth at the end of the last century, which seems to indicate that they considered life force universal in character. But Fersen believed that by an action of mind he could draw it out of the air and absorb and store it in his body.

Baron Fersen's affirmation was, "The Universal Life

Force is flowing through me now . . . I feel it." There was a pause between the two parts of the affirmation to let the flow accumulate. While making this affirmation, he had his pupils stand with feet as far apart as was comfortable to maintain, and extend hands and arms at the sides level with the shoulders. His belief was that the four limbs extended out beyond the astral body, or etheric double, and touched the flows of force in the air about the pupil, picking up the charge as radio antenna picks up the broadcast waves from a station. There soon came a tingling in the hands, which might or might not have been caused by the accumulation of the surcharge, but it was expected and the affirmation said it was there, and George obliged. (Or, the circulation in the arms may have been slowed down so that the tingling came for that reason.) At any rate, the surcharge of mana resulted, and could be demonstrated.

The late Dr. Oscar Brunler, the distinguished scientist and Radiesthetist, was a very helpful HRA. He demonstrated a method he had used which was even better than the Fersen method, although based on the same disputed idea that the force was in the air. His method added enough physical exercise to the operation to cause an automatic start in the accumulation of more mana and deeper, faster breathing. He stood with feet fairly close together and raked the air with widespread fingers, reaching up as high as he could, standing on tiptoes, and raking forward with a circling movement which swept past the sides of his ankles (the body being bent to reach the ankles) and ended with the hands and fingers brought on around and up behind him as high as possible. This raking circle was in this way about three quarters of a full circle. At the end of each raking motion he relaxed his arms and hands a moment and brought them back while he straightened his body, lifted the arms, and repeated the raking stroke. This was done vigorously several times, while the mental picture was strongly held that the life force was being gathered and a large extra amount of it stored in the body.

Dr. Brunler's method, coupled with the affirmation, "I am now accumulating a large surcharge of mana," repeated with each swing, is excellent. But, once George learns the art, he will respond without anything more than a mental request from the middle self. Some people carry a normal charge of mana which is high, others carry a very low one, but all can accumulate a surcharge which may be tested.

The test that Baron Fersen used and taught was simple. A well-charged person can, if he imagines and pictures that he is doing so, cause the mana in his body to concentrate in his hands, and there become magnetic in its action. His hands, made to become human magnets in this simple way, can then be placed lightly on the shoulders of a friend who is not surcharged (the friend standing facing away) and when the hands are withdrawn slowly, they will pull like magnets, often pulling the friend after them with enough force to throw him off balance. Certain persons are far more easily pulled in this way than others. By putting on a surcharge each time in advance and then testing a different friend, a sensitive one will be found who will respond to the pull more readily than others.

78

I have told elsewhere of an experiment which I carried on after studying with Baron Fersen in Honolulu, and practicing a bit at accumulating a surcharge. I had successfully exerted a strong pull on several friends in the class, but I was not sure that suggestion or even imagination might not account for the pull. To make sure, I arranged with an acquaintance in the class to make a test on his dog. We took turns accumulating a surcharge, standing behind the dog, placing hands on his rump, and drawing them slowly away. The dog was pulled after our hands no matter how he clawed at the matting to resist. The strange part was that we felt no pull at all on our hands. (This fact is still hard to explain, even in terms of Huna. However, it is possible that the aka-mana in our hands protruded as we pulled our hands away, retaining a grip on the dog in some way, and, under the command of the low self, used up the force in the invisible aka projections to pull the dog backwards. Spirits, with nothing but their aka bodies and mana taken from the living to fill them, can use up all the mana in a single sudden effort with the result that the living can be lifted into the air, tables or even heavy pianos lifted, or even entire houses shaken as by an earthquake.)

The kahunas, it will be remembered, used the symbol of water for mana. When they wished to accumulate a surcharge they breathed deeply and visualized mana rising like water rises in a fountain, higher and higher, until it overflows. The body is pictured as the fountain and the water as the mana. (They also could then send aka-mana into throwing-sticks which, when thrown over the heads of a line of fighting warriors to strike an en-

79

emy, would render the warrior so struck temporarily unconscious, much as the mesmerist in Hollywood, by projecting a surcharge along the line of his vision—undoubtedly with a projected finger of aka-mana—could send a man sprawling to lie unconscious on the floor.)

The magnetic pull test is one that demands other persons to try it on, and for this reason the HRAs needed a simple test that they could use when alone. One was not devised at once, but in time one was worked out that was satisfactory for most of those who had taught their George to handle a pendulum with fair skill.

In this test the pendulum is taken in hand in the usual way, but held over the left palm. George should be told simply and carefully that what is wanted is a report in code, through the pendulum, of the amount of mana he now has in his possession—that is, in the physical and aka bodies, interblended. (This will give the normal count, without surcharge.) In this code, as in all others, a convention must be established and well understood. The convention should be made to limit the count, as it takes a tiresomely long time to swing out a thousand counts. Suggest hundreds, for this reason and because we are aiming only at comparison with the count after a surcharge has been made. And swinging circles, which may be counted, instead of the former straight swings, will be an interesting change.

The procedure may be further shortened by using a convention in which you say, "Is the count over 300 swings?" and if one gets a "yes" at 300, but a "no" at 400, say, "Very well, let's start counting at 300." When the right number is reached George is to stop the swing with a slight jerk or wiggle of the pendulum. If you doubt the count arrived at, check with George on his finding with the "yes" and "no" method.

When the normal charge is agreed upon, a surcharge should be accumulated and another test made for increase of count. It is well to keep a record of the results of this practice each day, for with only a few minutes of daily practice, it can be seen that the surcharge becomes larger and larger. Anything over double the normal is good going. Four times normal is enough to send you and your George to the head of the class.

A number of the HRAs reported back to me that the pendulum swung, often in very wide circles, but that George just kept on swinging it endlessly, until their arms got too tired to hold the pendulum any longer over their palms. I had the opportunity on two occasions to run check tests with my pendulum and my George over the hands of HRAs who could get nothing but an endless count of swings. My George proved to be satisfactory at measuring for others, as he has been for me, giving us the normal count in each instance, and then the increased count after a surcharge was taken on. In both cases a little conversation, and perhaps a little silent converse between our two Georges, resulted in the exercise being understood and the erratic swings changed to give accurate counts. From this experience we concluded that the convention had not been understood by the Georges. They had caught the idea that the pendulum was to be circle-swung to indicate a charge of life force—which is a very simple idea to grasp—but had failed to understand their part in using a certain number of swings as the indicator of the normal charge, and of making increased numbers of swings to show the surcharge.

The individual with a low normal charge-level of mana has almost always found that he can sense the addition of mana after taking on a surcharge. It adds to the sense of wellbeing, of physical strength, or will and determination, and it sharpens the mind, makes memorization faster and easier, and the senses more acute. The latter feature is best noted in vision. The HRA test most favored is that of hanging up a colored picture, looking at it before the taking on of a surcharge and then again after the surcharge has been accumulated. Vision becomes clearer, and more, it is surprising how much wider a field one becomes aware of at one time, and how much more detail stands out and how the colors strengthen. One HRA who worked long and wearisome hours on his job found that if, once or twice, morning and afternoon, he paused to take on a surcharge of mana, he was immediately strengthened and greatly refreshed.

All the evidence shows that the mana is, indeed, the life force, and that with it, the life is strong, while without it, it fades. This is not exclusively an HRA or Huna discovery. Medical men have long known that if the level of vital force falls too low, the middle self loses its power to control the low self, and the low self, lacking guidance, becomes erratic, then neurotic or psychotic symptoms appear. And, if the level is far enough down, the victim sinks into a state of morbidity and depression that may end in complete insanity.

One cannot increase his aka body substance, or lose it;

but he can increase his mana charge with very beneficial results when it is too low, or more mana is needed for one purpose or another. Conversely, one can lose his mana and be progressively hurt by the loss, ending, if the loss is complete, in death.

However, the point that is most important when considering mana, is that when one has learned to accumulate a surcharge, it is possible to use it—with the help of the High Self—to perform miracles which range all the way from slow and simple healing to miraculous changes in bodily tissues and even in the fabric of the future.

For this reason, rather than to pause here to discuss the use of the mana surcharge in the hands of the low and middle selves, we shall go on at once to consider the nature of the High Self—in order that we may the sooner take up the work with mana and thought-form clusters in which all three of the selves work together as a perfectly balanced and co-ordinated team.

CHAPTER VII

THE HIGH SELF

The kahunas believed in, and performed their miracles through contact with, the third and highest form of consciousness in man—that which we call for convenience, the High Self. It, like the low self and middle self, is a spirit. It dwells in its aka body outside the physical body. It may be very close, or off at a distance. The aka cord always connects the low self and the High Self after the fashion of a telephone wire. If the three selves are working normally and freely together, the low self—at the request of the middle self—can at any time call up the High Self by way of the aka cord and give it a message.

The name that the kahunas used for the High Self was *Aumakua*, meaning the "Utterly Trustworthy Parental Spirit," also, "the god who is a father." It was not an ordinary father, as is shown by the root *au*, which means "older," and completely grown or evolved so that it is superior in strength and wisdom and in trustworthiness. *Au* also means "a cord," in this case the aka cord which connects it with its pair of lower selves.

Au, the root word, also means "an action of mind," and "a flow or a current, as in the sea," which symbolizes in the root the fact that the High Self performs an action with its mind in answer to our prayers to bring about *fulfillment*—but at the same time there must be a mana flow to it.   (A flow or current of water is a symbol for mana.)

Makua is "parent" or "father," and the root *ma* means "to accompany," pointing to the fact that it accompanies the low and middle selves through life as their guide.   The same root has the meaning of "to solidify," and this takes us to one of the most interesting beliefs found in Huna.   It is the belief that all of the events and circumstances which we ask in prayer that the High Self will cause to come to pass, are first formed in the aka substance as invisible molds of the events, by the High Self—it having the knowledge and the power (if given a daily supply of mana by the lower man)—and that, "solidified" or "materialized" into these aka molds is the physical substance.   When the "solidification" is complete, the requested event or circumstance of healed condition suddenly appears as a fact on the physical level.

It may be asked at this point, what does this concept of the beneficent powers of the High Self have to do with God?

The idea of one supreme God was the Hebrew contribution to the world's thought on this subject.   But in doing this masterly bit of reasoning, the reasoners accomplished for many branches of religion the wiping out of every level or form of consciousness between the middle self and Ultimate God, leaving a vast emptiness which is contrary to what we see of orderly evolutionary processes on earth.   We see the evolution of life through one elementary form to the next, through more and more complex forms, and on and on and on until the level of man is reached.

Each form of life, no matter how simple or how microscopic, shows plainly the possession of a form of consciousness that directs it, and a share of life force to enliven it. To stop with man and leap the unimaginable gap from his lowly mental and physical creative powers to that of a Highest Creator, is out of keeping with what we observe on every side—the orderly step-by-step evolutionary progress upward. The fact, of course, that the level above that of physical man is not visible to physical eyes, accounts in part for this failure to be reasonable.

The Mosaic God was, to make Him more acceptable, made very much in man's image. For those of little wit he was a benign old gentleman with a long beard and fiery eyes who was dangerous in his anger unless one did as he commanded. His commands were supposedly given to the priests and handed on to the trusting layman. Lacking commands given at first hand, the book in which earlier commands had been written down became "the Word of God," and woe betide anyone who questioned that Word. It made no difference that there were such "Words of God" in all religions, and that these do not agree very well on what the commands have been.

The kahunas believed that, as man had a trinity of spirits, there must be a trinity of Beings making up the highest God. These they called Ku, Kane, and Kanaloa, according to the Hawaiian legendary accounts, but they were considered to be so far evolved above the human level that they could only be personified as great men of magic power who created worlds and peoples and ruled over them.

The kahunas were very logical and wise in that they recognized the impossibility of the middle self ever being able to understand the nature of the High Self, or the form of mentation it uses. It followed that if we cannot understand the High Self, which is part of our own man and only one stage above the middle self in evolution, the possibility of comprehending still higher Beings or Ultimate God is very poor indeed.

They taught that all prayers must first go to the High Self for the simple reason that it alone is on the far end of the aka cord, and that no higher Being can be reached. However, there was the belief that, should the High Self not be able to bring about the condition requested in the prayer, it could—at its discretion—carry the prayer on to still higher Beings. Moreover, the High Selves do not exist as "lone wolves." They have a close, friendly, loving association called the *Poe Aumakua,* or "Great Company of Aumakuas," ready to do everything they can to help each other and, especially, to help their lower selves or the physical man to help the individuals over whom their associated High Self neighbors stand as guardians.

As told briefly in Chapter 1, one of the most profitable discoveries was that of finding Huna teachings in veiled and little understood statements in the Bible. By means of the symbols used, and by translating into the "sacred language" where the inner meaning is hidden in root words, these statements began to come clear. They revealed a common knowledge among the initiates of Biblical times and the kahunas in the far off Pacific.

Let us take, for one instance, the word Jehovah, used as one of the names for God in the Old Testament.

87

The meaning of Jehovah is "One who comes." We change the title, "One who comes," back into Hawaiian and get *kokoke*, and this gives us not only the outer meaning of "one who comes"—which was all that could be transferred in writing to the Hebrew scriptures—but also provides us with the roots from which to draw a good description of the divinity so named. And this, as will be seen, turns out to be really a description of the powers of the High Self.

Ko: "To accomplish, bring about, fulfill" (as answering prayer).

"To fulfill as an agreement" (or covenant).

"To obtain what is sought after."

"To put a law into force."

"To conquer or overpower" (to have great strength).

Koko: "To replace a bone" (as in instant healing), "to set a bone."

"Blood" (symbol in Huna of the life of the body).

"To fulfill." (More emphatic word than just *ko*. The High Self brings things to pass to fulfill the promise to answer prayer.)

Koke: "To be near, not far off, to come near to one."

"To be on friendly terms with one."

"To be attached to one."

"To favor one."

"To do instantly, quickly, immediately" (with the causative *hoo*).

There has been some groping about in modern Christian churches of the less orthodox type for a concept of "God within" or "indwelling God" or "The Father Who is within you." The idea has stemmed from certain New Testament phrases, perhaps especially from Jesus' words: "The kingdom of heaven is within you." We look into the Hawaiian language for words meaning "a god who dwells with or within one" and find *akua noho*, another of the several titles for the High Self. The inner meanings are supplied by the root words as follows:

An *akua* was any entity or being superior to the middle self in intelligence or power or other attributes. It was superior in its ability to judge, and counsel and guide and protect. *Noho* means "to dwell with one" or "abide with one"—as the High Self coming on call to abide with the low self and middle self. But, while it is with the lower pair of selves, or in contact with them through the aka cord of connection, all three selves are in a special condition or state of being, which is indicated by the second meaning of *noho*. This second meaning is a very important one: it is, "to have equal privileges" with the low and middle self. This points to the fact that it must have its share of the mana or vital force of the man to enable it to function on the dense physical plane, and also to do its creative work of shaping the future on the invisible level of its being.

Isaiah accurately sets down the Huna ideas of the High Self in describing it as "Wonderful, Counsellor." It is all this and more owing to its more evolved level of intelligence and higher knowledge. It is Guide as well as Guardian, if we will but open our two lower selves and allow it to play its natural part in our lives on this level.

Isaiah also calls the High Self the "Everlasting Father," and that brings us right back to the father concept in the word for the High Self, *Aumakua*. Centuries after Isaiah's time, Jesus stressed the "loving father" aspect of God to the complete exclusion of the jealous and wrathful God of his forebears. This was no oversight on the part of Jesus. As we have said, he must have been an initiate of the ancient Huna teachings. As such he was able to become actively united with, or "one with the Father" at will, and so able to enjoy the aid of the High Self in living the life of the three-self man.

Jesus called himself Son of Man, usually, but sometimes Son of God. When challenged for the latter, he quoted the ancient scriptures, "I said Ye are gods." He was speaking, as did the Psalmist he was quoting, from his High Self level.

Some of the HRAs with Christian backgrounds enquired about the necessity of always "asking in Jesus' name" when they prayed. "Ask it in my name," Jesus instructed, and so clear and so unusual a command seemed too definite to set aside as of no moment.

The phrase, "Ask in my name," can be translated back into the Hawaiian, and in this way the secret meaning is revealed. The "asking" is a "calling on," the one prayed to, in the Hawaiian idiom. The word used is *ku-he-a* or its alternate *ka-he-a*. In addition to the meaning of "to call," the roots of these words tell us how to call to the High Self in the Huna fashion. One extends an aka finger to touch the High Self and attract attention, and in so doing, one performs an act comparable with that of taking the telephone piece from its rest and dialing a number. The switch in the rest piece allows the current of electricity to flow through the wire and bring it to life. The wire or cord of aka substance that runs from the low self to the High Self is likewise charged with mana and made ready for use. The High Self has its attention attracted, and stands ready to receive the telepathic message or prayer which we send not in words only, but in clusters of thought-forms which represent words and thoughts when they have been pushed along the aka cord by the mana flow to the High Self "Father."

That takes care of the secret hidden in the "asking" or "calling upon" phrase. Next comes the secret hidden in the kahunas' word for "name." This is *i-noa*. In the roots of this word we find hidden the meaning of "to speak," indicating that the High Self will reply to our call, and the meaning of "to release one from restrictions of all kinds." This is the request that the High Self help us to make the contact with it by removing any obstacle which may be preventing the low self from sending the mana and the thought-forms of the prayer to it.

Still another root has a meaning which tells us what it is that causes the low self to fail to activate the aka thread or symbolic "path" to the High Self. This meaning is "to hurt another in some way," which, in the Huna system, is to commit a "sin."

In Huna there is one great sin which can be consciously committed, and only one: that of HURTING ANOTHER. The High Self is beyond the power of the lower selves to hurt, although it yearns over the lower man and longs always to have him live the good and hurtless life. It may be saddened when he remains sinful and, because of his sins, cuts himself off from the daily help and guidance which, under normal circumstances, the High Self gives.

Sins of hurting others, mentally or physically, or hurting one's own body by excesses, are things we are fully aware of and can stop committing. (There are other "sins" in the form of complexes and obsessions which we shall discuss in their place.)

Successful prayer, properly addressed to God by way of the High Self, or "In my name," as taught by Jesus, cannot be made while one is still guilty of having hurt others. Amends must be made for all hurts done others if that is possible; if not, good deeds done unselfishly for others must be performed as vicarious atonement for the hurts done those who can no longer be reached to be asked for forgiveness, and to receive such things as can be offered as restitution or repayment.

One of the reasons why the High Self was called the "Utterly Trustworthy Parental Self" was that it never interferes with the two lower selves and so robs them of their "free will"—which is their divine heritage and birthright. They are privileged to learn by experience, and they must be allowed to try their hands at living without interference from the elder and wiser High Self. This, naturally, can lead to learning the hard way, through bitter experience.

Some individuals have an intuitional type of "knowing" which tells them that there is a High Self, but intuitional sensing is impossible to share. One can only state the conviction that his own particular intuitions are valid, and this statement may or may not be acceptable to others. In *The Secret Science Behind Miracles* I went to some length to describe the mystical system found in Zen Buddhism which is aimed at gaining an intuitional or semi-sensual impression of the High Self as the "One Reality." I told of my own experience in getting this form of sensation and with it the conviction that there was a world of sorts which contained the perfect patterns of all things, and which contained the greater verities while having in it nothing to be sensed but an impression of "aliveness" or existence outside the body and independent of space, time and memory, but always bathed in light of one color or another. I felt that I was, temporarily, one with this light, a part of it.

It may have been similar experiences on the part of the first kahunas which caused them to symbolize the High Self as LIGHT. Also, the High Self was given the name of *Ao* or *Io*, "Light," and "Truth" or "The Real Truth and Reality." It was often addressed as *Ala*, which means "The Anointed One," but which also means "The Way" or "Path," both of which words are the symbols of the aka cord running from the lower self to the High Self.

In the New Testament these titles are preserved in their outer meaning only. Standing forth as one united with the "Father," and therefore permitted to speak as for the "Father High Self," Jesus said to those of his disciples whom he was initiating into the ancient Secret, "I am the WAY, THE TRUTH and the LIFE." The "life" in this case is the mana transformed by the High Self and returned to the lower selves as a healing and blessing force—as the High Self life force.

Jesus spoke of himself as the LIGHT of the World, and when he taught that only through him could the kingdom of heaven be reached, he spoke symbolically of himself as the aka cord "WAY" to the High Self— that being the one and only way by which contact can be made with the High Self in order to pray to it in the Huna manner. The Kingdom of Heaven is also the High Self, symbolically. The Anointed One, or Messiah (one in contact with the High Self as indicated in *Ao*) was the title used in the Old Testament frequently, and such references were pointed to by Jesus, centuries later, as prophecies of his own coming and ministry. These passages which refer to the "Anointed One" are thinly veiled allusions to the High Self and its blessed powers to help and save from troubles, and to forgive sin.

When Jesus taught the uninitiated, he used the outer meanings of words, just as did the kahunas during their stay in Egypt and in their later residence in Polynesia. To his disciples, however, he taught the Huna meanings hidden in the roots of the sacred language. In the New Testament, Matthew 13:10–11, we have a very clear statement concerning the inner teachings. The Fenton translation reads:

"His disciples approaching Him, afterwards asked, 'Why do You speak to them in parables?'

" 'Because,' He answered, 'it is granted to you to become acquainted with the secrets of the Kingdom of Heaven; but it is not granted to others.' "

In this literal translation the older phrase of the King James version is replaced and the word "mysteries" becomes "secrets." As Huna was the great "Secret," there is little chance to mistake the significance of this oblique reference to it as the system being taught.

Fortunately for mankind, the normal way of life is one in which all three selves co-operate and the lower selves invite the High Self to take its rightful part in the task of living—the High Self receiving its share of the "daily bread" or basic mana, and being asked always to use its superior wisdom and power to guide, heal, and shape the future in the best possible way.

The greatest single discovery in the life of any man or woman is that there is a High Self. The next greatest discovery is that in which the method of co-operating with it is learned and put to use.

In the normal life, the High Self automatically gives the daily guidance from behind the scenes, even if one is quite unaware of it being given. Things "just happen" right. Difficulties are avoided, and life is lived smoothly, happily and successfully. One serves and is given the "joy of the Lord" or the happiness that comes from helping others. At the same time, one evolves. The low self is trained and learns rapidly to be more and more like the middle self. The middle self becomes more and more "trustworthy" day by day, and so approaches swiftly the time when it can graduate into the next level of consciousness and life to become a High Self.

One who succeeds in uniting frequently with the High Self, by means of the contact made by the low self along the aka cord, is symbolically "yoked" to the Lord High Self. Jesus, speaking again as and for the "Father," taught, "My yoke is easy, my burden is light," and so the kahunas also taught in respect to the man cleansed and able at will to unite with his High Self.

The three selves each have a different form of mentation. The low self does the remembering. The middle self cannot remember, but it can use reason to arrive at a proper understanding of what is going on about it. The High Self has a form of mental ability which seems to include the ability to remember, to use a reasoning power far superior to that of the middle self, and to be able to see into the past and into that part of the future which has become crystallized.

Because of these differences in ways of thinking, it is impossible for the low and middle selves to understand the High Self fully. The best we can do is to try to understand as fully as our limited minds will permit, and go ahead from there—loving the god-like High Self and serene in the knowledge that it loves us at all times, no matter what we do or fail to do, and stands always ready to respond to our call and to help us when asked to do so.

We, the lower selves, are alone responsible for any limitations placed on the amount of help which can be given.

CHAPTER VIII

MAKING THE PRAYER OF THOUGHT-FORM CLUSTERS

The basic concept of prayer in Huna is contained in a number of words familiar and significant to one initiated into the lore, but lacking special meaning to an outsider.

The "cup" that is filled to overflowing is one of the excellent symbols because a cup can represent the thought-form clusters of the thoughts which one makes use of in composing the prayer which is to be made by the low and middle selves and sent telepathically along the aka cord to the High Self.

The filling of the cup symbolizes the "answering" of the prayer by the High Self. Also, this allows a very good additional symbol of how it does the answering. In sending an accumulation of mana up along the aka cord to the High Self to carry telepathically the thought-forms which embody the prayer and make a cluster or "cup," the mana is symbolized as water rising in a fountain. When it reaches the High Self it is changed to the form of mist or a cloud, and is used to bring about the circumstances which will give the answer to the prayer. After the passage of sufficient time (unless the answer is instantly given) the condition appears as a physical reality. This is symbolized as a downpouring of rain drops from the High Self to fill the cup. (A fine use of this cup and rain symbol is to be found in the

97

modern version of the Tarot cards assembled by Waite and referred to as the "Pamela Smith set.")

In Egypt and especially in India, the cup was replaced by the golden lotus, which is in itself a cup. Because the lotus rises from the pool on a long stem (this standing for the aka cord) and because it is floated on the water (symbol of the low self mana) it serves well to illustrate the things necessary to prayer. The Huna meaning of the symbols became lost at some time or other, and in India today the lotus has other meanings —although the phrase, "Oh, the jewel in the lotus," used in mantrams, indicates the mana symbolized by rain or dew falling in drops to fill the cup.

The kahunas in the dim ages made very sure that the cup symbol would not be mistaken. They did this by adding together the words for "squirt water" and for "a cord" to give *ki-aha*, the word used still today for "cup." The water "squirted" up the aka cord to the High Self, as indicated in this symbol, is, of course, the surcharge of mana. The cord is the aka cord of connection. The cup itself is the matrix or mold or receptacle into which the High Self symbolically pours the rain of blessings, the answer to the prayer, just as one pours material into a mold to cast an image.

It is the repetition of these symbols used by the kahunas which has made it possible to learn the secret lore at this late date. They used several symbols to cover the same meanings, as a rule, and in this way made certain that the secret contained in them should not be lost through changes in words or understanding.

Whether or not the kahunas were right in their firm conviction that the High Self must be furnished with enough low mana to enable it to mold things or conditions on the level of the invisible future into "answers," we cannot say without testing their beliefs to see if they are practical. The same may be said of their idea that the middle self must make the "cup" or thought-form matrix as a preliminary step—that is, visualizing the conditions to be brought about, before asking the High Self to do its part. What we do know, however, quite beyond a doubt, is what the kahunas thought and believed and what they worked on as *basic methods in prayer*. Their symbols which they took such exceeding care to leave behind them in a high state of preservation have guaranteed that.

Another symbol which was used even oftener than that of the cup or the lotus was that of the "seed." The thought-forms were invisible and too small to be seen, veritable dust motes of thought, but they could be symbolized neatly as clusters of seeds which could be sent to the High Self on a mana flow along the cord.

Once a seed is planted, it must be watered and made to grow. The daily sending of a surcharge of mana to the High Self was symbolized as water to nourish the seeds sent to the High Self and planted in the invisible Garden of Eden where all good fruits mature (but where there is one tree which bears the fruit of the carnal knowledge of evil—the complex—and if the fruit of this tree is put *inside itself* by the low self, there follows the expulsion from the Garden, and the good fruit —the answer to prayer—is no longer to be had and enjoyed).

It is interesting to examine the hidden meanings which the kahunas placed in their word for seed, *ano-*

ano. Not only was this a seed in the ordinary sense, but in the roots it had the meaning of something which *changed the state of things or changed the present conditions.* This tells us exactly what the High Self does when a prayer is sent to it, as, for instance, asking that an injured leg be healed. The mental picture of the leg in the healed condition is made and sent telepathically as a prayer, and this picture is the "seed." It is also (according to one of the several different meanings hidden in the word *ano*) *a likeness or image of the desired condition.* It is the *meaning contained in the words of the prayer* as they are spoken aloud while the prayer is being sent at the same instant by the low self telepathically. It is *something set apart for a special purpose—consecrated.*

This same word for seed also is the word for "now," and because of this we can understand the strange practice advised by Jesus, "Ask, believing that ye have received it now." *The seed is the mental picture of the thing desired, NOT of the present imperfect condition.* And the picture of the perfect or healed or corrected condition has to be *seen* as the perfect condition when the seed is being made. It is a now-condition in the making. Or, we might put it this way: one cannot make a picture of the injured leg and send it to the High Self as the condition to be brought about. The desired future must be visualized as actually NOW present, even if only in the body of the thought-form picture "seed."

The major work of the kahuna was to make prayers which would get answers, be it slowly or instantly. The word "kahuna" contains a root-meaning that indicates the microscopic thought-forms which must be made as the first step in prayer. This meaning is that of "fine particles, as of dust." Dust is a good symbol because it rises when stirred, and lifts as though on the way to the High Self. The same root word also means to "conceal," and this was the great secondary duty of all kahunas—the concealment of the "Secret" lore.

To get ready to make a prayer was a very important step. One had to decide with great care what to pray for, and one had to make as complete, detailed and perfect a picture in his mind as possible of the condition desired to be brought about. The picture would be real and perfect, and as perfected NOW, even though the condition might not arrive until a later time. Getting ready was called *ho-ano*, or "making the seed," and it also had the meaning of "solemnizing the mind" as in making ready to worship, and of "beginning a daring venture." Prayer is the highest form of venture, if we are to accept the Huna view of it.

In our HRA work our first experiments with the making of the Huna-type prayer brought to light the fact that the average person has almost no idea of how to go about producing a clear mental picture. Letters were sent in, as part of the record, to tell what prayers were being offered. In about half of these, the sickness or other condition which was to be removed was included in the prayer, and so in the picture sent to the High Self. In the case of a chronic ailment, such as a broken bone that refuses to knit properly, one does not pray, "Heal my *injured* leg," for the reason that the mention of injury causes that to be a part of the picture or seed.

In a very short time we began to go back to elementary things in order to learn to make a picture that contained only the desired condition—only the picture of the leg in perfect condition NOW, that is, as existing NOW in the picture-seed-cup state as healed and perfect. This was very hard to do, it must be admitted, because in the memory of the low self all memories connected with the injury to the leg and its injured condition were tied in by the many "association" threads of aka substance. Even in making the new picture, one could only with the greatest difficulty avoid starting his thought train on anything except the injury in the leg.

Our Theosophists and those who had practiced the exercises in concentration, meditation and contemplation, had the advantage of those who had never taken time to practice the fine art of confining trains of ideas to one single track and making that track lead to one, and only one, goal.

Any memory of a thing or event will contain its appearance, taste, smell, feel, temperature, place in time and space, and its rational relation to all connecting events. From this we see that a good mental picture of a future condition should be made to have all these aspects. To learn how the mind works in this respect, one has but to pause a moment and begin to recall the events of a few hours past or a week, month or year past. The low self usually presents first the impressions made by the sense of sight, then along with the time-space setting will come sounds, smells, tastes, feel, and so forth.

It will be observed that the visual image leads all the rest. The eye is the most highly evolved of the sense organs, and it seems quite natural that sight images not only should come first, but also be favored by the low self as the communication method easiest to handle in telepathy. As we have pointed out in our discussion of telepathic communications between two persons, the sending of a mental *picture* has been found much simpler than the sending of an impression of sounds, even sounds symbolized in words.

In our dreams we will find that George habitually takes memories or thoughts or impressions of a number of events and changes them into terms of visual impressions. In this way we will have a piano to represent music, a dog to represent the idea of the sound of barking and growling, a plate of food to stand for the satisfaction of tasting things, and so on. George, also, seems to believe that "One picture is worth a thousand words." In trying to learn what George had in his mind in dreaming certain dream sequences, the psychoanalysts have long since discovered that one does well to find out what the things are which have been thus changed into visual symbols.

What this adds up to is the fact that the best way to settle down to the work of making the thought-form clusters of the prayer is to use *visual* pictures for the framework. To these may be added such other sensory impressions as may be clearly and vividly imagined. Some of the things desired to be brought about through prayer lend themselves much better than others to the use of a variety of sensory images. A prayer for a bountiful meal would include almost all of the senses, while one for a night of deep and profound sleep would not.

Words to embody the picture of the thing prayed for should be selected with the greatest care and rehearsed ahead of time. So many words have several meanings, and George is apt to picture the wrong thing if a word appears to him to have a meaning unlike the one planned for use by the middle self. If he follows the usual custom and makes visual pictures to replace the words, as in a case where one prays, "Give me health, wealth and happiness," his symbol for health may turn out to be a prize fighter who has recently impressed him; his picture of wealth may be the money vaults of the bank on the next street; and his picture of happiness may be that of a neighbor's small dog wagging its tail ecstatically at the approach of its mistress. If these jumbled pictures are sent to the High Self in the telepathic exchange, it is obvious that only a jumbled answer could be given—if any.

To avoid such a failure, the picture of the health condition should be worked on carefully with the low self, and long enough to result in a visual image of *oneself* in a state of perfect health, able to do and enjoy and accomplish the things that perfect health would make possible. In the same way the pictures should be made definite and clear and to the point for wealth, as it applies to one individually, and happiness as it applies. (Or, in praying for another, a like procedure must be followed.)

It is not for nothing that we have given such careful attention in the box practices and the use of the pendulum to getting well acquainted with the low self and its vagaries. One cannot know his own George too well. This is illustrated in the report of a famous English investigator of telepathy who tells of dividing his group into two parts, then sending half of the group out of the room to confer and decide upon what should be visualized to be sent telepathically to the other half of the group. In one case the group in conference went into a kitchen and looked about at objects on the mantel and elsewhere to select one to be used. A blue china plate was selected, but when the image of it was projected telepathically to the other half of the group, a surprising thing was observed. Not only the blue plate was picked up, but it was evident that the low selves of the sending group had also elected to send other things seen in the kitchen. The clock on the mantel and a figurine at a distance from the blue plate were seen and mentioned by the receivers, also a table with the chair beside it and even a picture of a hunt scene on the wall. In later tests it was found that by much and carefully repeated concentration on a single object, the low selves were brought to understand that the one item was to be sent, to the exclusion of what other things might have been observed in the room and which might have attracted the low selves.

A mental housecleaning is needed, as the above example shows, to sweep aside and throw out the thought-forms which get in the way of those things for which one plans to pray. In the same way that one takes his George into his confidence and explains ahead of time what is expected of him in the box or pendulum exercises, or in accumulating a surcharge of mana and using it, one must have a sufficient number of heart-to-heart talks with the low self to explain in detail every step of the prayer method which it is proposed to use.

It is taken for granted that each one of us has some desire, some hidden yearning toward better conditions that he feels he cannot bring about without help. Before formulating his prayer, it is imperative that he take a straight reasoning look at that desire. If it materializes as an answer to his prayer, it might easily entail added responsibilities which, when thought over carefully, might impress one as being too heavy to bear. The larger the blessing, the heavier the responsibility, is often the rule. Health may be the cheapest in terms of responsibility, although most of us when we pray for health are faced with doing something strenuous as our part of bringing about the health condition. We may have to exercise more and eat less—and the majority of people prefer mediocre health to having to "help God help oneself" in this manner.

Sanity and normalcy are needed in deciding what one may ask in prayer. The logical middle self cannot believe for a moment that there is a single chance that the moon will be given as a gift in answer to prayer, and what we cannot logically believe to be both possible and probable will not be given. Disbelief prevents the making of a perfect picture of the requested thing as given and in our hands, here and now. Also, what the middle self cannot logically accept as a belief, the low self certainly will not accept. Its belief is the substance of FAITH, and if it disbelieves, it will ruin the prayer picture even before it sends it to the High Self.

As FAITH will be mentioned frequently as we go along, it may be well at this point to explain that, to the Huna initiates, "faith" was NOT just the act of complete BELIEVING. The word for "faith" in the sacred language is *mana-a-io*. Its first meaning is "to believe," but the literal meanings as seen in the roots are: (1) "To use a surcharge of mana" (root *mana* plus root *io*, the latter meaning "excess" and pointing to the surcharge or "excess" of mana.) (2) "To call for a thing desired," and "to reach out or extend, as the hand to touch something." This shows that one must reach out along the aka cord to "touch" the High Self in order to ask for the thing desired. (All from the root *o*.) (3) "To be real" or, with causitive *hoo*, "to cause to become real." (Root *io*.)

"Faith, if it hath not works, is dead," becomes clear when we know that the "works" part includes the sending of the mana surcharge to the High Self as a part of the over-all work of having the prayer made into a reality.

An excellent practice when formulating a prayer is to imagine oneself projected ahead in time into the conditions for which we plan to ask. It will be discovered that a number of obligations appear. If one asks for a new car, then projects oneself into the future and takes over the car, starts to drive it and pay for its upkeep in money, it may be seen that money for the upkeep must be included in the request for the car. This, in its turn, demands that one ask for a means of earning more money, and greater earnings demand greater efforts and expenditures of time.

One of the HRAs who had written in to say that she and her young husband had decided, after careful consultation, to ask for a six-room house with nice furnishings and with a fine large car in the garage, ended by asking for a comfortable apartment in a convenient location and a good used car. They got both. They were very happy with them, and they had little trouble meeting the modest bills as they came in.

In Honolulu, one of the HRAs decided to try to help a young man who had lost the use of his legs through polio. The two agreed upon the plan to ask restoration of the legs, and eagerly began practicing to make the prayers as they should be made. All went well and the useless legs began to tingle and show signs of returning strength. Then the young man suddenly became panicked by the prospect of having to get out and make his own living. He gave way to fear, and overnight his legs were back in the old useless condition. He had neglected to project himself into the future as a daily preliminary exercise and so get used to the idea of again assuming the obligations of health and normalcy. It was never learned which was the more dismayed at the discovery that he was being healed, his middle self or his low self.

The man who shoulders his full responsibility in life (and this is the man always standing ready to help others) has perhaps the clearest path to the High Self, because through his feeling that he has done all he can, he has the essential confidence and faith in asking help in the things he cannot do alone. Once when riding a remote trail in Wyoming I came upon a lone man crouched behind a fence, mending it and—as far as I could see—talking to himself. I drew up and said something like, "It gets so you have to talk to yourself out here, does it?" He stood up, grinning, and explained, "Not exactly—but I've got so I pray a lot out here. I was praying the horses wouldn't get out." I said, "And mending the fence at the same time?" "Yep," he told me, "that's the best way to pray, seems to me. Can't leave the fences down, and then ask God to keep the horses in."

Another thing to be thought over before making the prayer: the High Self is never party to a theft. If you ask to be given your neighbor's house you will not get it. Or if you ask for another just like it, without expecting to make the necessary effort toward getting it, remember that it takes the labor of many men for many days to make such a house. It is more than probable that the High Selves of the laborers and builders would not be willing to see their men robbed of their pay so that another could possess a house simply for the asking.

If there is any law that we can deduce by the simple act of looking around us, it is that as one sows, so one reaps. No sowing, no reaping. I have repeatedly encountered the attitude which says in effect that God has everything in abundance and therefore should give each of us everything he wants for the asking. (This is generally accompanied by a resentful unwillingness to take care of one's self, or make any effort to contribute to the welfare of others—and accompanied often by a jealousy of the "good luck" observed in the lives of other people.) This is a belief that is denied by all the experiences of daily life, and an individual who holds it will indeed have trouble getting his prayer acted upon by a High Self who knows that his man has not earned, and does not deserve, the benefits for which he prays.

When, after careful consideration of everything related to the matter, one has decided upon the exact things to be prayed for (at least in so far as the middle

109

self reasoning is concerned), one should consult the low self seriously about the decision. One explains everything to George, giving the reasons why this and that would be good. It may be well to explain why earlier ideas were given up. The future should be described in the most glowing terms possible, to convince George that the things to be asked for are good to have.

With this priming of George, one then relaxes physically and mentally, inviting George to go along while one imagines the prayers answered and the new life in the new conditions being enjoyed. In this exercise lies the opportunity to watch as through half-closed eyes what the low self does—how it reacts when no pressure is brought to bear on it to like or dislike the life in the picture which is visualized.

The little vagrant waftings of emotion of like or dislike, worry or contentment, pleasure, fear, etc., will be the signals which show the reaction of the low self. If there seems to be an irrational emotional reaction to some condition that the middle self considers desirable, it may be possible to talk the matter over with the low self, visiting aloud and explaining in detail why the disliked or disturbing imagined condition would really be very good. When well advanced in the practice and after contact and confidence have been well established between the two selves, it may be possible to ask, "Does this situation remind you of something that bothered you once before? Can you give me a picture or a recollection of what it was?" By waiting, relaxed, the low self may push into the focus of the common center of consciousness the very thing that caused the original disturbed reaction. If this happens, it can then be discussed, and it may be pointed out with patient arguments and examples that the imagined future situation and the old one are quite different, and that nothing in the old situation should be laid at the door of the new.

The final consideration in planning to make the prayer is its relation to others around one, relatives, friends and business associates (if involved), even business or social rivals.

If one prays for his own good fortune, he has his own High Self waiting to help him. If he prays for the good fortune of the family group, he enlists the High Selves of the entire family. If he plans and prays for the betterment of a larger group, he soon—if he works hopefully and strongly in the chosen direction—will have the help of the *Poe Aumakua,* or "THE GREAT COMPANY OF HIGH SELVES."

The same principle holds true if one plans to ask help to do something that may work an injury or hardship on others—in which case the help of the High Selves of others may be turned to active obstruction. The love of the High Selves for their man is the perfect and selfless love of the higher level. No matter how low and backward a man may be in the evolutionary scale, his High Self longs to see him learn life's lessons and make progress. Help given unselfishly to "one of the least of these" will enlist the help of the High Self of the unfortunate man.

As insects learn the lesson of the hive, so mankind learns that by combining and working for the mutual good, much is to be gained. There is strength through uniting and serving a common interest in family, in tribe and in nations. We still have not learned to work to-

111

gether as nations, but that lesson is the next one up. Any prayer which includes good for others has its chances of being answered multiplied many fold.

A word must be said about the widespread belief that one must not pray for material things. In the major religions of India the belief in Karma prohibits the desire for material things, even for life itself. Prayer, as we know it, is not used. It would make more "bad karma" and bind one more tightly to the "wheel of rebirth." The individual tries to escape from life by ceasing to desire anything. (Karma, as most readers may know, is an ancient religious doctrine joined with the belief in reincarnation, or successive physical lives. In it the accumulation of good or bad, as earned in past lives, determines the conditions of succeeding lives.)

The kahunas of the Bible and those in Polynesia may be identified as products of the same initiation, because they took exactly the same stand on such matters as karma and reincarnation. If they were aware of the ideas then current in India, it is plain to see that they rejected the belief in almost endless trains of incarnations. They concentrated their attention on the problem of living the earthly life of the moment, with the help of the High Self, in the best possible way. While they believed in an after life in the realm of spirit, it was taken for granted that a life well lived on earth would result in fortunate conditions after death.

Because of the loss of the knowledge of the way to make the Huna prayer, and because of the subsequent failure to get sufficient results through the use of prayers, there arose in Christianity a doctrine of hopelessness in which it was taught that the ills of earthly life were to be borne with patience and resignation, while every effort was made to insure a happier life in heaven. The kahunas believed it to be right, as well as possible, to have a good and happy life both here and hereafter.

The words, "Seek ye first the kingdom of God and his righteousness and all these things shall be added unto you," have been misconstrued because Huna meanings behind those words and others like them were unknown. This misunderstanding, which tripped up so many HRAs when they started to think about making ready to pray, must be cleared for everyone. In the ancient lore, the kingdom of God, or of heaven, is the High Self symbolized as a higher plane. In a like manner, the kingdom of earth is occupied by the low self with its companion middle self.

To "seek the kingdom" means (1) to learn that there is a High Self, (2) to come to a rational belief in its existence and in the fact that it is willing and able to help us, and (3) to learn by practice to cause the low self to contact the High Self by means of the aka cord, and to present the mana and the prayer.

In the simple words of Huna, one may say, "First learn to contact the High Self in its level above you, and if you can do this successfully, your prayers can be delivered and all things which you can gain through the use of prayer will be given you."

John the Baptist cried out that the kingdom of heaven was at hand. It is obvious that he did not mean that higher levels had come down to mingle with lower levels. What he meant, as a kahuna, was that the High Self was close at hand waiting for us to make the contact with it. But, warned John, it was necessary to re-

113

pent one's sins before the contact could be made. We must never forget that the making of amends for hurts done others is necessary before we can be rid of the feeling that we are unworthy to face the High Self—before the low self will give up its sense of shame and face the High Self across the length of the aka cord.

The old idea that one should give up living the normal life, or should sit with folded hands expecting God to know what we need and to supply our wants, is, emphatically, not Huna. Nor is it rational or even tinged with common sense. We are not put here to bend all our efforts toward getting out of the earthly life without living it and learning by our experience. We are put here to live and love and grow and progress. Exercise develops the muscles. Use develops the intellect. We have been given free will to be used, not to be discarded while we try to lay the responsibility for living entirely upon the High Self.

CHAPTER IX

CONTACTING THE HIGH SELF AND PRESENTING THE PRAYER

Some of the HRAs still wished to bypass the low self in prayer, still wanted to believe that their conscious reasoning middle selves could contact their High Selves directly, "if only we knew the way." When we began the work of translating passages from the Bible back into the "sacred language," it was the chief interest of these people that I find explicit directions for this way. One of them wrote as follows:

"I am sure the key lies in the words, 'Ask and it shall be given you. Seek and you shall find. Knock and it shall be opened unto you.' Do translate these phrases back into Hawaiian and see if there isn't something there that will tell us how to go about contacting the High Self directly."

The passage was investigated at once.

"Ask" means only "ask" in Hawaiian. No key there. But with "seek" and "knock" it was different.

In Huna, "seek" is *i-mi*. The roots give us the meaning of "begetting" or planting the seed-picture, and of pouring out water, the symbol of mana. In other words, when one has made his picture of the desired conditions, which must be sent on a flow of mana over the aka cord, it is then time to "seek" out and find the symbolic "kingdom of heaven," or the High Self, where the seed is to be planted and watched over by the "Lord" of that realm.

"Knock" is *kikeke*, which has the secret meaning of "to divide," and this is the symbol of dividing the surcharge of mana by sending part of it across the aka cord to the High Self.

The "door" which is to be opened when one "knocks" by sending the mana flow, as one "seeks" by making the "seeds" (or thought-forms) of the prayer and setting them floating on the mana flow, is called *puka*, in Hawaiian. This word means *to change something from one condition to another*, which tells us in Huna terms that the door is opened to the High Self, who alone can change conditions in answer to prayer.

I translated many other passages in the Bible concerning prayer. Jesus discussed very openly the matter of the need for prayer, but described the secret Huna elements and methods in words which only a student kahuna could understand in their inner meanings. The sixth chapter of Matthew is a source of much information concerning the Huna-type prayer, provided, of course, one knows enough of the secret meanings in advance to understand what is set forth.

Verse 1. "Take heed that ye do not your alms before men, to be seen of them, otherwise you have no reward of your Father which is in heaven."

The key here is in the word "alms," which in Hawaiian is made up of the roots *mana-wa-lea*. This tells us that what is given as "alms" is mana, and that it is presented to the High Self while we are using our mind (*wa*) in thinking-reflecting and reasoning, and that when we have presented the gift of mana while thinking carefully to send the thought-forms of the prayer, there comes pleasure (*lea*). The "alms" are not to be given openly to or before men, because they are gifts of mana given inwardly along the aka cord to the Father. The warning is appended, "otherwise ye have no reward of your Father."

Verse 2 is not pertinent to Huna, and verse 3 only repeats the assertion that prayer is a giving of mana, and therefore an inward action, not outward.

Verse 4. "That thine alms may be in secret, and thy Father which seeth in secret himself shall reward thee openly."

Another word for "secret" in Hawaiian is *nalo*, and its meaning is "hidden or concealed or invisible." It also has the meaning of the High Self when it "disappears in the distance and cannot be seen." Again we have the fact that the action is inward, and that the High Self may be at a distance and never seen, but that it may be contacted through the aka cord by sending the mana and thought-forms telepathically.

Verse 5 and verse 6 repeat the instructions to pray inwardly. Verse 7 warns against the mistaken belief that the High Self hears actual words, no matter how loudly they are spoken. Verse 8 adds a little more of the Huna secret in, "for your Father knoweth what things ye have need of before you ask him." In Hawaiian the word "need" is *pono*, which has the meaning also of having reformed, having made amends for hurts done others, having done the needful things before being "justified" and rendered ready to make the prayer.

This meaning puts an entirely different light on the difficulty mentioned earlier as one tripping up those

117

HRAs who asked why one must make a definite picture of what was desired to come to pass in answer to the prayer. They had argued that if all our needs were known before we could pray, then why pray? But, if it had not been necessary to pray, Jesus would not have told why and how prayer was to be performed, or who would answer the prayers and under what conditions. The High Self, without doubt, knows even better than the lower selves what the whole man needs, but does not override free will to interfere and give it instead of letting the lessons of experience be learned in the efforts to get needed things.

Our needs are known, but Huna tells us the further secret that unless we come to prayer only after having made amends and setting our house in order, our prayer will be of no use.

Pono is a very useful word in Huna. It has still another meaning of importance: it means to have everything properly done and put in correct form and order. This applies to the making of the thought-form pictures especially. They must be right, they must be for the good of all concerned, and they *must be of things possible to attain*—otherwise they are NOT *pono*.

In the verses which follow, known as the "Lord's Prayer," one has to pause to see what visual or mental pictures are required to turn the words of each phrase into a thought-form picture which could be sent telepathically to the High Self, and so be used as a seed or mold in creating the answer to the prayer.

It becomes immediately apparent that no such thought-form picture is intended in the opening line. It is simply a directive to show that the prayer should be addressed to the High Self who is looked upon with reverence by the lower selves.

"Thy kingdom come, thy will be done, on earth as it is in heaven," gives us through the outer and root meanings of the sentence translated into Hawaiian, "High Self, allow me to make contact with you, and to give you mana to be used to make the thought-form picture I give become a reality on the earth plane, just as the picture is now a reality on the level of thought-pattern-seed molds where you are." (The key words are "kingdom" or *au-puni* with its root meanings, then "come" or *e hiki mai* with seven different additional general Huna meanings and many more of significance hidden in the roots. "Will be done" is, in Hawaiian, keyed in the words *malamaia* and *makemake*, from the roots of which one finds that the "will" is "desire," and that such a desire creates, symbolically, by "causing something to swell, enlarge or grow"—which gives us again the "seed" or thought-form picture of the prayer.)

Verse 11. "Give us this day our daily bread," hinges on the play on words met in the Old Testament in which manna fell from heaven to nourish the Israelites —again a symbol rather than a historical fact. It was the mana, the vital force, the "bread of life" or the "water of life"—there were a number of symbols for the three manas of the kahunas. In this case the mana was the same as that which "fell from heaven" in the Biblical accounts. The mana sent to the High Self is of the low self, earth, earthly, but when it is returned by the High Self, it becomes "rain" or "manna"—a blessed nourishment. It is also the help and guidance and protection which can be offered only by the High

Self, and then only if it is allowed to have its full part in the life of the man. The low mana must be given to the High Self with the daily prayers, if work is to be done by it on the physical plane.

Verse 12. "And forgive us our debts, as we forgive our debtors" does not refer to the sins of hurt for which one must make amends and be set free inwardly before the prayer can begin. This refers to a different kind of sin—one of "missing the mark" or of failing to make complete contact with the High Self and get the prayer correctly made because of another grade of sin: the fixed or complexed tangles of unrationalized memory clusters lodged in the aka body of the low self. We shall be helped to get cleared of these, or "forgiven," if we help others to get free. This is a matter which will be taken up at a later time. Just now we are dealing with the normal condition in which the path is not blocked badly by complexes. (In verse 14 the same important idea is stressed.)

Verse 13. "And lead us not into temptation, but deliver us from evil; for thine is the kingdom, and the power, and the glory, forever. Amen," becomes "Do not cause the aka cord to be loosened (symbol of inability of the low self to make the contact with the High Self), or let us be caught in a snare (of threads—symbol of the complex), for we know that you are kind and perfect and beautiful and will always be so." "Amen" covers the definite ending of the work of sending a prayer.

It will be noted that, after a study of the Huna meanings hidden in the Lord's Prayer, we find that this is really not at all a form of prayer to be used as such in the Huna sense. It is a Huna formula listing the elements involved in prayer-making, and the steps which have to be taken. It contains almost nothing that corresponds to the thought-form picture, "seed" or "cup" of the actual prayer—these things are left to the individual to set about providing for himself according to his own needs.

So we did not find the "short-cut" to contact with the High Self for which we had searched. But we did find startling confirmation of the Huna method of approach to prayer. We were more than content to go on making our careful thought-form picture, getting George to understand and co-operate, accumulate the surcharge of mana, and send the prayer along the aka cord to the High Self.

Is there any way of knowing (lacking the intuitional "knowing") when we have made the successful contact with the High Self? Here are some physical sensations reported by the HRAs:

(1) A tingling sensation in all or part of the body. Some feel this as if it were raining a fine tingling electrical downpour from the High Self. Some feel it as a tingling in hands, or along the spine or in the genitals, or even through all the body down to the toes. This sensation may last a second or for a full minute or more. It usually leaves a fine sensation of wellbeing.

(2) A sudden great upsurging of mixed emotions of joy and love and worship. It is an emotion one cannot arouse at will, but which comes from the low self as the evidence of its joyous reaction when able to contact the High Self. (The kahunas believed that only the low self can create emotions, be they hate, fear or anger,

love or desire, but that once the emotion is created, it can be given to the middle self to share.)

(3) The last of the three sensations experienced by the HRAs upon making contact with the High Self, is a strange little feeling that comes in the solar plexus—from whence the aka cord probably goes up or out to the High Self. The same spot or part in the body, we are told by the kahunas, is the center of the low self mental-memory-mana activities. The same type of sensation is felt in "protruding a finger" of aka substance to contact something close at hand, or in sending a flow of mana across an aka thread or cord already connecting one's low self to the low self of another. Once one has learned to recognize this feeling, it will serve as a signal that the contact with the High Self is as complete as the blocked or unblocked condition of the aka cord will allow at the time. In addition to this sensation there is frequently one of having cobweb strands laid over the face or neck or hands.

What may be called the transcendent experience of contact with the High Self comes usually but once or twice in a lifetime. Suddenly the unseen doorway is silently entered by the low self and the contact is made. The mana is presented by the low self, and the whole man is flooded with joy. He may see the white light that forms as the High Self accepts the flow of mana and converts it into the vibration of light. He has an experience which will remain as a sacred memory and a conviction of verity for the rest of his days. Usually when this blessed reuniting takes place as the long absent Prodigal Son comes home to the Father in his house, all thought of asking for something is forgotten. It is enough, for that moment, to be at home again and to feel the joy of contact. But the comings and goings of the reformed prodigal soon become natural and regular. No longer is the fatted calf killed, and no longer are new garments brought to be laid on ragged shoulders.

However, if none of these sensations is felt for a time, one keeps trying for contact, always with a preliminary surcharging of mana. One holds ready the picture of the desired condition. But first there is a ritual before we present the prayer. The middle self does its part by meditating on and affirming love for the High Self, which the low self builds into powerful emotion. The middle self directs the drive toward the High Self until the contact is made. The *gift* of mana is then made to the High Self for its own high purposes of service and world betterment.

After that, the command is held over the low self to send on the continuing mana flow the picture we have so carefully built of what we wish to have brought to pass for us.

To make a precise and clear picture, the kahunas often composed a short prayer describing what was wanted in exact but brief detail. They repeated it three times in succession to make very sure that the picture remained the same and stood out clear and strong. They spoke aloud, as if addressing the High Self, knowing that the low self was carrying the picture along the aka cord to the High Self.

One well-made prayer may be sufficient, provided the one making the prayer is experienced and gifted with unusual skill. For most of us, the whole prayer action needs to be repeated daily until the answer is given. If the need is very urgent, one may "pray without ceasing," or as often as one can be rested and accumulate fresh mana.   There seems to be no limit to the ability of the High Self to bring about changes in conditions. Everything seems to depend on the amount of mana made available to the High Self, provided, of course, that the picture is well made.

Two people who are completely agreed on what the picture is to be, may work together, pooling their mana and asking their High Selves to work together to bring about the healing or changing of any condition or circumstance.   When one of the pair is ill and weak and lacking in mana, the one in good health can help greatly by supplying the needed mana to go with the prayer.

But not all of our prayers concern improvement in health or conditions.   Many of them are for guidance in a decision to be made, or a course of action to be undertaken.   We need *ideas* as an answer, not physical things that will be materialized.   How are the answers to be communicated from the High Self to us?

In *The Secret Science Behind Miracles* I told of how one man I knew well, "the elevator builder," described his sensations on contacting his High Self, and also how he received his guidance.   He said that on contact he felt or heard a sharp "ting-a-ling," as if an electric bell had buzzed inside him.   Three times each day he paused to reach out mentally for contact with the High Self which he had learned was there, even though he did not know just what it was, and always there was this signal when contact was made.   He relaxed mentally when it came, and waited.   If there was some danger to him or his men who were working under him, he would get a warning "hunch," and would be on guard. He might sense the danger as large or small, or close or distant in the matter of time. As the event drew near he would repeat his contact more and more frequently, often being given a mental picture of where to go to await the danger and, by being on guard, prevent injury or accident to his workmen, to himself or to the structure.

Neither from the kahunas nor from the work of the HRA have we been able to decide what form of communication is used by the High Self to give messages or guidance to the lower selves. Communications seem to come by way of the aka cord and the low self, when sent by the High Self, but the low self has a strong tendency to deliver the message in terms of symbols, or in the form of combined pictures with accompanying sound or other sensory impressions. These symbolic messages are very definite, and often come in a vivid dream. But the individual must learn to know and watch for dream messages of this type and from this source.

The High Self, as named in the word *Akuahaiamio,* or "the god who speaks silently," is indicated as one able to give an auditory impression of spoken words through the low self. This "still small voice" is the ideal communication, if one can get it. But few can, and these few are seldom able to be entirely sure that it is the High Self speaking and not imagination, or that what they hear said is not colored or changed by the low self as it delivers the message.

Perhaps the most common communication from the High Self comes in what the kahunas called the "rising of a thought in the mind." Experience tends to strengthen the belief that the High Self can cause thoughts to arise in our minds, perhaps by passing along seed ideas through the low self so that we feel that we have thought of things ourselves, but actually are getting ideas sent to us to give the needed guidance. This has been called "inspiration" when used in great art, or achievements which seem to transcend the human possibilities. Or, you will hear your friend say, "I had a hunch." Or perhaps, "I was impressed" to do this or that.

After an earnest prayer to the High Self, when a "thought rises in the mind" with clarity and compulsion anent the subject of the prayer, it should be accepted as an answer, and acted upon.

CHAPTER X

SUMMARY OF THE HUNA PRAYER METHOD

Because so much has had to be presented to make the Huna methods and concepts clear, it may be well at this point to review the several steps which are to be taken in making an effective prayer.

Before attempting the serious business of making the prayer, it is assumed that:

(a) One has become well acquainted with his low self, has found out something of its likes and dislikes, has established a teacher-pupil relationship with love, understanding and quiet discipline, and has made the low self understand that it is to take orders from the middle self.

(b) The low self has been taught to develop its own special talent for telepathy. It is experienced in sending thought-form clusters along the aka cords at the direction of the middle self.

(c) The low self has been taught to accumulate a surcharge of mana. If this has been done by means of exercises and careful testing, then a command to the low self to accumulate the surcharge should be enough, when one approaches the prayer time.

THE PRAYER STEPS

PREPARATION BEFORE MAKING THE PRAYER

1. Amends must be made for hurts done others. Or,

if this cannot be done directly, good deeds, gifts to charity and fasting will help convince the low self (as well as the middle self) that the books have been balanced, and that one is now deserving of help from the High Self.

2. One will have decided upon what is to be asked for, making certain that it is for the good of all concerned, and of hurt to no one. One will have projected himself into the future and imagined himself living in the new conditions. He will have made very sure that the low self is in full agreement that the desired condition is truly desirable, and worth the work necessary to bring it about. He also will have considered and accepted any additional responsibility the granting of the request may entail.

3. The plan will be made for a series of daily prayers on the same subject, always formulating the prayer in exactly the same way.

The instant or miraculous answer seems to require a very large amount of mana to enable the High Self to bring about the changes required on the physical plane. It is the exceptional individual who will be able to accumulate a sufficient mana surcharge and offer it with a sufficiently well-made picture of the desired conditions to get instant or nearly instant answers. Also, it must be remembered that some problems, especially those which involve the lives of others, take additional time to work out through a gradual change in circumstances.

4. Three or four unrelated things should not be presented in the same prayer action. For instance, suppose one wants perfect health, new work that is pleasant and useful, friends, and also the healing of an ill relative.

It is best to present each in a separate prayer, spaced at least an hour apart, after practicing a vivid visualization of each one in turn.

5. Visualize the end results which are desired, and do not be too specific as to how they should be brought about. This leaves the High Self free to bring about the desired condition in its own way.

It must never be forgotten that the High Self is the "Utterly Trustworthy Parental Spirit," and that it knows best what is good for its man. It cannot be forced or commanded to do what would be the wrong thing, by answering a prayer for something that would bring the wrong conditions, either for its own man or another. One does not try to compel the High Self to answer a prayer, nor "storm the gates of heaven" by following the very modern practice of affirming with all possible command of will that some set of desired circumstances is appearing as an actuality, here and now, whether they are good for all or may be hurtful to some. One asks, as of a living Father, that the prayer be accepted and acted upon—always with the proviso that it is something good and fitting and proper to be brought about.

6. One will have taken time to practice long enough so that a swift and easy contact can be made with the High Self at any time, even though a prayer is not made. Such practice is simple. There should first be an accumulation of a surplus of mana, then a quieting down and meditating on the nature of the High Self, the fact that it is veritable, and that it is always waiting, willing and anxious to be asked to take its full part in the job of living the happy and successful and helpful life. Its

love for its man and one's love for it will always be the central themes in every meditation, for one must arouse an emotional response of love in the low self—a response which can be felt and shared by the conscious self. This love is the magnetic force which draws the low self to make the contact with the High Self, and to desire to make its gift to it in the form of a sending of mana across the aka cord of connection.

Love ever desires to give and to serve, and the ideal gift from the lower man to the High Self is mana. Such a gift, given freely and without a prayer attached to the giving, is the ideal offering. It makes it possible for the High Self to bring about such things on the physical level of life as one may desire to help to accomplish. Through the High Self one can, with such gifts, help to bring needed assistance to others, even to serve on a world scale.

MAKING THE PRAYER

1. The picture of the thing to be asked in prayer is reviewed and brought clearly to mind. Nothing must be added or taken away from it after the first prayer of any series has been made, unless the High Self is asked to drop the entire prayer and begin afresh for some good reason.

2. Faith must be reaffirmed if anything has come up to weaken it between the sessions of prayer. A strong affirmation of faith is often needed each day before the prayer begins.

It is unwise to tell others what one is praying for, because if others thoughtlessly express doubts as to the outcome, the faith and confidence of the suggestible low self may be shaken. Such a suggestion of doubt needs much contrary affirmation of faith to counteract it. There must be a determination from first to last not to allow the slightest doubt of the final outcome to get a foothold in the mind. If necessary, special additional prayers for the strengthening of faith and confidence may be made.

3. The surcharge of mana is accumulated and the low self is told to hold it ready for the moment when contact is made with the High Self and the gift of mana can be made.

4. Sufficient meditation on the High Self is made (the body relaxed and easy whether standing, sitting or reclining) to arouse the emotion of love for the High Self in the low self.

The low self, having learned that the reason for meditation is to focus the thoughts and to allow it to make its contact with the High Self, will soon learn to respond with love and to make the contact almost immediately, also to start sending the gift of mana for that particular moment of prayer. There may come, as the gift is completed, a rush of the emotion of love and happiness which is the response of the loving Parental High Self. There may also be the sensation of prickling or tingling, which the kahunas spoke of as the "rain" or fall of mana changed to higher frequency and sent to bless the lower man. Or one may soon learn to know that contact has been made by some sensation or "signal" peculiar to himself.

5. Once the feeling of having made contact with the

High Self is noted, the low self is asked to send the prayer picture (thought-form cluster) on a flow of additional mana by the telepathic means.

The kahunas made it a practice to voice their prayer by describing the desired condition while recalling it as clearly and vividly to mind as possible. They memorized the short description, word for word, and recited it three times over, as a means of strengthening the "seed" while sending the mana to "water" it. The memorization of the description, after writing it out with thought and care, will have impressed the prayer picture on the low self very strongly and clearly.

6. When the picture has been described aloud or in silence, if speaking aloud is impractical, the prayer is ended with the same purpose and precision as it was begun.

One may simply say, "I give thanks, loving Father, and I now leave the prayer picture in your hands to build into physical reality in the future, just as it is already a reality on your level of being. Let the rain of blessings in the form of the High Mana of Light fall. I now withdraw from contact. The prayer period is finished. Amen."

7. The prayer, once made, is to be released into the keeping of the High Self until next time contact is made and fresh mana is to be offered, together with a restatement or additional strengthening layer for the original seed picture.

SPECIAL NOTES

Most of us have fallen into a very slack habit, early in life, of hurrying our prayers. We do this when half asleep as children, and the habit has a tendency to cling and cause us to voice empty words of prayer which are entirely useless. Another slack habit is that of drifting off into prayer and sleep. If prayer is to be effective, it must be made in orderly fashion and with eagerness, drive, and a strongly awakened and moving love. It is the will of the middle self which directs and controls the work, and this force is not exerted unless the conscious self is alert and is concentrating its full attention as it directs each step and superintends the low self in the part it is to play.

Another very bad habit is that of carrying all the doubts, fears and worries of the moment with one into the prayer period. Such things must be laid aside firmly so that faith may be reaffirmed and serenity reached for the meditation approach. Once one has learned to make easy prayer contact with the High Self, one may find it well to make the mana gift, then to affirm that this worry, or that, is being laid aside or given up completely. After the letting go of such worries, one then may make a simple verbal request (depending on the low self to send the thought-forms of the request to the High Self), such as, "Father, I have put away this thing which has bothered me. I now ask that you forgive and cleanse it away."

It has been the experience of the HRAs that a short period taken up with this letting go and getting assistance from the High Self to clear away the worries and angers and fretful moods of the day or hour, is often of great and lasting value. Such a cleansing of the low and middle self may be undertaken at any time, whether a full prayer is to follow or not.

There is work that needs to be done in the interim between prayer actions. The normal course of the series of prayers, when made Huna-fashion, is similar to the creative process we know so well on the physical level. First the seed is produced, and may be likened to the mental picture which embodies the prayer desire. The seed then needs to be kept watered and guarded with care for a proper period of growing time. We send the daily supply of mana to "water" the seed and the plant that grows from it. In due time comes the answer to the prayer in the form of the harvesting of the fruit of the plant. This seems to be a universal way of bringing things about. The egg is fertilized, cared for, and it hatches. The chick is then cared for and becomes a grown fowl. The seed or the egg, or the thought-form picture of the desired condition, cannot be changed once it has been selected—otherwise it could never produce the thing desired from it.

That is why a series of prayers, with the seed-picture carefully kept from change, once it is given to the High Self, must continue day by day until the harvest appears. The progress may be apparent to one during the growing period. One may see the gradual betterment from day to day before the full healing may be said to have arrived.

Just as one must live in the desired result when the prayer is made, so, when one thinks of the prayer and the desired outcome, it must be thought about as something already as real as the plant in the seed, the chick in the egg. This is as true a reality as either the ear of corn on the grown plant, or the chick when hatched and grown. The difference is in the time that must be given for the growth, not in the basic reality. Understanding this, one can think of the desired condition as being already a reality without insulting one's reasoning powers or intelligence.

Another essential thing to be done at all times from the making of the first prayer-action up to the time when the complete answer is given, is to take all possible steps on the physical plane to help bring about the desired condition. "God helps those who help themselves" is especially true here. Common sense and straight thinking win out. The idea embodied in the words, "Serene I fold my hands and wait," is not applicable when it comes to effective prayer. The three selves are partners in living, and each partner must do his utmost to bring about desired conditions.

Prayer, rightly and effectively made, is not a degrading business of begging. It is first a becoming worthy, and second, a building with all the power of reason and experience that can be mustered by the middle self. Third, it is an act of creation in which all three selves play their allotted part.

The past is beyond change. The present is slipping from our grasp. But the future is ours to mold in every way. With the great kahunas of old we can rise and exultantly cry, "Behold, I make all things new!"

Making new is making *hou* in the language of the initiates. See what secret steps the word reveals in its secondary meanings:

(a) *Hou*: "to make new." (To create the new conditions through prayer and work and planning.)

(b) "To extend, or reach from one place to another." (Symbol of the aka cord, and of making the contact.)

(c) "To soak with water." (Symbol of supplying mana to water the "seed.")

(d) "To repeat any act, to do over, do again." (Symbol of the repetition of the prayer daily so that the mana may be supplied, the picture held clear and firm and strengthened, in order that all things of the future can be "made new.")

CHAPTER XI

HEALING BY LAYING ON OF HANDS

In the Old Testament the laying on of hands was not used for healing, but as a part of the ritual or ordination. When the Levites were to be ordained as the priestly family to serve before the altars for all the people, the people themselves gathered and placed their hands on them as a part of the ordination rite. Following this, and all down the Christian centuries, the same rite has been used, but priests and prelates have been the ones to lay on the hands, not the congregation, as in the Mosaic times. This is, however, in line with the recorded command to Moses that he pass on to Joshua, as a new leader of a still later period, a "part of his honor," and that this was to be done through the laying on of hands.

In a less definite way we find the hands being placed on the head of one who is to be blessed. Food and drink were likewise blessed, and the hands placed over the food and drink. The implication is that in these rites there was thought to be something invisible but real transferred from the hands to the person or things thus treated.

Ordination could be a transfer of mana to carry a set of thought-forms to the low self of the one ordained. Or, by touch, an aka cord could be established between the one to be ordained and the one ordaining him. One in full contact with his own High Self might, presumably, be able to retain contact with the newly ordained priest and in this way have a means of keeping touch with him and helping him in his new work.

In Acts 6:6 we find that seven converts were selected to be sent to carry the new Christian ministry to other places, and that these were ". . . set before the apostles, and when they had prayed, they laid their hands on them." In 13:3 the same thing was done concerning the sending of other ministers, but with a slight difference in that they fasted as well as prayed before the laying on of hands as the final act of ordination. As fasting was part of the work of making general and impersonal amends in order to remove "sins" or the sense of guilt lodged in the low self, it is probable that the ones to be ordained also fasted, and that the aim of this work was to help them to clear their aka cords of complexes (something we shall take up later), and to make a full and complete contact with their High Selves. (This contact signaled the descent of the "Holy Ghost" which was the High Self.)

Jesus healed many times by laying on of hands. Also it is recorded that he touched the one to be healed, as in taking the hand of one to be raised from the dead; and at times he was touched, as in the instance in which the touch was only on the hem of his robe, but still was felt. In his comment, "I felt the virtue go out of me," we have further evidence of the belief hidden behind physical contact, that something was transferred from one to another and that it had definite healing power of a high order.

In the Early Church, healing was performed by laying on hands, and prayer. In some of the churches in modern times the same methods are used, but the Huna secret behind prayer and of the use of the mana has long been lost.

Not only in the churches did the laying on of hands play a large part in the direct healing, but in a similar way, without prayer, the "natural healers" of the many centuries plied their art. In many religions hands were laid on the sick, with or without prayer and with or without the use of holy water, fetish or chanting. In later centuries the "magnetic healer" appeared, convinced that he could draw a force from magnets into his own body and then transfer through his hands that same force to heal his patients.

The kings of a certain age and in certain parts of the world came to be credited with the power of healing through the touch of their hands—the "royal touch." The priests of Holy Church blessed cloths and amulets to endow them with healing powers when worn on the bodies of the sick.

With the discovery of mesmerism, which was an enlarged use of the force believed to be derived from magnets at first, but which was later known to be resident in the human body, "animal magnetism" healing by direct contact received a great impetus and a new school of healing developed rapidly in Europe. These early "magnetizers" did their healing work by means of the laying on of hands or by a contact through passes, the gaze of the eyes, or strokings. It is evident that they were able to cause mana to flow from them into the body (and so into the low self and its aka body) of the patient, and provide the life force to be used in correcting or healing.

Down through the ages the hand has been accepted as a symbol of power. Isaiah, whose utterances give every evidence of coming from a kahuna, had this to say in Chapter 40, verse 10: "Behold the Lord God will come with strong hand, and his arm shall rule for him." The word "hand" was inserted by the translators of the King James version, as indicated by italics (which was their practice when they thought such a word clarified the meaning). However, translating the passage into the "sacred language," we see that hand and arm have the same word, *lima*. When they spoke of one they could mean both or either.

But, as we delve further, we find that the secret of the direct healing by laying on of hands is hidden in the word for fingers, not the word for arm-hand. "Fingers" were *mana-mana*, which is a doubling of the basic word *mana*, and which doubles its strength, making from the low mana of the low self, the more commanding and powerful mana or "will" used by the middle self to control and direct the low self. *Mana-mana* also has the meaning of "to divide" or "to branch out," and while the fingers are formed by a dividing and branching out of the hand-end of the arm, this tells the basic and all important fact that the mana must also be "divided" in direct healing. It must be provided as a surcharge by the low self of the healer, and must be divided so that both the middle self and the low self may have enough to enable them to do their part in the healing. The final division is made by dividing with the sick person. Thus it is clear that it is the mana directed through the hands that all healers are using, whether they know it or not, in their work of healing by laying on of hands. (If prayer also is used, the Lord High Self must be given a share of the mana.)

After the magnetic healers, another school of healers arose, using suggestion in connection with the use of the vital force. Suggestion is the implanting of an idea, telepathically or by the spoken word, into the low self of the patient. Suggestion was supposed to have replaced all "animal magnetism," but the latter—the vital force or mana—still played a very definite part in such efforts. Almost no treatment in healing is without some element of suggestion, no matter whether it is suggestion intentionally given or not. The patient is usually receptive, desiring to be healed, and is more than willing to see in every manipulation or medication the probability that it will bring restoration to normal.

The kahunas always administered suggestion in mild form to their patients, while projecting mana through their hands. It may be well to give here a brief résumé of a kahuna's healing practices as seen and reported during the last fifty years before the turn of the century. They were the trained therapists of their day, working with all three selves of man.

They first took care that they had cleansed the patient of any sense of guilt left in the low self as a result of hurts done others or done against their own bodies by excesses. They made sure that the complex and the obsessional influences were also cleared away. (We shall discuss this in full later.) With such preparations made, they accumulated very large charges of mana, built the strong picture of the healed condition, and presented it to the High Self in asking for aid. Then they laid hands on the patient, often with some massage of any sick or injured part, sending in the mana and the strongly "willed" or charged thought-form clusters of the healed condition, and waiting with more and more mana being made available, for the High Self to set to work and make the healing complete.

When in the course of the treatment they wished to implant a suggestion, they did so by giving the patient at the same time a "physical stimulus." This was something which could be seen, tasted, felt, or otherwise sensed by the low self of the patient, and which, for that reason, made the suggestion much more powerful. For instance, they washed their patients briskly with water, sprinkled and scrubbed on with bundles of green *ti* leaves, the while assuring them that they were being cleansed of all the guilts left over after making careful amends for hurts done others, as well as of their ills.

While our aim in the HRA was always toward contacting the High Self, we decided to test the matter of healing by laying on of hands for minor ailments, using only that part of the kahunas' whole method of healing which is described above. We wished to make the test because we knew that many healers have produced results in healing by laying on the hands without recourse to prayer. We felt prepared to attempt this experiment because we had had time to train our low selves to obedience to our commands to accumulate a surcharge of mana, and how to send on it the thought-form picture we had prepared.

We followed the kahunas' method when we prepared

142

to heal ourselves or someone else, solely with the laying on of hands technique. We commanded the low self to accumulate a surcharge of mana, and to concentrate it in the hands while we made a strong mental picture of the healed condition. The mana and the picture were sent on command out of the hands and poured into the patient. An addition to this technique was tried by some. That was to reinforce the suggestion or straight command to the low self to bring about the healed condition, by using a physical stimulus as the kahunas had done. A salve or ointment was rubbed on the part being treated, or heat applied, or cold compresses, or friction or manipulation. But whatever was used, care had to be taken to make a strong picture of it in action to help along the healing.

One may speak aloud and repeat with "willed" firmness, a number of times, the command to bring about the healed condition. Such commands must be made so that they leave out all mention of the illness or defective condition. It is to be well remembered that one does not say to the low self, "Use this mana which I am pouring from my fingers into the *sore knee* to heal the *bruise.*" Instead, one says, "Take the surcharge of mana flowing into the knee and cause the knee to become perfect and strong and good and completely normal." I emphasize again that the thought-form clusters must never include the very thing we wish to get rid of, but must contain only the mental or aka molds of the desired normal condition.

The reports on the experiment that came in to me were rather astonishing. It seems that most of us have vastly more natural healing ability than we have ever imagined. Headaches vanished under direct treatment, pain eased off, fevers died down, strength returned, peace of mind was restored. The general tone or harmony of mana vibration seems to be improved by the gift of mana and strong healing mental pictures from the one who is healthy, and who acts the part of the healer.

Most people have never tried to heal, and so do not have the slightest idea what we can do with just a little practice. Every mother and father should help their children or members of the family in this way. Nor are physical ills alone to be treated. All hurts of an emotional kind will quickly respond. Mana with love cancels fear and anger. Courage can be greatly strengthened, and the entire mood of a child can be swiftly changed for the better. Restlessness can be turned aside, and relaxation and comfort and sleep can be induced. Pets respond to such treatments, and plants and trees have furnished excellent evidence of what love and mana can do when administered to them through the hands. The possibilities are endless.

Some doctors among the HRAs joined in the tests made of this healing method, and the ones—such as the Osteopaths and Chiropractors—who, in their customary therapy, place their hands directly on the patient, have had remarkable success in the use of the direct healing methods. Often they have used them as a part of their regular adjustments, but when their patients happened to understand Huna, the direct treatment method was used with the full knowledge and co-operation of the patient, and with even better than average results.

It has been our custom, in the HRA work of testing and proving Huna theories, to exchange knowledge with each other of anything being accomplished along our lines by others who know nothing of Huna. More of these reports will be recounted later, as we come to the points being tested. In this matter of direct healing we heard of a school of healers which teaches the theory that if the healer furnishes the power, God will do the healing—especially the adjustments necessary to put the bones of the spine back into perfect alignment.

The practitioners of the two main schools in this category try with their minds to cause the "force" to leave them and be "beamed" to the part which is to be treated. A few of these can cause a joint to become adjusted without touching it. Others place the hands over the joint and after a time exert a slight pressure. Frequently they accomplish results bettering those to be had when much physical force is exerted. In all cases their "beaming" of force and will to cause the adjustment is accompanied by prayer—which means, after all, that they may be contacting the High Self.

I proceeded to make a test of this reported healing on myself. I have a sacroiliac which sometimes needs adjustment, and, conveniently, adjustment was needed at the time in question. Usually, I use the kahuna methods which I know, but for that test purpose I used only the middle and low self therapy. I accumulated a good surcharge of mana, then stretched out on my bed on my left side, placed my right hand over the joint where the adjustment was needed, and assumed a determined attitude of mind—used "will"—to command my low self to concentrate the mana surcharge in my right fingers, over the joint, then to insert a finger of aka substance into which the concentration of mana was to be made to flow, and then to use the powerful aka-mana finger to put the joint back in place. My George, having had this joint adjusted at times by doctors, caught the idea at once. He had been well trained in the matter of projecting an aka finger through the card-board of the boxes, so he was well up on that part of the work, and, as the body is his own field of action and he knows it well, he was able in less than ten seconds to cause the joint to "click" back into place.

One thing that has been apparent from the first in the HRA use of the low self and the aka-mana under middle self coaxing or prodding, is the fact that healing is very much like memorizing. One goes over and over the thing to be memorized, making the thought-form clusters of verse or formula stronger and stronger, so that they are tied in more and more closely with each other and can be reproduced or remembered more easily and completely. Healing is something that should be handled in the same way as memorizing a long poem, unless it is a simple thing like causing the adjustment of a joint which can be done in one sitting. The picture of the desired normal condition is recalled and strength-ened and more and more mana is fastened to it. Even the emotion of confident faith can be generated by and in the low self through the efforts of the middle self.

The famous Coué, who gave us the formula, "Every day, in every way, I am growing better and better," had the right idea—repetition and more repetition with the constant thought that the healing or betterment was steadily going on. If he had understood the use of the

146

aka-mana and the thought-form clusters, his method might not have been forgotten so soon.

There is a marked difference between ordinary healing and replacement of tissues, and healing and replacement through a surcharge of mana and a willed command to set the low self working to make the correction. Some of the tissues in the body are considered by doctors to be of a kind that is not replaced by the body when injured—or, if replaced at all, has scar tissue substituted for injured cells. So far, the HRA work has not discovered where the limit can be drawn in the matter of the replacement which is possible when the extra mana is poured directly and often right into the part needing correction—accompanied, of course, by the proper instructions and commands to the low self—and, if possible, by a really impressive physical stimulus.

Of course, it goes without saying that when one gains the help of the High Self, the possibilities of healing are infinitely greater and more permanent.

I am going to quote a letter received some time after *The Secret Science Behind Miracles* was published. I insert it because it shows what an intelligent understanding, and putting to use, of the knowledge of accumulating the mana and sending it through the hands can do in healing. It shows steadfastness of purpose. Faith. I have never met the woman who wrote the letter. Though she does not say so, I feel sure she was in contact with her High Self during the healing, as witness her line, ". . . that scientific barrier which will admit no spiritual light." She did not become a member of the HRA. She had already tested and proved the kahuna

147

theory for herself.   I reproduced the letter in a bulletin, and it was a source of inspiration to the HRAs, it inspired them to keep on working.   Here is the letter:

"Dear Mr. Long:

"I have been wanting to share with you my experience in healing through the Huna methods, but felt that I should wait until my doctor would admit that it was a permanent cure.   Even though the cure was miraculous and impossible according to his standards, he insisted that it was probably a temporary phenomenon and that a recurrence could be expected.   *More than a year has passed* with no recurrence, so he has now reluctantly admitted that my condition has been cured, even though some aspects of the cure are impossible and just couldn't be, according to medical history.

"Fourteen months ago I was sent to the hospital with an eye condition which started with conjunctivitis, but developed rapidly into iritis, bilateral keratitis (both of which are considered incurable) and a corneal ulcer.   During the course of treatment before hospitalization, the ulcer had been cauterized twice, resulting in a very noticeable scar on the cornea.   I was informed by the doctor that cauterization was absolutely essential due to the fact that the ulcer had not responded to the various treatments, that it would result in a scar which would be with me as long as I lived, so I was prepared for that.

"To make a long story short, I was discharged from the hospital thoroughly discouraged as my vision had been quite badly and permanently impaired.   I was told to come back for an examination and a prescription for stronger lenses after the eye had had a month or two to adjust itself.   I had visions of myself wearing those thick-lensed jobs—which was bad enough—but to have my reading curtailed was the worst blow imaginable.

"While recuperating at home I read 'Secret Science Behind Miracles' and felt a surge of hope that really lifted me out of my doldrums.   Needless to say, I immediately began to practice the gathering of mana, directing it to concentrate in my hands.   I would then place my hands over my eyes and command the force to enter and heal.

"When I returned to the eye specialist for the examination, I said nothing to him about the improvement I knew had taken place.   He examined my eyes with every piece of equipment he owned, muttering occasionally that it was incredible.   Then he informed me that he would have to examine my eyes under drops before he could prescribe anything. After another examination under drops he was forced to admit that something had happened that he couldn't understand. He said there were no longer any APPARENT symptoms of the iritis or of the bilateral keratitis. More important was the complete disappearance of scar tissue. He pointed out that scar tissue has no blood supply and CANNOT be absorbed so it must be there even if it WASN'T. Best of all, after wearing glasses for seventeen years, my vision had improved to the point where I no longer needed glasses of any kind!

"The doctor kept questioning me about what I thought had taken place to effect such a change. I tried to tell him, but saw that I was getting nowhere with that scientific barrier which will admit no spiritual light. He just laughed and looked at me as though I were a mental oddity but of the harmless type.

"When he dismissed me, he warned me solemnly that I would undoubtedly have a recurrence within three months; that what had happened was strange but was most certainly only a temporary condition. That stirred the sixteenth part of my blood that is Irish and I made him promise to admit it was a permanent cure providing there was no recurrence within a year. He was so sure of himself that he agreed quite readily with a 'Just you wait and see' attitude.

"For physical proof to show to doubting Thomases, I have my old driver's permit stamped boldly across its face 'VOID WITHOUT THE USE OF PROPER CORRECTIVE GLASSES' and my new permit without it.

"I shall be eternally grateful to you and your book for this wonderful, wonderful healing."

I have permission to reproduce this letter, one of many such which I treasure in my files, but I feel it would work an injustice upon the writer to publicize her name and address (an eastern coastal city). All of these letters are interesting as healings, and in another way:

They remind us that the written word has no value whatever unless the ideas therein expressed are put to use and made a part of personal experience.

CHAPTER XII

THE TELEPATHIC MUTUAL HEALING GROUP

An experiment, based on the Huna theories of the aka cord and telepathic messages sent thereon, was launched among members of the HRA who wished to participate. We called it the Telepathic Mutual Healing Group, which was alphabetized, as is the modern habit, to TMHG in no time at all. Begun as an experiment to last and be reported upon for the period of only a month, the interest and results kept it going for years.

As has been said, the HRA was composed of people scattered here and there across this country, Canada, Europe and Australia. Our only means of meeting was by letters and the bulletins. There were many who felt the need of contact with others working along the same lines. And there were many with urgent needs, and whose confidence in the strength of their own prayers was weak. It is true that where one person can accomplish little, working alone, a number of persons banded together for a common purpose can accomplish great things.

There was no possibility of our getting together physically, as people do in a church or lecture hall. But why not get together telepathically? We had been teaching our low selves to use that talent which belonged to them alone. Here was a chance for experimentation along that line, but on a larger scale. Here was a chance to help those who needed help, if we could.

For many years there has been "absent treatment" practiced by modern religious organizations without the mention or realization of the involvement of the telepathic element. There has always been prayer on the behalf of friends and loved ones at a distance, and often organized prayer in which distant members of a larger group join at stated times.

I looked into the records of kahuna practices to see if there was a precedent or guide that might help us in planning our course. The ideal combination for healing, of course, was the kahuna and his patient. The kahuna concentrated all his efforts on one person before turning to another. But I found a most interesting practice in the matter of "braiding the aka cords" which suited our purposes exactly.

As set forth in earlier chapters on training the low self in telepathy, we knew that the thought-form message travels on an aka thread or cord projected by the low self and attached to the low self of the person to whom we are sending the message. We knew of the belief that High Selves of a tribal unit or group formed the *Poe Aumakua* or Great Company of High Selves. It was also believed that there was strength in union on the High Self level. The symbol for it was a rope, woven, twisted or braided from many strands.

A rope is much stronger than a thread, and the implication is that the aka threads or cords of many people leading to the many High Selves, if all animated for the sending of the mana and the thought-forms of the same prayer at the same time, will enable the High Selves to perform a mighty work of power in behalf of the community or assembly of low and middle selves joining in this form of prayer.

In Polynesia the temples were often large, raised, stone-paved platforms, and on the platform were several houses of thatch, each dedicated to a special purpose. One such house was set aside for the good of the tribe as a whole. It was the house in which, after proper preliminary ritualistic cleansing of the people who had gathered to make up the congregation, the priests hid themselves from sight and performed the mysterious final rite of braiding together the fibers of coconut husk to form a strong rope. Once braided, and symbolizing the uniting of the aka threads of all the congregation to provide the augmented strength—and probably exhibited to the people—the prayer was considered made and sent to the High Selves.

In Japan, where many things reminiscent of Huna have been retained in the older religions, the symbol may be found in the form of a strand of rope hung between two pillars before the temples. The rope is as thick as a man's body in the center, but tapers to little more than a single strand at each end, telling the lesson of strength in union in an enduring symbology.

From this idea of the significance of the rope or braided cord, our plan of procedure was evolved. I proposed to officiate at the center of things and do my best to perform the rite of "braiding" and to direct the mana, as it flowed in from all sides along the aka threads, to the High Selves. The participants in the TMHG were to send in to me along the aka threads connecting us, the mana and the thought-forms.

We know from our study of psychometry that an aka thread is attached to an object by the person handling it, and that later a psychometrist may touch the object, and his low self follow the aka thread to the owner, learning things about the owner which can be verified. Therefore, we decided to use, for our aka thread contact, letters and signatures sent in to me by those taking part in the experiment.

The letter was to state briefly the well thought out prayer (from which they were not to deviate). It was to be signed in ink, and the signature gazed at steadily for a half minute with the sheet held in the hands—in this way making sure that the aka thread would be attached to the sheet and signature. The letters were then to be sent to me and I planned to place them in a box and lay the palms of my hands on their edges during the minutes when we were to observe our prayer rite together. Before the appointed hour, however, I would touch each letter and concentrate on it for a short time to try to make preliminary contact through my low self and the aka thread.

We decided upon a set time daily for making our contact with each other and for the prayer action. As some HRAs could work only in the afternoon and others only in the evening, and as there was the time difference between various parts of the world to be considered, we set the TMHG periods at 3 P.M. and 7 P.M., California time, and it was left to the individual HRAs to calculate the time differences and arrange their own periods of observance to coincide with California time. Instructions as to procedure of the prayer-action were sent out to those who were to join me in the experiment. I append a condensed version of them which will serve to show how we went about the tests:

THE TMHG PRAYER-ACTION RITUAL is roughly divided into steps, as follows:

1. You will have your thought-forms of the desired condition all made and ready to be recalled on a moment's notice. At a few minutes before the hour strikes, assume a proper mental attitude of earnestness and then accumulate as large a surcharge of mana as you can. As the hour strikes, make a telepathic contact with your own High Self and the High Selves of the others by directing your attention to me at the center and holding the will to make telepathic contact through me as center from which rises the "braided cord" or united aka threads, to contact all the High Selves and increase the power of the prayer-actions for all who participate. Send love and blessings and mana, consciously, to the High Selves through me as center. Do this for two minutes, also asking and picturing world blessings, and offering mana for the use of the High Selves for their own purposes, whatever they may be.

2. At approximately the end of two minutes, relax and let me send to you my love and blessing and visualization of perfect conditions. I will also send a color, as an aid in developing your telepathic receptivity. Do not worry if you get no impressions at all. It has been our experience that the benefits are not lacking in any way because reception is poor or entirely lacking.

3. At about four minutes after the hour, set to work making your prayer-action in the usual way by recalling and visualizing in vivid detail the conditions which you wish to have the High Selves build into your future.

Imagine yourself as stepping into the new conditions, and doing all the things that you would or will do when they are materialized as realities—when the answer is completed by the High Selves. At these times it is good to picture others as also blessed with desirable conditions if your life is close to or dependent on theirs at any point.

4. As the end of the eight minutes draws near, endeavor to send, and say that you ARE sending the thought-forms of the desired conditions, together with a strong flow of mana to the High Selves by way of the center and the braided cord of connecting aka threads. That done, pause a few seconds and then end your prayer ceremonially and with definiteness, saying, "The prayer takes its flight. . . . Let the rain of blessings fall. (This is the return flow of mana made into High Mana which has the effect of revivifying and blessing us.) Au . . . ma . . . ma. . . ." (Or "amen.")

The experiment was carried on faithfully for the entire month, with reports being sent in during the period and at the end of it. Here is the report, again condensed from the bulletin, as it was made at the end of the test period:

REPORT ON THE TELEPATHIC MUTUAL HEALING EXPERIMENT
November 25th to December 25th, 1948

THE MATTER OF TIME was one of the main obstacles. Often some of us had to cut and run from social gatherings or home engagements to join in the work. Some were unable many times to make it at all. A surprising number found that they seemed unable to remember the time and forgot it until later (perhaps "George" was not interested). However, out of the large number who took part (about fifty or sixty), only a very few were unable to sit in on most evenings.

THE OBJECT OF THE EXPERIMENT was (1) to see whether or not telepathic impressions could be sent out by me from the Los Angeles center to a number of Associates at one time, (2) to see if the impressions could be picked up as sent or if they would be distorted and changed, (3) to see what effect working in this way as a group would have under Huna methods and beliefs, in healing body or circumstances, or in other unexpected ways.

SENT TELEPATHICALLY (by me for test purposes) were the numbers from 1 to 10, simple geometrical figures such as triangles, squares, circles, stars, cones, pyramids (solid instead of the simple outline in a few instances), the letter "H" (for "Huna"), and the color GREEN. This color was varied from light yellowish green to darker, brighter, and often light bluish green. There was also sent out the visualized picture of peaceful green valleys, fields and rolling green farm lands— to embody the idea of WORLD PEACE for which we all worked in addition to other desired things.

ON EACH WEDNESDAY NIGHT a well organized and fairly long established group of about fifteen persons, many trained in the use of suggestion for various purposes (not originally a Huna group, but with all members by then HRAs) joined me at the stroke of the hour in carrying through the steps of the experiment. I continued to send out the telepathic image as usual, to test

156

the difference in reception as it might be at a distance and close by. (No difference was to be noted.)

THIS GROUP, working with me as a unit, later in the evening, tried sending healing by telepathic means (and invoking also the help of the High Selves) to various HRAs in distant places. This was to test the idea that several people, working together as a group, might be able to exert a greater force than a single individual. Checks by letter (in some cases without letting the patient know in advance of the time and the plan) showed a marked benefit, especially in the matter of strength and restored feeling of wellbeing. In two cases the ones so treated felt so well on the following days that they tired themselves and were soon back to the former state. Members of the group also experienced this strange feeling of uplift and exhilaration the next day. (The problem of how to retain this effect longer or permanently seems to be tied in with the question of the mana in some definite way. In each instance the group had practiced accumulating a surcharge of mana to be used in a number of ways, experimentally, as well as in healing tests.)

MY PERSONAL FEELINGS AT THE CENTER were marked by the fact that they were very strong some nights and almost lacking on others. This has also been the experience of NEARLY ALL HRAs WHO HAVE REPORTED THEIR FEELINGS. The cause of this variation has not been determined. On nights when I felt little or nothing, the mental images sent out telepathically were picked up apparently just as well. On the first night, I took up the stack of letters which had

157

come in from far and wide, and worked through them, noting the names on them and reaching out mentally to my friends, one after the other, to establish contact telepathically through the aka threads attached to the letters and thus to them. As the hour drew near I felt a strong undercurrent of excitement as if sensing the attitude of expectancy of everyone waiting to begin.

As the hour struck, I relaxed and waited for the thoughts and mana directed to me to be felt. My hands tingled on the letters and, as I turned my mind to uniting all our threads and lifting them as one great "braided cord" (*aha*) to the Great Company of High Selves, of which our own formed a part, there came A QUITE UNEXPECTED feeling of being suddenly UPLIFTED AND CLEANSED AND BLESSED. I felt a rush of joy and love and a great desire to be allowed to help by doing my allotted part in the work of healing and restoration. The emotional reaction that marks the co-operation of the low self was suddenly very strong, and the joy of it all brought tears to my eyes. (Others reported this reaction on their part also.) In this emotional condition I sent back to my friends my love and the blessedness I sensed flowing to us from the High Selves. There was a mystical feel to it all, such as I have sensed in "Realization" under the Zen (Buddhist) system, and as I remember once sensing it in a Baptist revival meeting years ago. . . .

The next step was that in which we all made clear before us the pictures of wanted conditions. I pictured the perfect conditions of health and happiness and prosperity for all, and the world blessed with peace and abundance. In the next minute I presented my picture and felt the sharp tingle in my hands increase as our united mana and pictures flowed into the braided cord. At the end of the fourth minute I closed the prayer actions in the usual way, relaxing while I tried to sense any return from the High Selves. I sensed something dimly which seemed to fill me with new strength, and uplift and cleanse me anew. I soon went into my evening's telepathic healing work for individuals, much refreshed and with a greater feeling of faith and confidence. It was a very blessed experience, and one which when felt by the others has made us all eager to continue the work, even if many nights pass without such strongly felt rewards.

OTHERS REPORTED a number of times the reception of the things sent out telepathically, just as I had sent them, with almost no changes or mistakes. But in a majority of the reports there had been something added or changed. For instance, the triangle was seen set on a green shield which was bordered with gold. The circle was seen to begin to revolve and move and multiply. The green fields were augmented by trees with beautiful flowers, and the rows in the fields were amazingly perfect and straight and green. For some the green gave way to other colors, fountains and sweeps and rainbows of them. The solid pyramid and cone were both reported back. Simple stars became lighted and blazing, and at Christmas surmounted Christmas trees.

THE PART PLAYED HERE BY SYMBOLS indicates that the low selves were hard at work with us. The low self is known to add to what it picks up psychically, and to make symbols which, if we can get to the meaning hidden behind them, often reveal hidden things in the con-

159

sciousness below the threshold. The occurrence of such symbols lets us know that there was a reality to the reception and that it was not a figment of imagination.

THE HEALING RESULTS WERE EXCELLENT and the work in the test month seemed to help bring to a head self-healing work begun earlier, and healing efforts in which I have worked with Associates on their problems. Here are some comments gleaned from the letters: "I feel its benefit long after the appointed time." ". . . best I have been in four years . . . I feel so very little and humble, somehow . . . return thanks . . ." "When you told us that my wife had been treated by the Wednesday night group of nearly twenty, we checked back and recalled, singularly—or not—as it may seem, that she was lying in bed that evening at just about that very time. Out of a clear sky she called to me in another room to tell me that she was suddenly feeling better—much better. She cannot describe just what came over her at the moment, but states that 'something' seemed to calm her and give her a feeling of great strength, something that she had not at any previous time experienced." "Nothing yet." "I am feeling the benefit of the work and am hoping it will carry through the whole picture." "The first night I felt so relaxed that I fell asleep. I felt as if I were just floating out into space. (Note: This is a sensation that has become familiar to many by now.) The next night I saw such pretty green fields. . . ." "The first night I saw dimly, a sliding door that was pushed aside, which I took to indicate that the way was open for us. Last night there was shown a ring, with triangles set around the top . . . then streamers coming down like a rope, as they were intertwined." (Note: Others soon reported seeing the aka threads in a similar "braiding," and two saw them as of many and beautiful colors.)

"We three sit each night . . . Mother said that, night before last, she saw a big difference in her eyes. . . . We certainly are grateful for that." "The eyes improve steadily under Telepathic Mutual Healing Group experiment." "On November 23rd I received the lesson for the experiment, and learned part of the ritual. Next day I learned it all. In the morning of the 25th, I suddenly discovered that the terrific pain . . . had completely disappeared . . . either the treatment or just studying the instructions cleared away the pain . . . I am wondering." (Note: Undoubtedly she made contact with her High Self in practicing, and got a swift answer.) "I saw a double circle . . . like a ring, running with liquid, brilliant green fire . . . right in the center shone—like a diamond—a glitter of every color." "I had such difficulty in my breathing when I walked—if only for a short distance, and I would have to sit down to get my breath. Yesterday I walked two blocks and had no difficulty. I have not been able to do that for months, so you see how happy I am. . . ." "The growth has disappeared entirely . . . greatly puzzles the doctors. . . ."

ONE OF THE SURPRISING FEATURES of the experiment is the emergence of the feeling that, united in this way through the telepathic contacts, and making a united contact with the *Poe Aumakua*, we become a *group entity*. We are "braided" together like our aka threads, and seem to share the kind of unity or "oneness" known to the High Selves. We find ourselves united into a

161

"body" and sensing love and nearness and companionship. After this experience, which a number of us have felt vividly, we have come to know the inner meaning of the church or congregation as a mechanism to be used in contacting and in working with the High Selves—being guided, helped and healed—and, in turn, being given Service to perform on our levels of life at the behest of those of the Higher Levels.

As has been said, so satisfactory was the first test of the TMHG methods that we immediately continued into a second period, and then made this part of the work a regular rite at 3 and 7 daily, seven days a week without break.

As time went on, a prayer ritual was asked for, and sent by means of the bulletin. It was suggested that it should be changed to suit the needs of the user, and then be memorized for use. The thoughts contained in the prayer have a very great impressive force on the low self—a physical stimulus of a high order. After accumulating a surcharge of mana, on the hour, the prayer begins:

"I reach out now to contact MFL at the center, and to become a part of the Group now assembling for prayer. . . . With the Group I now reach out to contact the Great Company of Aumakuas, which includes my own . . . (Pause.) Beloved and Utterly Trustworthy Parental Spirits, cleanse me of all sins of hurts done others. Accept my pledge to refrain from hurts and to make amends for past hurts in so far as possible. 'Cleanse Thou my soiled face with the abundance of Thy Grace.' Cleanse this supply of living force that I offer as my living sacrifice to you. . . . I now send through the aka cord of contact, and through the braided cord of the Group through MFL at the center, this supply of mana. . . . Accept it with my love and joyous giving. . . .

"I now send the mental picture of conditions which I ask to be used as molds or seeds and filled and grown to realities in the future. I see a world at peace . . . a prosperous world . . . a happy world . . . a safe world. . . .

"I now present this picture of all in our Group being brought into the Light and standing in perfect health . . . with a bountiful supply of all things needed for happy living and Service. I see all of us, including myself, given the power to Serve, the means of Service, and the Joy of Service. I pledge myself to accept all opportunities for Service with faith and to the limit of my ability, that from small things I may grow into greater things of Service, and daily become more like you are—more utterly trustworthy in the use I make of the things entrusted to me. I will strive to do my part to become as I picture myself in the future, healthy, happy and prosperous—filled with the joy of life and Service—become utterly trustworthy in every thought and act and aspiration.

"I now present a special mental picture of conditions desired for myself (here visualize the desired personal conditions or conditions desired for others).

"The prayer now finishes. The mental images are released into your keeping to be materialized as soon as is possible, Beloved and Utterly Trustworthy Parental Spirits—Great Poe Aumakua. . . . Now let the return flow of mana fall, as blessed rain, to bring all good and all cleansing. The prayer-action is finished. I withdraw from contact. . . . Au . . . ma . . . ma. . . ."

When we entered the war in Korea I received many letters from anxious wives, parents and sweethearts of the men in the armed forces. They asked for help from the TMHG. So we inserted a paragraph in the prayer ritual, building a "Wall of Protection" around the soldiers whose names had been sent in. We placed a special prayer immediately after the mental picture of a world at peace. It was worded thus:

"I now present a picture of all the men linked with the group who are in the armed services. Each is surrounded with a Wall of Protection made strong by our High Selves at all times and constantly protecting them from danger in every way."

It is a fact that, at this time of writing, not a single man on the "Wall of Protection" list has been reported a casualty. Many have come through actions where others were killed or injured. One survived, unscathed, a plane crash in which a number of others were killed or hurt.

But such a fortunate result of TMHG prayer-actions was by no means universal. Though, through the years while the TMHG was in operation, letter after letter came in reporting results nearly miraculous, others reported slight results and sometimes a complete lack of benefit. Much seemed to depend upon the individual seeking aid through work with the group. The sending of the mana faithfully, day by day to the High Selves, and the careful and regular presentation of the pictures of the conditions desired, proved to have a building or cumulative effect. Also, the ability of one person to help another, something on the line of priming a pump with water, to enable another to pump for himself, seems to be necessary in many cases. One low self with faith and full confidence seems to be able to help the low self of another greatly.

For small groups, the ideal way to work together seems to be through the weekly contact meeting, with regular projects and with prayer-actions of the Huna type used in unison. The ritual just given is a very serviceable one and covers all the important points. Then, during the week, with some member of the group acting as center, the work on the hour once or twice a day can be undertaken, just as in the TMHG, and the strength multiplied by the association in all ways.

For those who wish to serve with absent treatment, the knowledge obtained by the TMHG in its experimental work with Huna can serve as a guide in theory as well as in practical application. The following report on telepathic communication between two persons with the object of healing appeared in one of the bulletins:

A SUCCESSFUL TELEPATHIC HEALING EXPERIMENT, with special research into the use of water as an adjunct to the telepathic reception, was carried out in May and June by HRA T. A. L., his home being in Los Angeles, and HRA Mrs. J. M. R., she being a resident of Madison, Wisconsin. The latter is gifted along psychic lines, accustomed to healing work, and given to feeling a downward flow of High Mana as a sparkling shower when contacting her Aumakua. T. A. L. had demonstrated some psychic ability and had used the kahuna method of gazing into a tumbler of water as into a gazing crystal to get visual images in answer to telepathic or other projections.

The date set for the test was May 23rd, 1952, at 7 A.M., California daylight saving time. Mrs. R. wrote to T. A. L.: "I should like to send you a healing radiation while the (telepathic contact and) current is strong. Of course, I may not be able to call forth a strong radiation at the appointed time, but perhaps the High Self will help. We might begin at seven and continue for nine minutes. You might even get a spoken message."

The experiment was carried out on schedule, and here is part of the letter of T. A. L. to Mrs. R., reporting on his reception: "Promptly at 7 A.M., I was ready, having prepared myself mentally for the message, and with the vessel filled with water. I sat passive and glanced into the vessel, awaiting the appearance of any sense of arrival of any message. There seemed an *absolute void*, then at 7:03 a scene appeared in the vessel of a lady with gray hair, light eyes, medium stature, clad in a dark jacket or maybe a vest, because the sleeves were of a light color and showed prominently, as her arms were outstretched upward in prayer supplication. (Note: The two persons making the experiment had never met.) She walked as though from one room to another, paused in the second room at a table, lowered her head and gazed as in deep meditation—and at the same time I became conscious of a pulsating vibration around my stomach. It lasted a full minute and within me surged the thought of release from tensions. I became very much relaxed and yawned. I could even see her lips move as if making a spoken statement, but could not sense the words. After a few minutes the action ended.

"It has been my daily obligation to have at hand some milk to alleviate the distress caused by my stomach condition. On my way to work I was in high spirits, as I had a strong feeling of wellbeing and promise of its continuance because of the healing vibration which I had felt. All day Friday there was no necessity to drink milk, nor was I disturbed in any way that day as I have usually been when 'tight' situations develop. Since then my stomach has been quite normal, and I have been able to eat and enjoy foods that heretofore had been taboo for me."

Mrs. R., in reply, and after expressing her pleasure and her gratitude to the Higher Beings for the healing, went on to give her check on the telepathic image seen in the water: "Your picture in the water was so true that it amazes me. Just as you described it, I walked from one room to another twice, while taking deep breaths and sending them to the top of my head as explained in *The Secret Science Behind Miracles*—to contact the High Self. Then I stood beside a low table and prayed with head bowed, next raising my arms, the right hand palm down and the left hand palm upward. I felt waves of gentle radiation and knew that you were receiving a healing. Then I asked that the healing be sustained. After the healing current was sent, I endeavored to send you the message: 'Accept thy healing.'

"Apparently the High Self—yours—ended the picture at this point. However, I continued with the activity by pretending I WAS YOU—and walked around the room, forgetting ME—WHILE I WAS YOU IN CALIFORNIA. I walked briskly, sensing vigor, and feeling 'wellbeing'—and complete release in health. I sometimes use this activity when sending healing, and find that it works! I spoke aloud and said—while I was YOU—'I'm strong and I AM HEALED!' Then I was back here giving thanks to the Universal Healer of ALL THAT EXISTS. Then I went about my usual duties. . . . Your description of the 'dark jacket with light sleeves showing' was right. I was wearing a dark housecoat and there were light sleeves showing below the dark sleeves of the coat."

CHAPTER XIII

CONTACTS MADE THROUGH SIGNA-TURES, ALSO SIGNATURE AURAS AND MEASUREMENTS

When the Telepathic Mutual Healing Group was organized, very little was known concerning the aka structure of signatures written in ink, except that in some way there was attached to each signature an aka thread which led back to the one who had signed his name and had gazed at the writing. We still do not know just how and why an aka thread fastened to a signature is retained by it better than a similar aka thread fastened to a plain sheet of paper through a touch and look. The fact, however, was well established by our telepathic experiments, and for that reason, the letters, each with its signature written in ink, were used successfully in establishing and maintaining contact with me at the center.

For almost a year, we of the HRA were forced to rely entirely upon the Huna theory of the aka thread or cord of connection simply because "it worked." The telepathic contacts were made beyond a question of doubt, as pictures, symbols and colors were being sent and being received, again and again. Then came two proofs of the validity of the theory of the aka thread contact, and much more light on the entire matter.

In 1949, Dr. Oscar Brunler, mentioned before as a

physicist of distinction, arrived from England to make his home in California. The HRAs of this area became acquainted with his work through his lectures, and because he became a member of our group. An outstanding contribution to our knowledge of the aka cord of connection, when running between a signature and its owner, was made indirectly through Dr. Brunler's earlier discovery that a signature held precisely the same vibratory rate or kind of radiation as the person who writes it. It is a fascinating story of discovery and one that deserves more than passing mention.

As recounted in another connection, for many centuries the psychic abilities of the low self have been put to use in such things as water dowsing with the aid of a forked twig taken from a living tree, or the use of a simple pendulum. In late years, such instruments as the Cameron Aurameter have been invented. In all cases, no matter what instrument is used, the idea is to furnish the low self with some mechanical means through which it can report its findings to the middle self.

For one who has sufficient psychic skill and training, it is possible to sense water under the ground *without* the use of willow fork, pendulum or instrument. A few years ago the press dispatches told of a boy in Africa who could "see" psychically into the earth, and who had made a fine reputation for himself by locating water, gold deposits and diamonds.

For the less able and less fully trained, the instrumental aid is of much value. The pendulum, because of its simplicity, and because it can swing in various ways or directions, has been a favorite crutch to help "George" tell his conscious mind or middle self what he has learned when instructed to make a psychic investigation of something, be it underground water and minerals, or the condition of organs hidden inside the body. As in our box tests, the low self can penetrate certain coverings, investigate what is underneath, and report by using a prearranged code of swings—the "convention."

In Europe the use of the pendulum has been commonplace for many years, and has been recognized as practical and legitimate, provided the user can prove his ability. In America, for a number of reasons, the use of the pendulum has been almost entirely neglected until the last decade when a slight interest in its use was stirred amongst some classes of "occultists" and some of the leaders in the "health foods" movements—the pendulum having been proven excellent as an aid in learning what foods were suitable for the operator of the pendulum and what were not. Unfortunately, many persons of the irresponsible element pounced upon the pendulum and undertook to use it for some form of fortune telling. That, of course, partly discredited the use of such an instrument even in the hands of proven experts.

In France, where the pendulum was widely accepted long ago, it was used by a certain M. Bovis in connection with a ruler 100 cm. long, to give readings in terms of centimeters when testing material things. He had determined on a convention, or code, in which his low self would make known its findings in terms of measurement on the measuring stick. 100 cm. or "degrees" was taken as the measure for a perfect egg, cask of wine, cheese, apple, bottle of olive oil—and later in diagnostic work for stomach, liver, eyes or teeth.

Anything, dead or alive, so long as it was physical and sufficiently material to contact, could be investigated by M. Bovis' trained low self to ascertain its purity or the state of health—the answer to be given in terms of centimeters by making the pendulum swing as agreed upon, when held over the right part of the measuring stick. The procedure was simple. A sample of the thing to be tested was placed on one end of the measuring stick, or the left hand of the operator was placed on the thing to be tested, as on a cheese or cask of wine. The right hand holding the pendulum was then moved slowly from the zero end of the measuring stick toward the 100 cm. end. The low self, as it had been taught, made the pendulum swing all the time, but in a diagonal or circling direction. Only when the correct place on the stick was reached for the reading to be indicated, did the pendulum begin to swing at exactly right angles to the stick.

To make his hand steadier in the holding of the pendulum, M. Bovis mounted a metal plate on a slotted board so that the measure could be slid slowly under the plate while the pendulum was swinging. On the plate he marked diagonal lines as well as lines to show the exact right angle, and the simple instrument worked very well indeed. He named it the "Biometer." Later on he evolved a fine theory in which he suggested that all things sent off radiations, and that his Biometer simply helped to measure the wave length of the radiations and report them in terms of his centimeter "degrees." He even went one step farther and announced that by multiplying his cm. reading in degrees by .065, one could turn the reading into angstrom units, and identify the radiations in terms of everything from infrared to ultraviolet light.

The Biometer was a great success. M. Bovis earned a living for some time as a special inspector for the French government. With his Biometer he could grade casks of wine or cakes of cheese—almost anything—and do it much better and faster than could be done by any other method.

From this to the inspection and testing of the various parts and organs of the body was a simple step which M. Bovis took without hesitation. His diagnostic ventures were so successful that doctors began to send patients to him when they could not determine the nature of some obscure malady. The use of the Biometer spread, and soon the inventor added several other devices to his list, all being simple instruments designed to allow his low self to describe the state of one's health in terms of some form of measurement, as in the degrees of a circle, and so forth.

Among the HRAs we were fortunate enough to have a member who possessed a complete set of the Bovis instruments, even though it was some time after the death of the inventor and the cessation of the manufacture of such things as his Biometer, Tetrameter, Radiographe and Dosimeter Jumelle. All were tested here at the center, and were found both practical and surprisingly accurate, provided, always, that the low self of the operator was properly trained and grounded in the use of the instruments and the convention of measurement to be used.

While M. Bovis was still alive, Dr. Brunler became interested in the Biometer and the theory which had been offered to explain that it was measuring radiations in terms of "Degrees Biometric," or centimeters which could be converted to readings in terms of colors. He purchased a Biometer and took it to England with him. There he learned to use it expertly and convinced himself that it was practical.

Being also an inventor and investigator, it was no long time before Dr. Brunler had increased the length of the measuring stick on the Biometer to a full 1000 cm., and was measuring radiations which he had found to lie in the range from 100 degrees Biometric upward toward the 1000 degree limit.

In this new range he identified radiations which seemed to come from the "mind" or "soul"—the very innermost being or "self" of human beings. For the sake of simplicity he called these radiations "Brain Radiations," but warned that he was not measuring the physical health of the brain or its tissues.

This was a great discovery. He was able to measure the *consciousness*, the *level of intelligence*, the *personality* and the *character* on the changed Biometer. By making a great many readings of different individuals and by classifying the readings according to his extended study of the persons so read, he was able to evolve a scale of measurements for intelligence and the general or over-all personality. Seeking for a way to explain the fact that some men had higher readings than others, and far greater intellectual endowments, he settled upon the theory that mankind is in a fluid state of mental or "soul" evolution. He postulated that, through a series of incarnations, men evolved higher and higher in the scale until they at last reached a definite goal. The nature of the goal was something not so simple to determine. He needed to know just how high a reading in terms of the Degree Biometric a person would have to reach through evolution before he had finished his course and moved on to something still higher.

In his search for limitations in the high degree brackets, he undertook tests aimed at getting readings from the great men of the past. Testing the things they had left behind them, manuscripts, paintings, statues done in marble and stone, he made the further discovery that the signature on a letter, a document or painting, carried in some mysterious way the same radiation as its maker, living or long dead.

He compared readings made directly from individuals, with readings taken from their signatures, and in every case found the two readings identical on the Biometer. Soon he was testing musty documents, writings in archives, paintings in famous galleries. By testing these signatures of famous men, checking the signatures written by them at various times in their lives, on into their old age, he found that the average of evolutionary growth during one lifetime was between one and six degrees Biometric. The latter was the highest he ever discovered, and a rare stride upward which seemed to have been made only because of much suffering.

The implication was made clear when he considered his further finding that the average reading of primitive men was around 200 degrees, and the reading of the most advanced stood not higher than 725. Allowing a degree of evolutionary growth per lifetime, the number of incarnations demanded would be about five hundred and fifty.

The highest reading which Dr. Brunler ever found came from a picture of a cloth reputed to have been used to wipe the face of Jesus when he suffered during his crucifixion. The cloth, supposedly, had been marked with the imprint of his face, and it was and is still revered in a famous church in Southern Europe. The reading was an even 1000 degrees Biometric. Dr. Brunler freely admitted that the relic might not be genuine, or that the reading might be colored by his own inner reactions, but he was, so he told me, inclined to place the limit of evolution at the 1000 degree point— at which point the transition would take place which would bring man to his goal, whatever that may be.

Among those great men of the past whose readings were taken from their signatures and which could be considered entirely reliable, the highest evolved ever found was the painter, writer and inventor—the all around genius—Leonardo da Vinci. His reading was 725 degrees. Below his level ranged the other great painters, and below them came the great composers. Next came the great writers, and then the great statesmen, followed by the generals. Men of science were found in these high levels also. Scarcely anyone under 450 degrees has ever become lastingly famous. The average person in Europe and America stands around the 250 level, while the men of less advanced countries average around 225. The lowest readings were around 118 degrees, and these came from those who were barely above the level of the imbecile.

The "personality pattern" was also registered on the Biometer, but not in terms of centimeters or measure, as in the case of the intelligence. Clockwise and counterclockwise movements, when the pendulum responded with circling movements, determined whether the one read was constructive or destructive—basically "good" or "bad." The will was also measured and registered in straight back-and-forth swings, these being to the right or the left of the ideal or upright mark on the plate of the Biometer (the right angle mark in relation to the measuring stick—although the latter does not come into the picture in measuring the personality pattern).

The puzzling matter of how signatures could carry the same radiation, and the *same strength* of radiation, as the body or mind of the one who had written the signature, was never satisfactorily explained, except in terms of the aka thread which allows the low self of the operator of the Biometer to "stick out a finger," follow the thread, and make contact with the writer of the signature, be he alive or long dead and "in spirit."

By accepting the Huna explanation that through the aka thread the low self can find and measure the maker of the signature, even if he is not in the flesh, we have additional proof that it is the *"consciousness"* or *"soul"* that is being measured, and not the physical body. More than that, we have here the proof that intelligence and personality characteristics reside in the "selves" that make up the man, and survive physical death. This conclusion permits the assumption that reincarnations must follow to explain evolution.

My personal experience, in using the Biometer, has been that when the signature is in the clip at the end of the measuring stick, and my right hand holds the pendulum over the plate ready to be used to convey the result of the investigation of the low self and to give its reading, there is a pause in which I feel nothing. I simply sit relaxed but attentive while I wait. Then, after a pause of perhaps from twenty to thirty seconds, I feel a very slight something in the pit of my stomach, and the pendulum begins to swing as of its own accord. I move the measuring stick slowly, so that the signature gradually comes nearer the plate over which the pendulum is swinging, and at first the pattern swings are given. They stop, and I again move the signature closer. It is now at the point where the highest grade of intelligence is to be found. The movement continues, closer and closer, the pendulum swinging steadily at a diagonal to the line on the plate that marks the right angle to the measuring stick which is sliding slowly along under the plate. Then, when the right distance has been reached, the pendulum gradually changes so that it swings exactly over the right angle line. When this is exact, I usually feel a very slight jerk in my wrist, and the pendulum stops. I then read the stick at the place where it meets the plate, and the reading is completed and I am ready to record it.

Some day we shall be using the Biometer as a matter of course, testing the very young to learn what personality pattern they possess, and what level of intelligence they have. As this personality pattern can be much improved, if less than good and normal, and as the will can be trained successfully, much can be done to guide the child in these directions of growth. As the intelligence level changes but a degree or two in the average lifetime, the child can be encouraged to take up training for the type of occupation that will best suit his level of mental ability.

There are a few things which still need to be learned about the use of the Biometer. The Brunler reading system still lacks a niche for the natural talents, such as those for music or art or mechanics. These need to be accounted for so that a child who is not at all musical, for instance, can be spared a musical training and given one that will better fit some other talent.

Most promising of all is the prospect that, given time, we can find the best way to measure the low self and the middle self separately on the Biometer, and learn their respective standings and natures. We may even be able to measure the High Self. In addition, it would seem possible to measure the degree of trouble which may be caused for an individual by the presence of complexes and by obsessional influences. The ability of the low self to measure things seems almost unlimited, and it is to be guessed that in the making of very difficult measurements, the High Self may sometimes lend a helping hand.

To get back to the signature and the aka thread connected to it, we come to a second set of proofs which were offered some time after work with the Biometer was begun:

One day, when HRA Verne Cameron was visiting me in the Study, and after we had run a series of tests on ivory figurines which had been worked over experimentally to make them into "ikons" (to give them artificial aka auras and make them centers for certain beneficial forces), we fell to talking about the use of signatures in making Biometric readings, and the question

179

was raised as to whether or not a signature had an aka body or "aura."

Using the Aurameter, Mr. Cameron began tests over a signature which I provided, and in a matter of less than a minute, he had outlined an aura over the signature that was like a thin and irregular fan rising from it and extending some two feet above it and trailing off to a six-foot point at the far end. At the pointed end it was guessed that the connecting aka thread led off to make contact with the distant writer of the signature.

Oddly enough, the Aurameter seems not to register the aka thread leading from a signature. It may be that it is too fine and slight to set up a positive or negative mana field to influence the head of the Aurameter, or it may be that unless the aka thread is actuated, as during a Biometric reading of the signature, and mana made to flow through it, the thread itself remains almost a nothingness in so far as substance or mana is concerned. (Tests will later be made on this point.) Almost all objects which have been held in the hands and concentrated upon with the intention of giving them an artificial aura have, when the work is finished, an aka cord of a peculiar kind which seems to take the form of a strong "beam" of force extending from the object in some direction and disappearing in the distance, or through the ceiling or into the empty air.

In any event, even if the aka thread is idle and provides no beam or indication of a force or mana flow, the signature definitely has an aka body. This can be accounted for only by supposing that some of the abundant aka substance of the low self of the writer is fastened to the writing, and that it remains there.

The most significant thing about the fan-shaped aura rising from a signature and extending from it forward and backward (but not downward) is that no two signatures so far tested show the same shape. Some are rounded and high at the top, some are low and notched and broken. The size and shape differ from one to another in endless ways. Each aura is as individual and unmistakable as a fingerprint.

Work must be undertaken to continue the study of this new discovery. While it is too early to hazard a guess as to the direction in which such studies may lead, it seems possible that in the general outlines and contours of the signature auras there may lie indicators which will tell us something about the individuals. Just what may be told remains to be seen. It might even develop that the lacking Biometric indication of special talent might be deduced from the aura pattern of the signature, once we know the meanings of the angles, turns and domes, or of the nicks and deeper indentations, or of the strange thin projections sometimes observed.

Not only are we recovering the knowledge of Huna and its uses, but we stand on the threshold of many new discoveries which will soon become landmarks as we press forward in this still little-explored field.

CHAPTER XIV

MORE FINDINGS OF THE HRA

Since we were organized for research, devoted not only to the testing and proving of Huna theories but also awake to what other people were doing and thinking along allied lines, information concerning all kinds of strange and little known theories, facts, tests and guesses came in to me. In no other field does speculation run as wildly as in that of psychology, religion and psychic science. Much of the material was of no value to us, but now and then we ran into something that was very much worth looking into.

Early in our research our attention was called to the work of Mr. L. E. Eeman, of London, and we found his discoveries and theories of great interest and value—particularly because they had to do with what we call mana. A correspondence ensued, and Mr. Eeman eventually joined the HRA. What he had discovered was that the vital force could be made to run, much as does electricity, from a positive to a negative pole. In his work he found the human body polarized right and left, and so was able to make the vital force run along an insulated copper wire from the right hand to the base of the spine, and from the left hand to the back of the head.

This changing of the normal flows of vital force (mana) in the body, he found, caused a state of relaxation which was a great help in getting off to sleep. He called it the "relaxation circuit," and once having made his basic discovery, set to work to see what else could be done by carrying the mana flows here and there on wires. He hooked several people up "in series" as one might a number of batteries, and observed the effect. He tried the wires in "parallel" and invented tests of many kinds.

He discovered that, together with the flow of mana along the insulated wires, there was carried from one person to another such things as bodily poisons. A person suffering from infection and fever, when hooked up in circuit with a well person, transferred some of his fever and discomfort to him. This had the strange effect of helping the sick person to recover, even if it did make the well person temporarily ill, but the actual germs of the infection were not transmitted to the well person.

Equally surprising was his discovery that a person who had once recovered from a disease such as typhoid fever, measles or smallpox, and who had supposedly developed proper antitoxins in his blood, was a great help to one suffering from such a disease. In the circuit the recovered person apparently sent through the wires, along with the mana flow, some of the substance which provided the immunity.

This was all very unscientific and mysterious. Wires are not pipes, and, so far as physics and mechanics were concerned, such transfers were impossible. But, like other impossible things, they happened, were proven, and demanded an explanation.

With the help of medical men, Mr. Eeman continued

his experiments and soon was making a direct test on medicines, drugs and poisons of many kinds. His method was simple. The person volunteering for the test was asked to lie down on a cot with the wires arranged in the usual "relaxation circuit" hook-up. Then one of the wires was cut and the ends fastened to two electrodes which had been thrust down through the cork of a bottle into a solution of the stuff to be tested.

In his excellent book, *Co-operative Healing*,* Mr. Eeman tells in detail of over seventy tests which were made and of the reactions to the substances introduced through the mana flow into the body of the one submitting to the tests. Great precautions were taken to avoid suggestion or telepathy. The physician joining in the experiment had the substances placed in bottles and given code numbers so that only after the effects had been observed could the substance be identified and its usual reactions on the human body be compared. In all cases the subject developed physical or mental reactions in the same manner as if he had been dosed with the substance placed in the circuit. The tests were conclusive proof that something actually went from the bottle to the person, and a new field was opened in the matter of the administration of medicines.

Naturally, the question was at once raised as to just what it was that had traveled along the wire from the bottle. Obviously, it was not a part of the solution in the bottle, so it must be some form of radiation given off from the substance. Mr. Eeman, after years of con-

---

* Obtainable from Mr. L. E. Eeman, 24 Baker St., London W 1, England. 15 shillings.

184

sideration, concludes that the substances give off some form of energy radiation, or "dynamisms."

A possible explanation is furnished to us through Huna. The kahunas believed that all things or substances had corresponding aka or shadowy bodies (the "etheric" body of modern psychic science). They further give us the idea that the aka body is a duplicate of the thing it represents, and that the aka body comes as the first part of the creation, the physical as the second, and that there is a definite amount of consciousness and mana tied in with all things, otherwise they would not exist or retain a special form.

If we accept the idea that the medicines in the Eeman circuits had corresponding aka bodies, then it is easy to say that the aka body material of the medicines was carried on the mana flow to the body of the one being experimented upon. That simplifies the problem greatly, and one is left to inquire whether the entire effect is on the aka body of the subject, or, through the aka body, indirectly on the physical body.

In his writings, Mr. Eeman brings up the question of whether all infectious diseases may not have, as a part of their spread, some relation to the travel of toxins along wires. If this is so, he suggests, the mental state of the one subjected to such infections might be sufficient to repel them.

Another proof that the aka (or "etheric") body exists, and that it is not injured when the body is injured or even when death comes, was supplied by the Eeman circuit experiments with drugs. A man who had lost both of his legs was placed in an appropriate circuit with metal bands placed where his feet would have been, and the results were exactly the same as if real feet had been there. It was then suggested that the man imagine that he had drawn his knees up and that his theoretic feet were no longer down in contact with the wire terminal bands. He did this, and the effect was as if the circuit had been broken.

At the end of over twenty-five years of research and experimentation, Mr. Eeman discarded the wire in his circuits and replaced it with silk or wool cords. These worked just as well, and as they are not conductors of ordinary electricity, the difference between the vital force and electromagnetic or chemically produced electricity was made very plain. Dr. Brunler had also given up using wire, and had conducted the radiations from a head band on his subjects to the end of the ruler on his Biometer with a silk cord when making his tests.

It is to be seen that the original idea that the vital force was like electricity and that it could be conducted as a current through wires, was an erroneous concept. More than that, since the wires of the Eeman circuit can be replaced with silk or wool, or even with cotton cords, the question is at once raised as to why the ordinary clothing of a person does not set up a circuit between the poles of the body. The effect of "short circuiting" the vital force through the clothing, makes the entire theory begin to fall apart as irrational. However, Huna again comes to the rescue with an explanation.

Huna gives us the basic belief that the low self causes all flows of mana, and that the perfect conductor of mana is aka cord substance, not wire or cloth. The low self, being readily influenced by suggestion, will obligingly cause a mana flow along cords or wires if the suggestion is given to it that it will do so. However, as mana flows only through aka substance, a "finger" of aka will be projected along the wire or cord and the mana made to flow through it—the visible cord being only something that shows the low self where to extend its aka cord—as from hand to head, or from hand to bottle and into the medicine and then on to the head. Having seen the cleverness of the low self in its expert handling of the aka-mana combination in a thread or cord, and its use of its consciousness, it is no longer surprising to learn how it can work in new fields, once it has been given the idea of what is wanted of it.

Another of the unsolved problems which the HRAs took up was that of whether an object, like a certain very old Babylonian "prayer bowl," had retained in its unglazed clay a radiation placed there centuries ago. Or whether the strong influence exerted even today by the bowl was due to the fact that an enduring aka thread still connected it with the priest, for centuries dead, who had performed the rites over the bowl when it was made, giving it its strange powers.

The bowl in question is the size and shape of a soup bowl, and around the inside of it had been imprinted in the writing of the Babylonians of the time, a prayer for the protection of a local Israelite, his family and his domestic animals. Nothing is known of how the bowl was treated by the priest before it was given to its new owner, nor about the efficacy of the enchantment accompanying the bowl. The bowl had been covered by the dust of centuries, and not until a few years ago was it dug up and placed in a museum in Sydney, Australia.

It was part of a display set before the audience by a lecturer from the museum who described the ancient civilization. One of the HRAs was present, and she listened with much attention to the translation of the inscription on the inside of the bowl and to the description of the use of such bowls for healing and for protection from disease or disaster.

After the lecture, and while holding the bowl in her two hands, curious to know whether its power might still be awakened and used, she was surprised to feel a sudden tingling in her fingers. Guessing that she had, by her desire, enlivened the power in some way, she mentally asked that she be healed of a painful condition which had defied the efforts of doctors to heal over a period of many years. In a moment or two the pain left her, and the fissure was later found to have closed. It remained closed for many months. Later, her husband visited the museum and obtained permission to touch the prayer bowl. He also was apparently cured. (That the cures were not permanent seems to be due to the fact that the complexes, which may have caused the conditions, were not removed, and in time caused the conditions to return.)

All things, so science tells us, radiate a force of a characteristic kind, and in the radiation expend their life force and either change to some less active substance or suffer the peculiar form of "death" which is characteristic of their level of being.

There can be no doubt that there is a natural radiation rate from the clay in the prayer bowl, but this seems to have had a new and very different potential added to it. We would certainly say that some substance must have been added that gave out the higher radiation frequency which could bring healing.

As healing with such superimposed radiations demands that there be consciousness to guide the healing action of the radiations, one must look either to the low self of the one healed (although it has failed to use the mana at its disposal to heal its own body), or to some living or spirit entity connected to the bowl by an aka cord—and still able, when contact is made, to exert the guiding influence which might cause the indwelling or in-built radiation energy of the bowl to go into action and make physical changes in bodily tissues so that healing may result.

Working on this problem, some of the HRAs undertook to experiment and discover whether or not a healing "ikon" comparable to the prayer bowl could be made through actions of mind, prayer, and ritual blessing—even with the invocation of certainly friendly spirits of the departed. One of our English HRAs possessed an ikon over four hundred years old. It was in the form of a carved reproduction of Jesus on the cross, cut on the face of a heavy slab of dark wood and embellished in colors and silver. It had been made in Ethiopia and had been obtained there through the friendship of a native artist.

Through this crucifixion ikon, contact could be made almost at will with the spirit of an Ethiopian woman, long dead, but one taking an active interest in the new owner. This spirit furnished help of many kinds, and gave advice as to where to travel and what was to be done. She had directed the owner to find my book, *The Secret Science Behind Miracles*, and after he had read it, he was advised to go to various islands of the Pacific to investigate native beliefs, and especially, to study native images of other days.

Under the guidance of this spirit, the work of making new ikons was undertaken. Several materials were tested, and in the end it was decided that natural ivory was the best substance for the purpose. A small figure of a Japanese woman was obtained for the first test, one carved from African ivory. Later, the figure of a dancing Hindu god was obtained, carved from Indian ivory, the two making a male-female pair.

These little statuettes were ceremonially washed, blessed, and placed in contact with the crucifixion ikon for a period of time. In the end they were declared by the spirit to be finished. To one was attached a female spirit, and to the other a male. Both figures, when tested with the pendulum, now showed a very marked increase in strength of radiation energy. They were eventually sent to me and were tested by Mr. Cameron with the Aurameter, as remarked in the previous chapter. They were found to have much larger auras than similar untreated objects, and both had beams of force extending from them, making it probable that in the core of the beams were aka cords connecting them to the spirits assigned to work through them.

Another experiment in the making of a type of ikon was undertaken long before the organization of the HRA by a distinguished Englishwoman who is a powerful natural healer, an artist, and a well known expert in the use of the Bovis Biometer in the diagnosis of physical ills. She had worked with marked success to treat oils and canvas used in painting her pictures, then blessing and impregnating the finished pictures to give them healing radiations.

Her test of the potency of a finished healing picture was to place it in contact with a patient who, while gazing at it steadily, was given a Biometric reading. When the patient would register a reading of 600 degrees or better, the picture was considered finished and ready to be put into use. In use, it was hung on the wall and those desiring healing came and concentrated their gaze upon it for a time. Through the gaze contact is established with the picture and its radiations, it is supposed —but it is probable that the picture acts only as a place of anchorage for the ends of an aka cord leading to the healer herself, and through her, perhaps to her High Self. At any rate, these healing pictures have proved highly efficacious. One of the finest of these "potentized" paintings was sent as a gift to me, and has been tested with the Aurameter and pendulum. It has a strong aura and a heavy beam extending outward from the upper half of the canvas. After receiving these gifts the TMHG work was conducted in my study before the picture and the two ivory ikons.

One test project of the HRAs revolved around studies of the electronics or radionics type of instrument used for diagnosis and treatment by some medical doctors and by many chiropractors. It was decided that none of these instruments had need of being plugged into electric outlets, and that all depended—just as do the Biometer and pendulum and Aurameter—on the psychic ability and training of the operator, and on the contact with the patient, or something connected with him, which would furnish an aka thread contiguity. For this, a drop of blood on a bit of blotter has been the favorite, although saliva on the blotter has worked equally well. The setting of many dials did nothing in the instruments we studied but change the length of the total amount of wire running from a patient through the instrument and to the "rubbing block" or other indicator which is used by the operator to replace the pendulum of the Biometer.

What healing benefit there may be given from the instruments seems to come, as from the healing picture, directly from the operator, not from the instrument. The dial settings give "readings" in terms of numbers, and these replace the degree reading in centimeters of the Biometer. One maker of a famous instrument of this type understands the Huna theory, and has accepted the fact of the aka thread as the means of contact with the patient for all away-from-office treatments.

Another HRA, an English doctor of exceptional training and psychic ability, has abandoned the use of the Biometer and electronics instruments, and now uses nothing more elaborate than the tingle in his fingers to get the message from his low self that will help him diagnose the ills of his patients and determine the right medicines and the right amounts needed for dosage. As did the kahunas of old, this modern physician takes advantage of all possible healing aids. After his diagnosis he adjusts joints or administers medicines, as the case may require, and uses his marked natural healing powers in combination with prayer. It goes without saying that his results are far above average.

There were many other things investigated by the HRAs, some of which were promising, some of which turned out to be blind leads. We had, among us, a solid core of highly intelligent people, open-minded to new ideas but not to be blinded by the "mysteries" with which certain false prophets lead on the credulous. They had become HRAs in the first place because the Huna theories seemed to them based on common sense, though they needed verifying.

It is as if one could put oneself back in time to when men looked on lightning with awe and fear, and had no explanation for it other than that it was an act of God, and meant potential destruction. Then if we could live also in the time that men learned to harness this dread force, to make it work for them, actually to *generate* it, we might have a comparison with this study of ours. We have had to convince ourselves of the validity of the idea that we are composed mentally of three selves, that there is an aka-cord connection, and that we can and must generate a strong mana flow along the cord. Only then can man begin really to use his full powers.

But all is not perfection yet, by any means. We encountered the greatest problem of all, which will be reported on next, together with our attempts at a solution.

CHAPTER XV

THE PROBLEM OF THE UNANSWERED PRAYERS

It must be said that, from the very first, we were made aware often of the individual HRAs who were unable to contact their High Selves, and that often no results were obtained through the efforts to use the Huna method of making the prayers. Also, there were the failures in the TMHG work to be considered. In the first place, we must acknowledge the fact that some people are so constituted that they will try a method for a little while, then lose interest and drift on to something else. There are others who just cannot "find time" to train the low self, or even to get into the right attitude of mind and accumulate the surcharge of mana before they pray. Then there are those who want someone from outside themselves to perform a miracle for them—and immediately, with no work on their own part. But, with all such accounted for, there is still the problem of the people who try earnestly and sincerely, whose need is so urgent that they can and do find time to pray, but who cannot seem to reach their High Selves.

In my book, with which all HRAs were familiar, I had reported the observed prayer-actions of kahunas which achieved such amazing results. I told how they went about their healing work by helping their patients to get rid of their feelings of guilt, requiring them to make amends. How they helped to remove the things which were "blocking the path" and "eating inside" (complexes), and then, if present, any spirits who had been exerting influence in the life of the one to whom they had attached themselves. Also, they dealt with spirits who had not attached themselves to the patient, but who periodically did things to cause him trouble, usually in an effort to avenge loved ones who had been hurt by the one attacked.

I told of the mana surcharge taken on until it was so large and strong that it could be used by the kahuna much as the modern shock treatment to dislodge obsessing entities. I told of a supermesmeric use of the same power to administer suggestion, with the aid of a physical stimulus to make the suggestion even more powerful, and to force its acceptance by the low self.

These were the methods. But we found it difficult to learn to do as the kahunas had done. The best kahunas were trained psychics who could sense spirits causing trouble. We could not. The use of suggestion was looked upon by some with natural suspicion, and an attempt to interest a group of eighteen hypnotists in experimenting with the "mana shock method" proved useless. Also, it was not revealed just what steps the kahunas took to remove the complexes, though their root-words and symbols showed a deep knowledge of the presence of these trouble-making things in the low self.

The reader will probably read all the way through this report before pausing to see whether or not he can use the Huna prayer method, as it has been explained. However, it should be said here that the only way to find out whether or not one can use the method, or whether there is a "blocked path" to the High Self, is to try—to take the training steps and see whether or not answers are obtained to the prayers which are correctly and carefully made. If answers are not forthcoming, the next steps to be taken will be found in the following section of the report. If one inspects the first and earliest religious writings, it will be found that back in the dim beginnings of history, men had begun to pray and were already wondering why prayers were sometimes answered and sometimes not.

The Bible is especially valuable in this respect, as it is filled with passages relating to prayer and the methods of making prayers. In the ancient religious literature of India the problem was not set forth as clearly because the doctrine of karma more or less forced the people to believe that it was better to suffer, and so to repay or wear out their karmic debts, than to try to get help from the gods through prayer for the things that caused them to suffer.

Propitiation of the gods was, of course, as old as the concept of "gods" or superphysical beings. Sacrifice was the most common rite of propitiation, and next came penance and self-punishment for acts classed as "sins" against the gods. Self-torture, wearing hair shirts, self-mutilation, fasting and vows of silence or abstinence, were all part of the propitiatory efforts. Certain men came to be the ones to officiate at all sacrificial rites, and gradually they appear in the pages of history as a class apart, the priestly class. They, and they alone, were supposed to be able to tell whether or not the gods were angry or were pleased. They soon arrogated to themselves the right to administer or grant forgiveness for "sin" as direct and authorized agents of the gods. Even today this office is administered for the Supreme God.

The scapegoat is no longer burdened with the sins of the people and driven into the wilderness. The slaughter of animals on the altar, the sprinkling of the congregation and temple furnishings with the blood, and the burning of the flesh—all these things have passed for the most part. But still it is the *outer meaning* of religions which has been preserved. The inner meaning has long been lost from those religions of old into which Huna had been introduced as a secret body of knowledge.

In modern times much has been done to try to get away from the savage rites and concepts and the priestly arrogations of divine privilege, and many theories have been offered which run all the way from a complete denial of all material reality—including sin—to the expanding of the idea of God to one in which Diety is Vast Impersonality.

Today, as in Christianity at the time of its inception, the most widely accepted explanation of why prayers are not answered, is that the one making the prayer is not deserving of an answer. "Sin" is thought to be the thing that makes one undeserving.

The standard steps to get oneself cleansed of sin and so become worthy of having prayers answered, may be set down as follows:

(1) Stop sinning.
(2) Make amends for sins committed.
(3) Ask forgiveness and hope to receive it.

These three steps have been followed with care for

up to twenty centuries, and still prayers are all too often left unanswered. This has been painfully true despite the doctrine of the vicarious atonement, which, if accepted as applicable to the individual for his own cleansing, is thought to make amends for any and all sins. Obviously, something is missing.

It has long been suspected by students of religious history that something must be very wrong with our understanding of what was taught in both the Old Testament and the New, in so far as prayer and its frequent failure are concerned—and this includes our *understanding* of sin, amends, atonement, purification, prayers for forgiveness, and such rites as baptism, conversion, the confessional, and so forth.

We have to go to Huna for the correct concept of sin, and then we find that sin is, basically, not just breaking a "law" proclaimed by some prophet as having been laid down by God, though the Ten Commandments were necessary social laws for a primitive people, providing a moral basis for life, and stand today as still basically useful.

Sin is much more than that. It is far wider, deeper, and broader. Sin is, as we find through Huna, *anything that is bad for the human being or his fellows.*

To hurt others is a sin. Not only physical murder, but hurting others mentally and emotionally is a sin.

To hurt God is impossible. Man is too weak and small to do this. And breaking a man-made "law of God" means nothing if it hurts no one.

But anything that prevents the low self from acting to make the contact along the aka cord with the High Self and delivering the prayer (thus "blocking the

198

path"), is bad because it cuts man off from God—cuts the low and middle selves off from the High Self, breaks up the team of three selves, makes the entire life less than normal, and prevents the High Self from helping the lower pair of selves. (As has been stated before, the High Self seems pledged to allow the lower pair their use of FREE WILL to a large extent—to permit them to blunder and stumble and suffer and sicken in order to learn by experience.)

The BAD done which is of such a nature that it hurts others, may be reclassified according to Huna as:

(1) The "sin" of bad done others by malicious intent and with a full knowledge that it is bad—but, nevertheless, with a sense of guilt and a resultant twinge of conscience. This will cause the low self of this sinner to "flee from the face of God" as a child flees from a parent when it deserves punishment and fears it will be given. A low self filled with (a) guilt, (b) shame because of its acts, or (c) fear, will NOT make contact with the High Self or try to send a prayer by way of the aka cord.

(2) The naturally bad person who hurts others maliciously but who feels justified in doing so, and who suffers no sense of guilt or shame, but feels triumphant and worthy of praise for having "overcome" others, will NOT have his low self refuse to make the contact with the High Self. NOR WILL HIS HIGH SELF CUT HIM OFF. His prayer for help in the good things he may do, will be answered. "God is no respecter of persons," and in this case the "wicked flourish as the green bay tree" for a time, but their punishment comes in the form of the slowing down of their evolution upward. This will seem very hard for many to reconcile with the

"Justice of God," but one has only to look around to see the wicked prosper and suffer no twinge of remorse or shame. One's sense of affronted "justice" can only be healed by realizing that our concept of "sin" must be changed from all the customary beliefs and made to rest on one test alone. DOES THE ACT CAUSE AN INDIVIDUAL TO BE CUT OFF BY HIS LOW SELF FROM HIS HIGH SELF? If it does not, he has not sinned under the classification which we are forced to consider in order to understand why prayers are not answered. It all rests on and revolves around the question of what may or may not cause the low self to refuse to contact the High Self. The matter of justice, human or divine, or of karma or ultimate retribution has no part in this premise from which we approach the problem of unanswered prayer.

Once this point of view can be accepted as a fact, or even as an assumption (while leaving the matter of justice entirely out of the picture for the time being), one can go on to look into the list of things that prevent the low self from doing its part in prayer—the things which are quite apart from the kind of Bad acts we have noted above.

The low self is affected by only two things:

(1) What it senses at the moment with the five senses, as what it sees, hears, feels—painful, fearful, good, bad, or pleasant impressions.

(2) What it remembers of the times or events in the past when it has registered events or happenings—has remembered or registered by making *thought-form clusters* with which to record and remember.

This brings us to the two kinds of memories. The one made in the normal and natural way has as part of it the MEANING or RATIONALIZATION of the event and its RELATION TO ALL PREVIOUS EVENTS of which the man has knowledge, or which he anticipates, fears or hopes to see develop. All memory thought-form clusters are, as made, connected with all the other memories which ARE RECALLED DURING THE PROCESS OF DECIDING WHAT THEY MEAN IN RELATION TO ALL THINGS FORMERLY EXPERIENCED, read about, imagined, or otherwise touched upon.

As indicated in the translations of their ancient words, the kahunas used the symbol of the spider's web with flies caught in it; each fly was a memory, and all flies were connected by the strands of the web with all other flies. In the center lay the spider—the man made of low and middle selves—aware of the presence of each fly and able to run out to inspect it at any time. The thin strands of the web stood for the aka thread, and the normal memory was one tied to all other memories in a rationalization process as it was made, thought over, and considered.

This in turn brings us to the other kind of memory— which is made and stored WITHOUT BEING RATIONALIZED. This set of thought-forms will not be tied in correctly with other thought forms, and because the middle self DID NOT DO ITS PART AND RATIONALIZE the memory as it was being made, the middle self never has that particular memory given back to it as one recalled. It is an outlaw memory. It is deformed. It is something that the low self knows is not normal and not right, and of which it is ashamed or afraid.

A low self which harbors a sense of guilt because of

bad deeds done by the low and middle selves, will not face the High Self across the aka cord. In exactly the same way it will not face the middle self with the shame of an unrationalized memory weighting it down—making it feel that it has dirty hands and that it must hide the black thing at all costs. In this trait the low self is more stubborn and obstinate than can be imagined. It hides these outlaw memories like a crafty criminal his loot, and, like the criminal, it crouches hidden from the middle self at night when the middle self sleeps, and considers its ill-gotten loot, sorting it, trying to RATIONALIZE IT IN ITS OWN ILLOGICAL FASHION.

The result of this effort to put right the outlaw memories results in a worsening condition. In the hiding of the "black sack" where it keeps this loot, the low self works and compares and comes to all kinds of illogical and irrational conclusions. (The reasoning power used by the middle self is impossible to the low self.)

One outlaw memory cluster may slowly be tied by the low self, using aka threads, to several other chains of linked or connected, but normal and rational, thought-form clusters which register the memories and meanings of events. As a result, the individual, although the middle self can recall none of the unrationalized memories, will seem automatically to react to certain events thus connected with the outlaw memory, as if he were slightly demented. He may react in any or all of several ways:

(1) He may fly into a rage or may be filled with unreasonable fear or some other form of emotion which seems suddenly to well up from inside him and to be too strong to control.

(2) He may be unable to think normally, rationally or at the usual speed when some event which is tied to the outlaw is confronted. He may find a blank in his memories right there, even to the degree of amnesia.

(3) He may suddenly imagine things to be entirely different than they actually are. He may imagine a friend is an enemy or almost anything at all. He may imagine that he, himself, is vastly superior all of a sudden, or that he is so put upon that his very life is a continuing misery.

(4) He may react physically, jerking, trembling, becoming hysterical or paralyzed or blind or deaf and dumb—for a short or long period.

(5) He may show no outward reaction such as these, but may develop physical ills of all sorts. (Physicians now know that a large part of human sickness comes as a result of involvement to a greater or lesser degree with this trouble which we are discussing.)

In addition to the abnormalities in reactions to events, physically, mentally, emotionally or in matters of health, there is one other very important factor to be kept in mind at all times. This is the fact that there is, tied up with each memory cluster, a certain something that gauges the amount of mana which will be automatically used or "exploded" when that particular memory cluster is touched or activated by some circumstance.

Most memories arouse almost no emotion on the part of the low self, and so use up almost no mana as they are recalled. Emotion uses up mana faster by far than anything else. All of us have witnessed the effect of an emotional storm which has depleted the vital force— sometimes even to the point of physical collapse.

If an outlaw memory has been made by some event

which caused the low self to get out of hand because of anger, fear, grief or hate, almost the same very large amount of mana used in the original emotional explosion will be recalled and used as the memory is triggered. If the middle self was unable to function when the original emotion caused the low self to grab the bit, so to speak, and bolt with the man, leaving all reason behind and out of the picture, the same thing will happen on a slightly lesser scale when the memory is activated.

Because of this waste of mana, the individual whose low self may be inwardly seething with outlaw memories, all tied together in a wild tangle, may find himself chronically exhausted and ill. We all know the bedeviled persons who are constantly expressing their hates and fears and black suspicions which are irrational for the most part, but to which they cling despite all argument, desperately and almost insanely. As a matter of fact, such persons are psychotic or neurotic to the extent to which these outlaw memory tangles afflict them.

A person who is only slightly burdened with outlaw memories is able to go through life fairly well. Most of us are entirely unaware that we have these burdensome memories, and in no way do we suspect that our physical ills, our "bad luck," our angers, hates and illogically "set" ideas and beliefs are caused in any way by the outlaw memory clusters. Least of all do we suspect them of being the cause of the failure of our prayers.

Unfortunately, most of us are unaware that the lesser mental troubles are caused by the outlaws. We decide only when things become serious that we are suffering from some "mental illness," and we go to a doctor, who sends us to a psychologist or a psychiatrist. One greatly burdened in this way tends to tie up—and use up—more and more precious mana in reacting to the outlaw memories, and as the mana level sinks, the middle self loses its control over the low self. The mental illness may become so marked that the person must be placed in a mental hospital for treatment.

The kahunas had three words for the three levels of the state of severance from the High Self which was caused by the low self when it harbored deep feelings of guilt, shame or fear, or heavy loads of outlaw memory tangles. These words were:

(1) *Ino:* to hurt others, to be wicked and BAD willfully.

(2) *Hala:* to have a normal number of outlaw memory tangles so that only a part of our actions or reactions are off-normal. This word also means to miss the path one should take. This "path" is the aka cord, and to miss it is to have the low self refuse to send the prayer to the High Self. It is to miss the mark in trying to hit the thing aimed at. (Check the New Testament: "Miss the mark of the high calling," in which the calling is the prayer to the High Self.)

(3) *Hewa:* to make a mistake, to think or act or react wrongly, to be mentally deranged to some extent. To forget. Also, this word has the meaning of "missing the right path," as has the word *hala.*

The symbol words used by the kahunas to indicate this thing that cuts one off from the High Self—this unrationalized memory tangled with its many aka threads—appear all through the Bible. Here are some of them:

Thorns, thistles (the cursed things God caused to grow in the soil which Adam was forced to till after being driven from the Garden because of his "sins").

The dragon, the serpent. Any ferocious wild beast—particularly a lion.

A snare, which is made of a thread, cord or rope, symbolic of the aka threads and the tangle of the outlaw memories ("sins") which tempt or capture or otherwise hold one captive.

A "stumbling block" of any kind. A cross of any shape.

All of these symbolize the fixations and obsessions—the outlaws which trip us up. If there are many outlaw memories, they will BLOCK THE "PATH" OR "WAY" OR "ROAD" OR "HIGHWAY." (A straight path or a straight or stretched cord is the symbol of the opened path; while a "crooked" path or a tangled cord, one *not* pulled tight, is the symbol of the aka cord which is entirely or partly blocked, or which the low self will activate only at rare intervals to send a prayer to the High Self on the command of the middle self.)

The kahunas used a wooden cross in the form of an "X" on the path leading to a temple. It was the sign of taboo in Huna. The temple itself signified the "place of the Most High." The cross placed on the path was a warning that the uncleansed must not proceed. Later we shall take up the symbology of another form of cross.

Dust or fine particles of dirt symbolize the thought-forms, as well as do seeds, as mentioned before. But in the case of the outlaw memories these fine particles of dirt are looked upon as something that makes one unclean, which soil our hands or especially our feet. One needs to be cleansed of them before being fit to face the High Self, by way of the low self, in the action of making the Huna-type prayer. (The word Huna means fine dust particles, as well as "secret," and this shows how important the kahunas of old considered the understanding of the thought-forms. These are symbolized as acting in clusters, the "seeds" of the prayer, and forming other clusters in the outlaw and unrationalized memories which cut man off from the High Self.)

A net of any kind is a symbol often used because of the intermeshing of the cords as between associated memories, and at times the fish caught in the net represent the memories which become entangled and removed from their normal state. The fish are especially good symbolically because they are usually hidden, and are hard to find and catch. However, when brought to the surface, and deprived of water (mana) they are killed (rationalized or re-thought and made harmless).

The mana which is tied up with the defective memories is symbolized by ice or snow or cold. It is frozen water, and is as set and fixed (so cannot flow, symbolically) as are the beliefs and ideas contained in the defective memories—the latter being held to stubbornly by the afflicted low self despite all arguments presented by the middle self or by others.

Trembling, shivering, shaking with fear, therefore, are symbols of the mana and the memory tangles which hold the man captive. "Fear of the Lord" causes the low self to try to escape parental punishment by refusing to "go before the face of the Lord" or the High Self, and fear and guilt and shame interlace so that one interchanges with another.

In short, what can prevent our prayers from being answered is the unrationalized memory which we have learned to call "complex" or "fixation." It is also the guilt sense caused by having committed the sin of hurting others.

We can stop hurting others and make amends for hurts already done. That is comparatively simple for most of us because we live fairly hurtless and helpful lives.

To get the memory tangles to the surface and to rationalize them—that is the major problem.

CHAPTER XVI

THE PROBLEM OF THE BLOCKED PATH

In our HRA approach to the problem of unblocking the aka cord "path" to the High Self by bringing to light and "draining off" or rationalizing memory tangles, we began with a close study of modern findings concerning what Freud called "fixations," and what later psychologists called "the complex." (As is well known, Freud stubbornly held to the theory that the instinctual sexual urge was the basis of all troubles in the "unconscious." However, it is possible to use his term, "fixation," in a broader sense to cover all memory tangles.)

Freud defined the word "fixation" thus: "One instinct or instinctual component fails to accompany the rest along the anticipated normal path of development, it is left behind at a more infantile stage. The libidinal current in question then behaves in regard to later psychological structures as though it belonged to the system of the unconscious, as though it were repressed." * "Complex" is defined as "an emotionally colored idea or idea pattern that has been repressed." † We shall use the terms interchangeably, and they will be understood to refer to the stumbling blocks of Huna phraseology. The word "rationalize" is used here as mean-

---

* *Freud: Dictionary of Psychoanalysis,* edited by Nandor Fodor and Frank Gaynor.

† *Words: The New Dictionary,* Grosset & Dunlap.

ing, "To make rational; also, to endow with reason." ‡

In gratitude to Freud and the psychologists who followed close in his footsteps in exploring the human mind, it must be admitted that, had they not first postulated the subliminal or subconscious part of mind, and discovered that it held unrationalized memories which cause a variety of mental and physical ills and irregularities, we might not have been able to understand even in part what the kahunas meant by their phrase, "things eating one inside," nor the symbolic words of the Biblical kahunas who spoke of stumbling blocks, thistles, thorns, serpents and secret sins.

In passing, it is interesting to note the fact that the early missionaries in Hawaii, in the years between 1820 and 1860, even with kahunas at hand able and willing to instruct and help them to an understanding of Huna, failed entirely to grasp the idea of the subconscious or low self as distinct from the middle self and High Self. Of course, the subconscious was not yet known in the Western world, so the difficulty is easily understood. (The kahuna words for the three selves were, respectively, *unihipili, uhane* and *Aumakua,* but the best the missionaries could do when compiling a dictionary, was to translate all three words "some kind of spirit.")

Fortunately, the complex had been identified some time before my study of Huna began in earnest, and the barrier to full understanding was lowered. The verity of the fixation is well established by now, and, while the kahunas were more specific in describing the aka threads, the thought-form structure, and the tie-up of mana with

‡ *Webster's New International Dictionary.*

the complex, the modern view of the matter is very similar.

Freud, being a medical doctor, became interested in the patients who came to him with distinct symptoms of some neurotic or psychotic trouble, often accompanied by physical symptoms of illness or abnormal muscular functioning. He gradually evolved a method of treatment for these cases which depended on the finding of the complex held in the subliminal part of mind (our low self), and the rationalization of the unrationalized tangles. The subliminal was found to be secretive and stubborn to the extent that it would not allow the fixation memory units to come to the center of consciousness as recalled memories, either by invitation, coercion or through the use of suggestion and hypnotic pressure. He fell back largely on the observation of the dreams of the patients in his care, and upon careful studies of the circumstances surrounding the appearance of such reactions as might be laid to the presence of the fixation in the subliminal.

Other workers joined Freud in his research, and soon there was built up a table of symbolic correspondences intended to show the relation between the dream and the complex—for instance, that when there was a dream of a potbellied stove, it indicated that the subliminal self was thinking symbolically of the womb from which the man had been born. Each person, no matter what his characteristics, was thought to have in his subliminal almost identical sets of symbols to use for the same things and experiences in dreams. The arguments given to back up these slightly preposterous claims were none too

211

good, and the part played by suggestion, even though this was supposed to have little or no part in the process of dream study, was seldom properly evaluated.

Freud's insistence that sex frustrations were at the root of most fixations, caused later investigators to differ with him on many points. Jung and others added to the theories and leaned slightly more toward adding the Superconscious in some form to the picture; but the methods of Freud remained in more or less general use. Dreams continued to be observed, recorded and studied for their significance in order to learn through them what was buried in the subliminal part of the mind. Where dreams were few and far between, the method was augmented by "free association" of ideas on the part of the patient, who—in a relaxed physical state—would tell the analyst what came into his mind automatically as an associate idea whenever a certain thing, person, place or event was mentioned. The play of imagination, when allowed to run free, such as in picturing what random ink blots might suggest to the viewer, was included in the methodology.

One of the later additions to the system of treatment was strange indeed. The analyst created an artificial complex by thinking up some possible situation which, had it been actual, might have caused the patient to form fixations. This event was then related to the patient with the strongly urged belief that it had taken place in fact, and, more important still, that it had been the cause of the original fixation which was bringing about abnormal physical or mental reactions. How much the element of suggestion entered into such a procedure was seldom stated, but good results were often reported.

One of the defects in the methods used by the analysts has been that too much effort was given to finding the complex, and too little to a general renovation and correction of the over-all attitude of the patient toward life and his fellow human beings. It seems not to have been realized that defective thinking on the part of the middle self was often a thing that prevented the complex from being found. For instance, the many hates and fears of the patient may have come from wrong ideas about people, things, religions and the like. These might be in need of study and correction. Of course such ideas can be the result of the complex. But all too often, the doctor has made the mistake of thinking that seemingly illogical hatreds and fears had their roots in some complex when, in truth, the educational life-experience of the patient had been to blame.

The greatest defect of the system, however, has been its lack of a clear understanding of the necessity of correcting the morals of the patient. A man's mental structure is "a house built upon sand" if the individual is not made to see that envy, greed, senseless anger, and the taint of dishonesty are wrong and are contrary to the good of his fellows. Nor has the part played by a sense of guilt apparently been given full recognition, whether this sense is lodged as a complex in the subconscious or is something shared by both the low and middle selves, especially when the vague thing called "conscience" smites the patient.

Freud was forced to recognize the "conscience" as a very important factor in melancholia. This is a condition in which the individual suffers greatly from what Freud described as over-severe punishment by conscience, which is used as a whip by the "super-ego." Freud's super-ego concept was anything but a glimpse of the High Self as he examined his patients. It was something he thought of as the result of the pressures of moral teachings, which caused a repression of unconscious urges. The super-ego was to be deplored, as was all influence of religion.

There are many psychoanalysts practicing today who follow Freudian principles only, not taking into account the later valuable work of Jung, who recognizes the religious impulse in man as at least valid. These doctors apparently have felt themselves bound by the materialism of science, and for that reason have carefully refrained from advancing any theory which might resemble current religious beliefs. Religion has meant, to most of them, muddled thinking and confusion. Moreover, it was supposed by churchmen that the Bible made no mention of the subconscious or the complex, and for this reason, even today, attacks by religionists on psychoanalysis are not infrequent.

This is a strange state of affairs. The analysts know full well that many fixations which they are called upon to treat stem from the wrong religious teachings—from fear of eternal damnation. On the other hand, the results obtained by the analysts have been so slow and so uncertain in coming, that many of them have taken to making full use of a patient's religious beliefs and of his faith in God, in offering treatment. A happy medium has been found in churches which have opened clinics for the treatment of their members and who have staffed them, in addition to the religious advisers, with psychiatrists and psychologists.

What neither the analyst nor the average churchman recognizes is the part played in mental abnormalities by the influence of spirits. This influence may be so slight that it is mistaken for the natural bent of the patient, or it may be marked but not recognized for what it is. Even in cases of complete insanity—where obsession is so evident that it has been named "obsessional insanity" —the scientific standing of the psychiatrists will not allow them to give a moment's heed to the possibility of spirit interference. Most churchmen, even with the Bible filled with mention of evil spirits and demons who cause sickness and insanity, have gone over to the side of science in this matter.

Despite all of these defects and limitations, however, it must be freely admitted that much very good work is being done for many people, and that the finding and removing of complexes, if nothing more, often results in marked improvement, even if the progress in this narrow corner of the field has been painfully slow.

The dissatisfaction with the slowness and uncertainty of psychoanalysts, and the almost complete failure by churchmen (comparatively speaking) to get healing for minds through prayer, resulted a few years ago in a strange revolt by amateurs. They broke away from the professional analysts and the religionists to try to improve upon the conservative theories and to invent newer, faster and better analytical methods—especially methods which one amateur might use to help another.

Outstanding among these revolutionists was L. E. Eeman, of England, whose relaxation circuits have been discussed in Chapter XIV. He began experimenting and writing on psychoanalytical lines as early as 1924, and made some very interesting discoveries. He evolved a system of locating and removing fixations, named it "Myognosis," and described it in articles and lectures as well as in his book, *Co-operative Healing*. He did not hesitate to add the element of religion and of the Superconscious to his theories—and for that reason, in spite of the excellent demonstrations which he made of his methods, gained little recognition from psychiatrists.

The revolt against the slow and reactionary phychiatrists and the psychoanalysts of the Freudian school was turned into new channels in mid-year of 1950 by a layman, L. Ron Hubbard, a writer of science fiction and one who had been a battle casualty in the Marines. Mr. Hubbard had, much as had Mr. Eeman, been led into a study of the mind and its nature by his own difficulties. He had spent some time inventing and trying out various methods of adminstering mental therapy, and had evolved a set of theories to match his methods. Whether or not he realized that there were numerous people in America who were ready to revolt against the older theories and therapies, it is hard to say, but as soon as he published his book *Dianetics*, and offered leadership, hundreds flocked to his banner.

Dianetics may have owed its great appeal to the fact that it offered a therapy for everyone, not just for those who had recognized mental quirks, psychoses or neuroses. The theory was advanced that everyone had "engrams" (something similar to a complex) to a greater or lesser extent, and that each engram tied up with it a part of the mental strength of the individual. It was promised that when the engrams were found, brought to light and broken up through the new methods, the great release of mind power would make one thus "cleared" much more able mentally than before. These results were to be obtained in from forty to fifty hours of application of the methods. Such application demanded nothing more than a careful reading of the book by two people, after which they could "audit" one another, it was said, and thousands of amateur auditors were soon experimenting with the new method.

It was found that the promised release of more mental energy and the healing of ills of a psychosomatic nature were not being as widely realized as had been anticipated. It was evident that training and experience were needed after the book had been read. Meanwhile, Mr. Hubbard, to fill this need, organized schools in which students might be audited and be taught at first hand to use the new auditing methods. The demand for the services of trained Dianetic auditors was already so great that the six-weeks' course seemed to many to be an excellent and simple way to enter a new profession.

A few of the HRAs were attracted by the possibilities and promises of the new therapy. Some tried auditing their friends and being audited in turn. Some hunted up the newly trained auditors and submitted themselves to the treatments, and some enrolled in the schools and became professional auditors.

In the HRA Bulletins the new therapy was discussed at length and reports were given from time to time on the experiences of the HRAs who had tried out Mr. Hubbard's methods. At first the reports were uniformly hopeful and often enthusiastic. Then a doubt crept in, a feeling that the Dianetics methods did not live up to their promise. Mr. Hubbard himself was among the first to realize this, and he began to revise his theories and ways of encouraging the recall of events (often prenatal) which he believed to have caused the engrams. New techniques were frequently announced and made available through short printed releases.

While Mr. Hubbard was revising his conclusions from month to month, other laymen, most of whom had taken the Dianetics professional course and had gone to work as auditors, formulated theories of their own and offered therapy in a slightly different form.

The "Eidetics Foundation" was one of the new groups founded by former Dianetics auditors. In this group the approach was based on Gestalt Psychology and the subconscious was not recognized, therefore the engram, which was so reminiscent of the complex, was replaced by other concepts. Naturally, with no subconscious, there was no super-conscious.

"E Therapy" was the contribution of Mr. A. L. Kitselman, another of those who had taken the auditing course. However, "E Therapy" was something that Mr. Kitselman had been formulating for a number of years on the side of theory. He had been a student of religions and psychology, and it was his belief that whatever it might be that prevented a person from being at his best mentally or physically, could be removed by "God," in whatever form one might think of Him. This Divine Being, which he designated as "E" to make it fit all forms of religion, had but to be requested through prayer to take charge and to correct conditions by correcting their psychic causes.

It is difficult to evaluate these new therapies, as they

are in a state of growth and experimentation. Constant changes in theory as well as practice are appearing, and new terms are coined to fit the new ideas in a bewildering manner. Since the prime interest of the HRA was to discover whether or not a better method of removing blockings of the path was becoming available, we shall have to await a more settled period when their methods shall have been tested and proven.

From the standpoint of Huna, we agreed that, like psychoanalysis, they were not working with the *three selves*, and therefore their work was bound to be incomplete. The extremely important matter—to Huna—of the mana was completely unknown. In some of the methods there seems to be an effort to cause the ones treated to give up old hates and fears, to try to better their attitude toward life and toward those around them. But there is not the strong forceful teaching of the kahunas in this part of the work, nor the insistence on amends being made to those who have been hurt.

One thing that Mr. Hubbard has been discussing in recent writings which sounds promising is the influence of "demons." The Eidetic Foundation group is also working along that line. In this respect there is a definite step toward agreement with Huna, and away from the limitations of science which have prevented modern psychiatrists from such recognition.

There seems to be a definite fear on the part of the originators of the new therapies that they may fall into the same pit which has so long awaited the Christian revivalist-healers, who would by now have replaced most of the doctors in the land if their healings had been permanent in more cases. Any healing which does not remove the cause of the trouble, be it physical or psychic or the result of spirit influence, is but a temporary aid. This is what the revivalist-healers fail to understand. Even the primary work of aiding the patient to rid himself of old hates and fears, jealousies and envies, is done for only a short preparatory period (if at all) before actual healing is attempted. And, of course, the complexes are not recognized, and not removed. Apparent healing may be obtained, and often is, but when the complex which caused the trouble in the first place is not removed, it is but a matter of time until the healing has "worn off" and the malady is back, usually worse than before.

An example of this difficulty—and a very real one it is—was brought painfully to our attention in the HRA in the case of T. A. L., who was healed by telepathic contact and prayer by Mrs. R., as has been related in an earlier chapter. T. A. L. was entirely free from his painful stomach condition for a time after the healing took place. He could eat any type of food without harmful results, and was convinced that his healing was permanent. But without warning, the trouble came back, and, greatly disappointed, he was forced to visit his doctor and ask for treatment. It is evident that as long as the *cause* of these troubles is not removed, the healing will not be permanent.

The auditors of the Dianetics type fall into the same pit of a lack of permanency in their healings in some cases. This comes about through a lack of understanding broad enough to cover the religious aspect of the problem. The complexes and the spirit influence, no matter how described and renamed, cannot be audited and removed so that they will stay out of the way unless the patient is entirely desirous of giving up the old hurtful ways of life and going over to the kindly and helpful life. And above all, he must make contact with his High Self and keep the path open.

No system of mental therapy can be complete which does not take into consideration the almost universal impulse of men to recognize some form of Higher Being and to look up to it worshipfully—to look to it as the possible source of help in time of trouble. Psychologists still argue the question of whether there may or may not be some basic instinct behind worship of a Superior Power. But it is very possible that such an instinct is as real and as urgent as Freud found the sex urge to be, or as others consider the instinct to survive or the drive for recognition or dominance. I have seen primitives stand lost in adoration of a spectacle of great beauty, giving every evidence of an impulsive reaching out and yearning for something in that beauty which is beyond and higher, which is truer, nobler and more real.

Man cannot live without hope, and, when all else is gone, he can still have hope of survival and a future life if he is allowed to have a faith in a Higher Being who will not fail him. Any therapy which does not build upon such hope builds poorly. More and more this is being understood as psychiatry enters the churches to help in the healing ministry being offered for troubled minds. But, not until the significance of the "demons" of the Bible and the obsessing spirit "eating companions" of the kahunas is recognized, can the psychiatric part of the ministry be complete.

CHAPTER XVII

ARE FIXATIONS BROUGHT OVER FROM FORMER LIVES?

ARE THERE UNSUSPECTED SPIRIT OBSESSIONS?

In all forms of psychoanalysis, as has been said, the operators depend not only upon dreams, but also upon the thoughts which occur as the patient (in a relaxed physical condition) allows his mind to wander at will, one idea calling up another by free association. The things that come into the minds of patients under these conditions are like waking dreams, and are studied in the same way as dreams while asleep, to discover in them symbols or other clues which may help to identify the memories of events which have caused complexes.

The patient often imagines scenes, people, places and experiences which are almost as real to him as his dreams, and he describes these to his analyst as he would his dreams. Because of the vividness of these impressions, and because they often seem to be so true to life, there arose a very interesting perplexity. Were these waking dreams to be considered figments of imagination, or were some of them memories being recalled of events and circumstances related to the past lives of the patient?

Freud inclined to the opinion that both night and day dreams, of the kind mentioned, were based on imagination, and were not experiences. As such, he set about analysing them both as "psychological structures" in which might be hidden symbols which would point to the origin of the complex or fixation. Later, when Jung broke away from the Freudian principles, he seemed to think this theory hardly good enough to explain the matter. Jung suggested that each of us may inherit through the genes a portion of the "racial memory," and because of this may seem to remember events in our own past lives which actually took place in the lives of ancestors of the race. These memories were supposed to be common to all of the race, and not actual and individual experiences of any one patient. This theory seems to have interested him enormously, for he is spending his declining years in research through legends and medieval writings to try to find the meaning of symbols and archetypes in the history of the race.

Other analysts have been speaking and writing of the evidence they have found that events lived through in past incarnations of the individual were being remembered. The investigators of the Psychical Research Societies had already broken ground in this direction, and many of them had become convinced that reincarnation is a fact and that memories from past lives are sometimes recalled. Mr. Hubbard, in his latest research (called *Scientology*) takes this stand.

Let us take up briefly one of the most recent and convincing reports on tests aimed at exploring the combined question of past incarnations and fixations carried over from them. These tests were made around the year 1945 by a famous medium and investigator, Geraldine Cummins, working and writing with Dr. R. Connell,

in England. (See their book, *Perceptive Healing.**)
Miss Cummins found by the use of psychic senses that
many strange illnesses and mental quirks in various
members of a certain old family in England seemed
to arise from memories brought over from past lives.
This family was Jewish, and the terrors of persecution
made up most of the memories lasting through from
other lives, especially the life immediately previous. I
quote from the book:

"This narrative (one telling of a special instance in
the life of one patient), it is submitted, justifies the assumption that in assessing the actions of others the
memories handed down to them from the past should
be investigated and appraised before any final judgment
can be passed on them. The fears, the persecutions, the
nights of horror, the torture chambers, the silent graves
of friends and relatives unjustly slain—any such experiences from the life adventures of ancestors could
undoubtedly extend their influence out of the past and
affect the actions of descendants in the present, particularly if such descendants suffered from some minor
(mental) shock or trauma of an analogous nature.
Thus an act of cowardice, as it is popularly conceived,
may well have been initiated by some terrible and in-
sistent urge out of the forgotten past which, unknown
and unexplained, has condemned many a man to the
opprobrium of his fellows.

"The psychological as well as the physical attributes
are inherited, modified or aggravated, as each generation passes, according as the genes that carry them are

* *Perceptive Healing,* by R. Connell, M.D., F.R.C.P.I. and Geraldine Cummins. Psychic Book Club, 5, Bloomsbury Court, London W.C. 1, England.

dominant or recessive. Terrors, quite incomprehensible to some of us, have their roots nourished by forgotten horrors. Dead hands stretch out of the past and mold the present. Into the future they extend their clutching fingers and twist and distort our decisions and destinies. And we, blind anthropoids, too often think the decisions are ours and ours alone—that the successful achievements of our lives are entirely of our own fashioning. That the crimes and failures of others are matters for unqualified condemnation."

The transmission of the end results or reactions caused by terrible experiences, from parent to child, is commented on by the writers in the discussion of another case:

"One cannot contemplate the present agony of the human race without endeavoring to assess some of its consequences in connection with the generations that are yet to come." Dr. Connell tells of assisting a male child into the world after the First World War. The father of the child had experienced "nine months of work in a German coal mine. He was a prisoner of war. During that period he was in a coal mine he never saw daylight; suffered unspeakably, physically and emotionally; fear haunted him. Until his son reached the age of 10 years he had such a horror of all visitors that he always hid under a bed or a table when strangers came and whenever the doctor was called. His illnesses were nightmares to both. He was born with a terrible fear complex dominant, and even now, 20 years later, and in spite of the most careful upbringing, he has a haunted look. A daughter, born four years later, took after her mother and had no such heritage."

In some schools of psychoanalysis it is thought that from the moment of conception there is some way in which the embryo senses and remembers words spoken by the parents, especially if there is much emotion or some pain felt at the time of this recording. The facts seem to bear them out, and Huna can give an explanation:

Only the low self, in its aka or shadowy body, is connected with the embryo. As the middle self does not begin to play its part in the infant until some time after birth, all words and other impressions are remembered by the low self and it alone—with the result that such memories are not subjected to the correcting light of middle self reason. They thus remain in the form of blind and hidden memories which later cause strange fears or other mental reactions. In nearly all cases, the urges to action, caused by these fixations, tend to cause physical ills if the urges are frustrated and beaten down.

In the case of the boy mentioned above, it could be explained that while he inherited through the genes the mental characteristics which might respond to similar fears, the real cause of his terrors may well have been the pictures drawn with much emotion by the father in the presence of the pregnant mother, in recounting his experiences and terrors. The low self, being illogical, would react to the words literally as compulsions, not related to actual events or to their place in time.

One possibility which appeals to us in our study of kahuna methods seems to have been overlooked by most students of these matters. That idea is that the spirits of the dead attach themselves to the living and force upon them memories of their own lives in the flesh.

Psychologists have studied such manisfestations and have classified the attached spirits as "split-off" parts of the resident spirit or personality. Under the influence of hypnotic suggestion the "secondary personalities" (or spirits, as the case may be) have been brought to the surface and conversed with. Many of them have their own memories of life in the flesh, and almost always they try to influence the person whom they victimize, forcing thoughts and emotions and impulses on them, or at night taking the body on sleepwalking expeditions. They often remember their death pangs in earthly life and their sicknesses, pains and sorrows, and cause symptoms or emotions corresponding to them to appear in the one to whom they have tied themselves and on whose vital forces they feed to give themselves strength of will to exert a form of hypnotic command in many cases.

It seems natural that the spirits of ancestors should select members of the following generations as their victims and hosts. This being the case, we might account for memories and compulsive reactions which are forced upon the living, and which—because the source seems to be their own inner self—causes the belief that experiences from a past life are being carried over from their own past life or lives, not the earthly life of some attached spirit ancestor.

Modern psychiatrists are fully aware of all of the outward appearances of spirit influence beginning with the very slight and intermittent influences and ending with complete obsession. However, as it is taboo to be so unscientific as to admit that there might be such a thing as a spirit, or as survival after death, or as a set of memories brought over from a past life, the symptoms which have been known for many centuries and which have been laid to spirit obsession, have been neatly re-catalogued and given new names. Under the heading of "Obsession" in the *Freud Dictionary of Psychoanalysis* already quoted, this point is well illustrated:

> *"Obsession:* Obsessions are always reproaches re-emerging in a transmuted form under repression—reproaches which are invariably related to a sexual deed performed with pleasure in childhood. . . . Two components are found in every obsession: (1) an idea that forces itself upon the patient; (2) an associated emotional state."

It will be seen that Freud made careful note of the *compulsive strength* of a thought. He, of course, related it to a repressed sexual thought—but certainly, in obsession it could have been forced on the patient by a spirit. He also noted the change in the emotional state of the patient to fit the compulsive thought. The question is left open as to whether the thought aroused the emotion, or—which would be more probable if it came from a spirit—whether the emotion also came from the spirit and was not generated in the patient. Obsessive acts and ceremonials were assigned by Freud to the unconscious part of the mind because, despite reason and logic, the patient is unable to resist the urge to do certain things.

In the mental hospitals of today (aside from patients whose brains have been injured by disease or such poisons as alcohol), schizophrenia, or "split personality," accounts for the majority of cases. Shocks, stresses, strains, fixations—almost anything that weakens the individual on the mental and "will" level or by taking too much of his mana—may allow the "secondary person-

228

alities" to make their presence felt to a greater or lesser degree. Shock treatment by electricity, insulin or other drugs is a popular remedy and while hard on the patient is often effective. (The kahunas used a mana shock treatment method long ago, as mentioned before.)

Of all the medically trained psychiatrists, only one, as far as I know, actually recognized obsession for what it is. He broke away from the hindering scientific traditions of his profession to break ground in finding a better means of casting out these "evil spirits" or "devils" which were so well known to the kahunas of Polynesia, and which are so often discussed in the Bible.

This man was Dr. Carl Wickland, an American, who during all his later years gave his time and attention to the obsessional angles, and was denied either recognition or a hearing. However, he did pioneer work of an advanced order, obtained excellent results in many cases, and left a remarkable record of his findings, theories and methods in his books, the best known of which is his *Thirty Years Among the Dead*. His method was to drive obsessing or attached spirits out of, or away from, the patient by a shock of static electricity. The spirit was directed to enter the body of Mrs. Wickland (who was a psychic) and there it was talked with, persuaded to leave the patient alone, and handed over to good spirit "guides" to be cared for or forced to change its ways. It was an entirely unscientific method, but many cures were made and much help given to sufferers.

Since the kahunas of the healing orders were either trained psychics or used a psychic as an assistant, they were constantly on the lookout for spirits which had

229

fastened themselves to the living and were causing some degree of illness or mental trouble. These spirits, because they invariably drew mana from the living to strengthen themselves, were called "eating companions" by the kahunas, and in all efforts to heal a patient they were watched for, and if found, were removed, just as were the complexes. The observed technique for the removal of evil spirits was, as related before, the accumulation of a very heavy shock charge of mana and the use of it, coupled with a type of mesmeric suggestion, to dislodge the obsessing spirit. Also the High Self of the kahuna was furnished with sufficient mana for its aid in the operation when asked for help. Always there was available, too, the powerful co-operation of the *Poe Aumakua*.

The complexes and evil spirits, "things eating one inside," were lumped together in the same classification of sin as were deeds of hurt done others, or mistakes in good conduct. And, it is important to state again, all these elements which went to make up sin were basically bad because they caused the low self of the ill or troubled or obsessed person to refuse to make the contact with the High Self. Since refusal resulted in a blocked path to the High Self, and in order to obtain healing it was necessary to open the path, the first essential was to correct the things that caused it to be blocked by the low self.

We find in the New Testament many references to the work of casting out evil spirits as a healing practice. Little is known of the early training of Jesus, but from what he did and what he taught, it is evident that he was a member of the highest healing order of kahunas. As he healed, and as he taught his disciples to heal as part of their ministry, his teachings are of the greatest value in the reconstruction of the ancient lore at this late date. He and his disciples stressed the part played in illness by evil spirits, and drove them out of patients in order to bring about healing. Sometimes the evil spirits were called "devils."

In the Old Testament the word "devil" appears only four times in the King James version. In the original Hebrew the words used were *sairim* and *shedim,* both used twice, and meaning respectively (as given in the Revised Version) he-goats, or satyrs, and demons. The Devil, in contrast, was a fallen angel, Satan, the "Prince of Darkness," who was believed to be just a little less powerful than God. He was given the title of "The Adversary" and "The Tempter." In the New Testament Jesus is said to have wrestled with Satan and to have been tempted by him in his guise of "Prince of Darkness."

A little of this confusion can be cleared by going back to the older religion of Huna. In it beautiful and very effective symbols were used to present basic ideas which ranged from magnificent and vague concepts such as those involved in the theory of Creation, and the common basic concepts such as those of the three selves of man, evil spirits, sin in general, and so on.

The Creation of the universe was, in Huna, symbolized as a titanic struggle between Light and Darkness. Both were symbolized and personified. Light was Supreme Intelligence and Good. Darkness was lack of in-

telligence, stupidity, inertia, and the breeding and re-
siding place of evil—of all that was adverse to Light
and Goodness.

The personified Darkness was overcome by the personified Light, and Creation was the result. However,
the struggle was not ended. All through the long upward progression of created things, including man, the
struggle between Darkness and Light continued as the
conflict of great overshadowing elemental powers, and
as fragments of those powers lying in the hearts of men
and continuing the struggle on a smaller scale. The
Darkness was, symbolically, broken up into small parts
which were able to enter and direct all men who were
evil, also all spirits of evil men—these remaining evil
and bound to earthly levels after physical death. On
the other hand, the Light was represented as the High
Selves, one for each man, to be his Light and to guide
him out of the ways of darkness.

One of the most rewarding efforts along this line of
seeking to understand the composite nature of sin, came
in the work of translating the baffling meanings behind
the story of the Garden of Eden into the Polynesian
language. Most people today understand that this is an
allegory, not a statement of historical fact about specific
people and a geographical place. It is the story of
Everyman who "falls" from his natural state of contact
with his High Self. The story has been found not only
in Biblical writings but the world around, told in many
languages and with many versions. It was common
property of the civilizations which centered in the Near
East centuries ago. That it originated with the kahunas
of old there seems little doubt, for in any dialect of the

Polynesian tongue it gives up Huna secrets which are foreign to any other language, people or philosophy.

In the Garden of Eden, as the story was recorded in the Old Testament, there stood one tree which was set aside and its fruit forbidden to Adam and Eve. The serpent tempted Eve to eat the fruit, she persuaded Adam to partake of it, and they were expelled from the Garden.

Now "fruit" is *hua*, and its secret meaning is (1) to be much addicted to evil, and (2) to quarrel, be angry, to envy. The "serpent" of Genesis (like the Satan of Job, the Hillel of Isaiah, and the dragon of both Isaiah and the Apocalypse) is understood as symbolizing the first cause of sin, death and evil—and so, the revolt against God, the Light and the Good. They are all "sin" symbols in Huna, and the word *moo* covers them all. This word means any kind of a reptile, and has the secondary Huna meaning of "to dry," which is the symbol of taking and wasting the "water of life," or mana.

The serpent, then, was a spirit of the "eating companion" class. We know this because it stole and squandered mana from the low self—dried him out, according to Huna symbology. This serpent tempted Eve. The word for "tempt"—*walewale*—means not only "to tempt," but also "to entrap" and "to snare." This is important in understanding the Huna meaning of the story because the snare, the trap or any form of net, whenever mentioned in describing any part of Huna, is the symbol of either an "eating companion" or obsessing spirit, or of a complex.

As modern botanists assure us, the apple was not yet developed in Biblical times. It was first used by painters of imaginative pictures depicting the Garden of Eden in Europe much later. It is not stated in Genesis that the tree bore apples—it was simply "the fruit of the tree of knowledge." In the Polynesian version, however, every evidence is given that the story originated in some tropical land. The tree was described as a breadfruit tree, and near it grew an *ohia* tree, both tropicals.

Ulu is the word for breadfruit, but it has a surprising number of Huna meanings which tell directly or by the use of symbols, the nature of the "eating companions," what they do to their hosts, and what they force their hosts to do. These meanings show us what was considered the gravest of the sins of mankind:

(1) "To be influenced to a greater or lesser degree by spirits of the dead." (At worst, to be completely obsessed by them.)

(2) "To grow, as in size and strength." (This points to the increase in strength of the spirits when they draw mana from their victims—"dry them out.")

(3) "To grow, as more angry or more evil." (The spirits, once they are tolerated by the victim and allowed to feed on his mana, grow more and more powerful and more able to force their evil impulses on the victim. They become more and more able to obsess him and gain more complete control of his body.)

The *ohia* tree, which in the Polynesian or Huna version of the story stood beside the breadfruit tree, gives us more meanings which corroborate those hidden in *ulu:*

(1) "To force, to compel, to restrain." (These describe very well the methods and abilities of "eating companion" spirits, in relation to their influence on their hosts.)

(2) "To be deceitful, evil, sinful and wicked." (This tells us the nature of the spirits.)

234

The "sin" of Adam and Eve was that of harboring evil thoughts so similar to those of the evil spirits that they were in agreement, or of like minds. The spirits were, for this reason, allowed by the low selves of the man and woman to attach themselves to them. Very soon they began accepting their evil ideas and impulses as their own. Thus they were driven from their allegorical position of sinless goodness—or, in other words, from the condition of natural and full contact with their own High Selves.

In the Genesis story, the serpent was cast out and a curse was placed upon him. Adam's punishment was that he was forced to live by the sweat of his brow, and farm the land which God cursed so that it grew thistles and briers. Thistles, thorns and briers, it will be remembered, are, in Huna, symbols of either "eating companions" or complexes. (The kahunas seem to have used the same set of symbols for both, no doubt because the two produced the same symptoms in their patients.)

The Garden is the ideal and normal condition of life when one is free from any of the blockings of the path which come under the heading of "sins" in Huna. The word for "garden" is *kihapai*. Its secret meanings are to be found in the root words of which it is composed. These are:

(1) Root *ki:* "To squirt water." (Symbol of sending the accumulated surcharge of mana to the High Self along the connecting aka cord. This can be done only when the individual is in the ideal or normal condition in which his path is not blocked by one of the forms of "sin.")

(2) Root *pai:* "To be tied in bundles; to be in clusters." (Symbol of the clusters of thought-forms or visualized picture of

the thing desired. These clusters are sent with the mana flow over the aka cord to the High Self in the Huna type of prayer.)

(3) Root *ha:* "To breathe heavily." (Symbol of accumulating a surcharge of mana. Such accumulation usually is accompanied by heavier breathing.)

(4) Roots combined in *hapai:* "To lift up." (This is the symbol of sending or "lifting up" the thought-form clusters to the High Self.)

The Genesis account tells us that after Adam and Eve were expelled from the garden because of their sins—because they had allowed the serpent to tempt them successfully—God placed "Cherubims" with "flaming swords" to the east of the Garden to guard or "keep the way of the tree of life."

The word for "sword" is *pahi,* the roots of which, *pa* and *hi,* give the meaning of "drying out" and of "purging away something." The secret is that the ideal condition symbolized by the Garden is protected by the High Self against the intrusion of evil spirits. They are kept from being strong enough to control the living by themselves being "dried out" or prevented from obtaining mana. The purging is also "to flow away," and furnishes a check on the first meaning in that mana, symbolized as a fluid, is made to leave the spirits if they have some of it in their possession (as they would have if found obsessing a living person). The work of driving them away and rendering them weak and harmless was carried out by the High Self. The "way of the tree of life," which was to be guarded, symbolizes the aka cord. It is the thing that is to be kept unblocked and open. The evil spirits are to be kept from causing such a blocking.

From the kahunas we learn the great truth that if we go to the end of life and die without being cleansed of our fixations, we take them with us. On the other side they hang like millstones around the neck and prevent clear understanding which would normally allow one to go on, and progress as one should in the evolutionary stages toward perfection. The fixations and unreformed evil in one's nature hold one to the earth level and tend to make one become an "eating companion."

There are many rites in the Catholic Church which can be traced back to Huna origins or to a source in Huna ideas and beliefs, even if the meaning of the rite has been partly lost. One of these is the rite of Extreme Unction, and the Catholics make every effort to perform it with the intention of giving a last and final cleansing to those who are about to die. The rite of the Confessional with that of Absolution should, if properly understood and administered, clear away (and keep cleared away) the fixations from the path of the individual during life, and he should go on freed and sane and unhampered at death. The Church has also the rite of Exorcism for the removal of the "eating companions," and in every case the rites are performed with the use of "holy water," even though it is not now understood that this symbolizes the calling down of the High Mana for cleansing purposes and presupposes the aid of the High Self—who, beforehand, must have been provided with a sufficient supply of low mana to work with.

In Tibet there has existed for centuries a written ritual which has often been called "The Tibetan Book of the Dead," to compare it with the better known one of ancient Egypt. Both of these writings were aimed at assisting a dying person to progress properly from life into the state after death. In Tibet it has been the custom to have these ritual instructions read to the dying by a priest—the recital continuing for some time after death, under the conviction that the dead can hear and follow the directions given for their entry into "Bardo," the hereafter.

In both rites stress is laid on the great value inherent in a life properly lived while on earth. The state after death is seen as a continuation of life and of the same inclinations. If these inclinations are not good, trouble can come swiftly on the other side, it is believed, for evil spirits lurk there who are inimical to those caught on the lower planes of the hereafter. If there is any truth in all of religion, one must conclude that the condition after death depends much on the moral progress during life.

The belief in obsession, or "eating companions," is no longer fantastic, thanks to a century of work in psychical research and the many proofs found for human survival. The complex or fixation has been rediscovered in modern psychology.

The alarming incidence of insanity in our time, coupled with ill-informed treatment of the victims in most institutions, would seem to compel an examination into the probability of obsessing spirits in at least some of the cases. Psychiatry has proved that is is possible to restore some people to sanity by removing the complexes. Why not go on to the study of those patients very obviously obsessed by a spirit outside themselves?

CHAPTER XVIII

THE VARIOUS DEGREES OF FIXATION AND OBSESSIONAL INFLUENCE, WITH A SELF-TEST CHART

The reader may feel by this time that he has been led to look into dark depths of possibility which do not concern him. While the darker depths may not, still there are—as has been explained—many degrees of darkness or of those things we have considered in the last chapter. And, even if one is convinced that he has a clear path, it is well to make sure. Moreover, it is important that we inform ourselves, so that we may be better prepared to help others who are in need of help but who do not realize their need.

Psychoanalyst Dr. Lawrence S. Kubie tells of the great need for *preventive* psychiatry in an article in the *Bulletin of the New York Academy of Medicine* in September, 1952. He urges that steps be taken to inform doctors and laymen so that they can assist in the work of educating the public to the end that the symptoms of fixation troubles may be recognized early and treated promptly.

Dr. Kubie tells the story of a girl who, at the age of eleven, developed a stubborn stomach-ache, and was taken to a hospital. An intern there recognized it as something due to mental or psychic causes, and recommended that she be taken to a psychiatrist. This was not done, however, and the stomach pains recurred in the years that followed. By her 35th year she had undergone nine abdominal operations and had received some 5600 hours of free medical treatment. At last she went to a psychiatrist, because the doctors had found no physical cause for her complaints. It was too late to repair damage done, or cure a patient who had become a hopeless hypochondriac. Dr. Kubie asserts that this is not an exceptional case. It merely illustrates the need of preventive psychiatry.

He offers doctors a simple test to help determine whether or not a patient may be suffering from psychiatric disturbances. "If a patient can use common-sense advice effectively, no more is needed, and our patient cannot have been very ill. When [common-sense advice] rolls off the proverbial duck's back, then that duck is ill, and needs technical help as early as it can be brought to bear."

While we have been discussing illnesses mainly, the blockings of the path may cause other things in one's life which are equally as oppressive. From the point of view of general happiness or success, nothing can be more deadly than to be cut off from the High Self and to lose its help and guidance. We need to do all we can for ourselves and for others, to make sure that full and normal contact is attained and kept. It is with this in mind that the following classifications have been made to give a clearer picture of the things which block the path in different ways and in varying degrees.

(1) Those blocks we know we may have, and which consist of our hates, fears, greeds, intolerances—all of which we act upon and all of which cause in us a sense of

guilt because we are living less perfectly than we really know how to do. We seem unable to put aside the hates, fears and other "temptations" which cause us to fail to live up to the "mark of the high calling," or the ideals of the religious or moral teachings which we have accepted as right, proper and altogether good.

(2) The second class of stumbling blocks which close the path along the aka cord to the High Self contains the low self's half of the same hates, fears, greeds, and especially, sense of guilt caused by responding to these "sin" impulses. As the low self is not logical, it will have tangled and jumbled fixation-complex units or thought-form clusters of a large part of the memories of times when the man hated, feared, was greedy or unkind, and so forth. As we all have a strong urge to justify ourselves for what we do that we know inwardly is not kind or good, the low self accepts all the justifications of the middle self—but, because it has guilt senses, it does not stop there. It keeps working with the guilts, greeds and memories of the non-good acts, deep in the hiding of the "black sack" of its memories, sorting, matching, trying to get better justifications. It ends with fixation tangles which are of such a nature that when triggered, they may explode to the surface in the form of sudden emotional reactions and urges which cause us to do still other hurtful things, and to say bitter things which give us further reason to be sorry.

These "temptation" blockings are often triggered by something that strikes even slightly at our pride or sense of personal importance, or at our false structure of self justification for things we have done to others in the past. At this stage they can generally be brought into consciousness by self-analysis, or by the help of a friend, and the path made clear.

(3) In class three we come to the fixations so deep that they cannot be recalled without the help of a trained person—a doctor or a psychoanalyst. Here, far more than in the first two classes, there tend to be bodily ills caused by the pressure of fixations. And when the bodily ills do not furnish a complete outlet for the goaded low self, the neurotic and psychotic mental symptoms may be added to the trouble. These fixations may, as we have already noted, possibly originate in past lives or in prenatal periods, early childhood, or at times of mental or physical shock when memory tangles are formed.

(4) Class four is one not recognized except in Huna and in the Huna backgrounded sections of the Bible. Mental and physical ills of this class come from spirit influence. In modern terms these are the "split-off parts of personality." In Huna they are spirits which attach themselves to the living and, to a great extent, live on the mana of their hosts. They are able to inject their own thoughts at times into the consciousness of the low self, and even more often their emotions or moods.

It must be remembered that the physical causes of mental ills, large or small, are to be considered. Poisons in the system, glandular disturbances or failures, diseases which affect the brain or nervous system—all of these causes are in the province of the physican to treat.

In our HRA work we found that the use of some of the many test charts now available in books and journals was excellent in helping to determine whether or not fixations or eating companions were present, and to what extent they might be coloring one's life. (It is true that the person most afflicted with blocking of the path is least aware of it, as a rule. Set habits of belief and of reacting to certain ideas or situations are often tied in with fixations which make the habit difficult to change. All habits need close inspection—suspicious inspection.)

The test charts are all based on ideal ways of reacting to conditions or situations—ways which have been proven by experience to be best for the individual, the family and the community. By comparing one's own reactions with those outlined in the charts, one may gain a fair idea of whether or not fixations are present, and to what degree one has been caused to think and act and react *below* the ideal standard of normalcy. Here is a condensation of the main points in several charts which HRAs have found beneficial:

SELF-EXAMINATION CHART FOR FIXATIONS, OBSESSIONS AND HABITS

(1) The normal person has, more or less, the following characteristics: A faith in some form of Higher Being or Power and confidence that he is being watched over, that his prayers will be heard if he asks for the right things, and that his sins are more than balanced by good deeds. Is steady. Is courageous and confident, kind and thoughtful of others. Likes and understands people, being able to understand their failings and pity their weaknesses instead of blaming them hotly. Has a great sense of personal responsibility and loves and cares for his family. Strives to do more than his part in community projects. Is cheerful and quick to smile. Can

243

converse with people and get his ideas across simply and clearly. Is not given to worry, anger, fear, doubt or suspicion. Can see the other fellow's side of a question —even one of politics or religion. Is neat, efficient, healthy.

(2) Next down on the scale, the normal good characteristics as listed above show a slight lack on a few points, or there may be a general lack of positiveness in most of the desirable and normal characteristics. Intolerance may show slightly, there may be more selfishness, less interest in the other fellow, and more of a tendency to emotional outbursts, worry, doubt, jealousy, envy, suspicion. The self-confidence is not as strong, faith is weaker, there is less steadiness, and there is slight confusion evidenced in the thinking—this resulting in a little difficulty in getting ideas across clearly, and in conversing freely. The health is not quite as good.

(3) Here the departure from the normal is still more marked. A few points of defect begin to stand out plainly. There may be focal points at which the forces of the several largest fixations meet to cause explosions when events "trigger" those fixations. These explosions take the form of reactions which can be recognized as too large or too small in comparison with normal reactions to the same situations or events. The man may be maudlin in his expressions of love and solicitude for some members of his family, or, on the other hand, unwarrantedly harsh, severe and selfish. He is obstinately set in his own opinions, and has little patience with the opinions of others.

(4) At this point the straight flow of thoughts

(which depend on a proper flow of rationalized memories) is filled with gaps left in the flow by memories which have been blocked off, and by memories partly tied in with the fixations and thus partly blocked off. This causes thinking to be slow and the individual to arrive at wrong conclusions when there is the slightest emotional content in the matter under consideration. This condition causes a further lack of confidence and builds doubt in the place of faith. Emotional outbursts of resentment and anger are frequent. Or they may smoulder most of the time, resulting in such a lowering of the mana supply that the individual tends to avoid association with others, to talk little about anything except in an argumentative tone, and to be generally suspicious, antagonistic or dull. The health is not good and he is prone to have accidents and losses and to blame these on anyone except himself.

(5) Here the fixations overbalance the normal reactions. The emotions are often badly out of hand. Self-confidence is at the lowest ebb. There is no sense of protection on the part of a Higher Being, but, rather, a sense of continual condemnation. All the world seems against the individual. He is fearful, often given to grieving over things in his past which should long since have been laid aside. He is inflexible in his thoughts and tends to repeat over and over in his attempted conversations the statements of his fixed opinion. He cannot consider other or contrary opinions rationally for a moment. No matter how reasonable the arguments presented, or how he seems to be convinced, he is soon back repeating his former statements. He pities himself and longs for pity. He retreats from people, but

wants to cry on the shoulder of any friend who will tolerate such continual outbursts. He is filled with mysterious pains and ailments, and his strength is at such a low ebb that he is usually "tired out." Or, he may at times have bursts of unreasoning exhilaration, exaggerated faith, and exaltation followed by depression.

(6) At this stage the individual is close to the danger point. The mana supply is so low that the middle self cannot get enough to build up its "will" to control the low self, and the man no longer takes an interest in anything but his own self and condition. He is not too much interested in even himself. Whether real or imaginary, he has more ills and troubles and persecutions than can be recounted. He does not want to be helped. He simply wants to be left alone to wallow in his groundless miseries, hates and fears.

The classifications given above are subject to a thousand variations to fit the condition of the individual in matters of health, or natural physical and mental endowments, social conditions, environment, education, accidents of life that have brought good or bad to him, and so forth. The value of the generalization is that it shows the model on which the classifications are built.

The higher the person is on the scale of the chart, the more apt he is to make an effort to get rid of his fixations —and the more drive will be put into the effort. The lower one is, the less will he wish to change himself— the reaction being "So what?" after the first slight showing of understanding and enthusiasm.

Worry, and all the little doubts, fears, feelings of uncertainty and lacks of confidence, are classed as "anxiety" by the psychiatrists. The majority of us are sufficiently complexed to show some of these symptoms. As a result of these slight reactions to fixations, we usually have a few bodily ills. Small as these fixations seem to be, they can carry considerable weight when taken as a whole, and may keep us from trying to pray, or prevent what prayers we make from reaching the High Self.

In so far as the eating companion spirits are concerned, the things they make us do through their influence on the low self, or prevent us from doing well, or doing partly or at all, will appear as if a part of the resident low self. For this reason, any departure from the ideal or normal state indicated in the chart may be partly due to the influence of one or more spirits who have been attracted to us by our own attitudes.

The Lord's Prayer, when compared to the Old Testament sources and the Huna meanings hidden therein, gives us, instead of "Lead us not into temptation, but deliver us from evil," the meaning of "Guide us away from the snares or fixations, and deliver us from the evil ones or spirits."

CHAPTER XIX

CLEARING THE SLIGHTLY BLOCKED PATH

In our experimental work of trying to discover what was blocking the path of the individual in prayer, we always started with a careful check to see if it was a matter of habits of thought and deeply prejudiced beliefs which the low self was reluctant to change. That is something which a man or woman can find out working alone, if he or she will examine such beliefs honestly. All blockings are certainly not as difficult to expose as the outlaw memories and the complexes.

In making the Huna-type prayer the usual blocking reported was that no emotion of any kind was felt at the moment that the High Self should have been contacted. We well know from our study of the beliefs of the kahunas that where there is no faintest shade of emotion, enthusiasm, desire, fear or love—no emotional reaction of any kind—the low self is not doing its part in the work. We had to remind ourselves that when the low self gets to work, it produces emotions of one sort or another. It is this upwelling of emotion which we customarily think of as coming from our conscious mind or middle self entities. We say silently to ourselves, "I like this, or I like to do this." Or we may say, "I do not like to do that." All likes and dislikes are tinged with emotion, otherwise they are automatic actions to a large extent. And this emotion has its origin in the low self.

Attention may be classed with the emotions. If the low self is interested, it will like a thing that is to be done, or perhaps be sufficiently impressed by its importance that even if it is a very unpleasant and difficult task which must be performed, it will pay strict attention and do its best to help perform the task from beginning to end.

It is hard to define the sensations which come from the low self when it is in action and is doing its full share of the work in any undertaking. In games it is enthusiasm, enjoyment and attention intermixed. There may also be an admixture of the competitive spirit, or of the will to hunt and capture, or to defend successfully against the attack of others.

When the "blank wall" is faced as one tries to pray, it is the complete lack of any emotion. However, there were reported by different HRAs certain slight sensations which were clues to the low self attitude: a vague fear for one, a sudden emotion of aversion for another, many times a conviction that the whole thing was "something that won't work." In some cases it was not a sensation so much as an inability to keep the attention of the low self fixed upon what was wanted of it. The attention seemed to slip, and in a moment other thoughts were pushed into the mind—such as urgent recollection of the daily chores, or things which should be done or which it would be pleasant to do. The excuses presented by the low self for not doing its work were endless. Sudden impulses to call up friends might come, or worry would start from fear that something was

249

wrong in the kitchen, or in the outer office. One HRA found that when he tried to get his low self to contact the High Self, he would almost invariably begin to itch furiously so that his mind was entirely distracted. The low self proved to be most ingenious and evasive.

The HRAs tried many different experiments in their efforts to get to the bottom of the trouble and find out why the low self was reluctant to co-operate. It was found that the simplest method was to talk it over with the low self, by way of the pendulum. Those who had taken time to get well acquainted with their low self were able to get most illuminating information by the asking of simple questions which could be answered by the "yes" or "no" of the pendulum, or by the diagonal "doubtful" or other movements which had been agreed upon as having certain meanings. The main trouble turned out to be the fact that some quite characteristic belief on the part of the illogical low self was blocking its desire or will to help make the prayer.

One HRA, after much questioning, got to the heart of her difficulty in praying for healing of a certain condition from which she had been suffering, by discovering that her low self did not wish to make the prayer with her because it thought it was useless. The reason for this conviction was found to be that many times prayers had been made in the ordinary way, and nothing had come of them. Such faith as the middle self had come to have in the Huna method of prayer was rendered useless by the stubborn low self.

Fortunately, the low self can be won over by arguments and reasoning, if there is no major fixation which blocks the path. In this case the HRA found that by going back to childhood training and faith in God, the careful reapproach to the matter of prayer could be made and the lack of faith cleared away. The report to me was in a simple, easy and very personal conversational form which I repeat here:

You still believe in God, don't you? (Low self answer by way of the pendulum:) Yes.

That is good. Then you also believe that God can answer prayers, do you? Yes.

(Several instances of answered prayer were recalled.) Do you remember how glad and thankful we were for these things? Yes.

Do you believe that we should pray to God through our own High Self? No.

You know we have a High Self, do you? Yes.

But you think we should pray to God direct? Yes.

Is that because we were taught that when we were little? Yes.

Do you believe we must pray through Jesus to reach God? Yes.

Do you think you feel God when you pray? No.

Do you feel it when you pray through Jesus? Yes.

You contact the High Self often, do you? Yes.

Can you tell the difference between contacting Jesus and our High Self? Doubtful.

Of course you can't. All prayers go to the Christ Within that you were taught to believe in, and that is the High Self. Do you understand that? Doubtful.

Then I'll explain it all to you. Listen carefully. (There followed a careful and forceful presentation of the fact that the High Self is the Christ Within for each of us, and that it alone can take prayers to God if that is

251

necessary.) Now do you understand that we must contact the High Self and give it our thought-forms or pictures of the things for which we pray? Yes.

Then are you ready now to contact our High Self, send mana to it along the aka cord of connection and send with the mana the pictures of the things we wish to pray for? No.

Is that because you think we are praying for the wrong things? Yes.

Do you think we are asking too much? Yes.

Would you pray for our daily bread? Yes.

Would you pray for jam on the bread? Doubtful.

Do you think we don't deserve jam? Yes.

Do you think we deserve healing? No.

Is this because you think one should pray only for wisdom—seek first the Kingdom of Heaven—and expect all other things to be added unto us? Yes.

Do you believe that because we were taught that way when we were young? Yes.

Do you think it is wrong to tell in our prayers what kind of things we'd like to have added to the gift of wisdom and spiritual grace? Yes.

I see. You still hold to the old habit of thinking formed in our childhood. There is a new and better way to pray, and I thought you had paid attention and had understood it. Now tell me, wouldn't you like to have jam on your bread? Yes.

Do you believe that God can give us jam as well as bread? Yes.

But you said we do not deserve jam. Well, do you feel we are so wicked we deserve only punishment? Doubtful.

Do you think being sick is the punishment we deserve? Doubtful.

Do you want me to stop eating—just fast and pray all the time until we die? No.

Do you want us to get so sick we die? No.

Do you believe that God has only love for us? Doubtful.

Do you believe that God is love? Yes.

I see. You still go back to the things we learned when we were little. Now you listen to me and pay strict attention while we go over everything and I give you the truth of the matter and explain what we have been learning here of late. (There followed careful explanations.)

This will illustrate the type of questioning used when habits of thought and the inclinations of the low self cause the blockings. Often the questioning and lecturing and requestioning will have to be continued for a number of sessions before the troubles are unearthed and the low self won over to the new beliefs. In the above case the effort was entirely successful: the prayers were finally correctly made, and they were answered.

Among other things which HRAs found by communicating with their low selves as to why they did not help with the prayer making, were the following:

(1) A feeling that unless one prayed for others and helped them to get needed things, one did not deserve being helped.

(2) A feeling of fear of God and High Self, usually caused by a feeling of guilt, unworthiness or shame. (The fear might have been formed in childhood and have become a habit of thought and reaction.)

(3) Refusal to help with the prayer was found in one case to be caused by a deep dislike of a certain ultra-pious relative who had forced religious observances on the HRA in question in early life.

(4) A feeling of vague general fear and anxiety becoming strong when the needs and lacks and tangles in social conditions were sharply pointed up by the assembling of the prayer. Because of these inner worries, the quiet and "solemnized" condition needed for making the complete prayer action was almost impossible to attain.

(5) Inertia or laziness on the part of the low self. It did not want to make the effort to help the middle self in its desires. This state was, in one bad case, a complete lack of interest in life. In two other cases the trouble was caused by memories of former experiences in which failure had come after long and strenuous efforts to succeed in some way or with some person in correcting social tangles or relationships. Desire had to be aroused once more, with an element of ambition, and sufficient renewal of confidence and faith in the High Self and God to go ahead and make fresh tries. In one instance the low self seemed unwilling to make the prayer because it would entail a subsequent effort to start the ball rolling in the direction of bringing about the answer to the prayer. In other words, the low self felt that the thing desired was not worth working for.

(6) A feeling that old hates and grudges were better to hold than to give up in order to clear the path and get the prayer made.

(7) A feeling that to pray and get healed would cause the loss of loving care and solicitude on the part of

other members of the family, and force the individual to shoulder responsibilities happily evaded by illness.

The part played by *habits of thought and belief* proved to be much greater than was expected. The low self was found in almost all cases to be in need of a rather complete working over to break down and correct old belief habits, those beyond which the middle self had progressed.

In correcting dogmatic religious beliefs of earlier life, it was found that the low self places great reliance on the printed word. As in learning things at school, repetition, more repetition and constant review and drill helped replace old ideas that blocked the work. The reading and rereading of the parts of *The Secret Science Behind Miracles* or of the HRA Bulletins which clearly explained and made logical the Huna concepts were invaluable, as well as of other material covering similar ways of thinking and believing. Especially convincing were the repeated readings of explanations of the Huna meanings in parts of the Bible—this, because the low self had once been grounded in its belief that the Bible was to be accepted without question.

Such readings of the ancient secret lore as found in the Bible were also of great value in helping the middle self to come to an understanding of what was real and genuine and what was added dogma, for there is much of Huna in the Bible. The rule to be followed was that only the actual words of Jesus were to be trusted in the New Testament. After his death a mass of dogmatic theology was invented and added, as were rites and doctrines which, like the many misconceptions surrounding the earlier ideas of blood sacrifice, were evidently inaugurated to impress the people and make the teachings work better. That they seemed to be needed, can be laid to the fact that the Huna teachings and the initiations to pass on the teachings, were either stopped or were too difficult for the masses to accept, even if there were those able to give them.

Almost any person who has been brought up in Christian circles will find in himself dogmatic beliefs which are held by his low self long after his middle self has renounced them. Many have found that their low selves became filled with fear at the thought of questioning the commonly accepted dogmas of their religion. (This can amount to superstition.) Old and invalid beliefs have usually been far easier to change by explaining the true meaning behind them than by any effort at flat contradiction. If the middle self in convinced, it must in turn teach the low self as carefully as if requiring it to relearn a long poem which, wrongly written, had to be unlearned in many lines in order to relearn it as it should have been in the first place.

It was observed that some people who were never able to go forward in the prayer work seemed to be blocked by selfishness and greed or intolerance which they did not acknowledge. Such things could not be called to their attention without offending them deeply. Such an attitude sometimes was shown unexpectedly by a chance remark such as, "Why should we be taxed so that people who have never saved a cent can retire on a fat pension—when they should jolly well be made to keep working instead of lying around twiddling their thumbs?" Another revealing remark was, "They ought to shut down every factory in the country and starve those union fellows until they learned to be glad of the chance to earn two dollars a day for twelve hours six days a week like our pioneer fathers had to do." (These are actual quotes.)

The teaching of the great kahuna, Jesus, was that there must be love and mercy in our dealings with others and even our thoughts of them. Any attitude of mind that denies compassion to others is almost certain to be accompanied by a sense of guilt or unworthiness in the low self, even if it is deeply hidden. Almost all of us have had some early grounding in fair play and common decency, and where the conscious mind flouts it, there will be conflict with the low self in which it is ingrained because it belongs to the earliest memories. In almost every such case which came to our attention, there were physical ills which seemed to defy all medical or prayer aid.

The matter of making amends for hurts done others was a basic part of the kahuna methods for clearing the path, and we can see the reason for it as we study low self reactions. One may forget in the rush of a busy day that he spoke irritably or unfairly to wife, child or employee yesterday. But his low self does not forget the hurt look of the person so addressed. It will not be satisfied until its man has made a forthright and humble apology, erasing all hurt from the injured person.

When such amends have not been made in the long time past, the low self still harbors a deep-seated feeling of guilt. When one becomes aware of this, yet does not discover just what person or persons he may have injured, or if the chance for making personal amends has passed, a period of making general amends is necessary. General amends are really physical things done to impress ideas on the low self—physical stimuli. Exerting oneself to do good in an impersonal way, and giving of contributions to a good cause until it hurts, are excellent ways of appeasing the low self.

Sometimes the low self feels that his man deserves punishment for these long past deeds of hurt. Here, again, the physical stimulus can be used to advantage by performing a penance such as fasting, denying oneself his smoking or other pleasurable habits for a time. Such general amends were prescribed in my own case in Hawaii many years ago when one of the few surviving kahunas of the time was making me ready to be helped. As I was working hard at the time, she did not impose a complete fast—only going without food or cigarettes until one o'clock for three days. A contribution was made to the Salvation Army, which did good work locally, and because the low self becomes impressed with the great value of money from its earliest days, such a gift—if large enough to hurt—is very impressive. In my case my low self was well impressed at the end of the third day that we deserved help from any and all Higher Powers. The help was forthcoming at once— and with jam on the bread.

One of the great teachings of Jesus was that direct atonement to one formerly injured could be exchanged for general atonement in which a sufficiency of good deeds done here and there balance the score. "Inasmuch as ye have done it (a kindly act) unto the least of these, my brethren, ye have done it unto me." Each of us makes his own payment, but when we have a deep sense of guilt and cannot make amends directly, as to one long dead, we can substitute good deeds done for the benefit of those around us.

A great truth was proved once more in our HRA testing: there is no "Royal Road" to the High Self— the "Kingdom of Heaven." The rich and powerful, like the poor and weak, have to go through the same process of cleansing the inside as well as the outside of the symbolic "cup" of man. The outside of the cup is the middle self, and its beliefs must be examined and reformed to meet the test of hurtlessness which is basic in Huna. If this repentance or reforming can be carried to the point at which non-hurt becomes positive, and can include the sincere desire to help others—to love one's neighbors—even to a small degree, so much the better.

The low self is the inside of the cup, and no matter how clean we have made our middle self attitudes, the prayers will not go through to the High Self along the aka cord if the hidden and habitual beliefs and attitudes of the low self are not cleansed or made to conform with those of the middle self. "A house divided against itself cannot stand."

Habits of thought are very strong, perhaps stronger than such habits as drinking and smoking. The low self is hard to grasp and hold and force into new lines of thought and action. The HRAs have had their "backsliders" just as all other groups in which a new way is proposed and accepted by the middle self, while the low self is not immediately taken in hand and steady and patient efforts made until its habits of thought and belief are corrected. We must be "born again" in this respect—and in this life, not waiting and hoping that we shall automatically evolve and progress in a series of future incarnations. The spiritual gains made here will be carried with us into the life—or lives—ahead.

In the HRA we searched for a method which could be used by one person alone as a substitute for psychoanalysis, in which a second person must help to locate and remove the outlaw tangles which are difficult to surface. Attention was fastened for a time on the "writing out" method popularized by an English layman, E. Pickworth Farrow. In his book on the subject, *Psychoanalyze Yourself,** Mr. Farrow tells how he had failed to get mental and bodily healing after trying the services of several analysts—none of whom, it appears, were themselves cleared properly. He had then set to work using a simple method in which he sat for periods of about fifteen minutes each day and wrote out whatever came into his thoughts as he let his mind wander.

He found that the subconscious slowly responded to his desire that events causing fixations be recalled and presented before the focus of consciousness so that they could be thought over and thus rationalized and changed to harmless memories. In his book he reported the slow and steady progress made in this way, one incident after another being recalled, although theretofore entirely forgotten, and his mental and physical ills gradually becoming healed as a result.

A few of the HRAs undertook to test the method and in time were able to make their reports. The results obtained were far from uniform, as might have been ex-

* *Psychoanalyze Yourself,* by E. Pickworth Farrow. International Universities Press, 227 W. 13th St., New York.

pected, since each HRA had his or her own life experiences and resultant fixations with such symptoms as matched them. Outstanding was the fact that when the low self was encouraged to select the thing to be written down, it soon began to push into the mind memories of the past, and as this went forward, there came to be more and more memories of things and conditions long forgotten.

Things which had ceased to be of any importance to the conscious self were discovered still to be very important to the low self, and in many cases surprisingly and even laughably so. Old hopes, old ambitions, old fears, affronts and desires, all came to the surface, and the odd part of it was that they came up with such strength and freshness that the HRA was often swept away by them as he was when they were new and vital to him. The freshness and power of the revived memories of "drives" and desires and plans and compulsions were in some cases so strong that things long since given over as proper to drop, were on the verge of being taken back to be acted upon. Old schemes for making money, or of reforming politics or the economics of the world were among the list of things that suddenly returned as seeming both possible and good to attempt.

This tendency of the low self to give back the bright old memories as well as the darker ones of fear and sorrow, caused me to issue the warning in the HRA Bulletin that anyone undertaking the use of the method should see to it that nothing in the way of an unusual action or undertaking or response should be allowed or considered without first laying the matter before a trusted friend who was not caught in the flood of old

261

"drives" and who, therefore, could point out the fallacy of doing anything about them—of reacting.

In one case an HRA used the writing down method for over 2000 sittings, going back bit by bit, reviving her old drives, until she came at last to the very strong religious drives of her early girlhood. Although she had long since left the old religious views which had been impressed upon her, and gone on to explore the metaphysical lines of thought and the religions of India, she reverted completely to the stage in which she had lingered a short year or two as a girl. Not only did she resign from the HRA as from a "heathen organization," but she wrote long letters to convince us that we should give up Huna and go back to the severe dogmatism of the religion of her girlhood.

On the other hand, some HRAs had better results and were able to avoid being caught in the rushing drives by swiftly re-rationalizing them on the emotional side and removing from them the false glamour or the fear which they contained. Also, interspersed with the other memories were those of events which had caused physical ills later in life. One instance of this was in the case in which an HRA had recalled the long forgotten fact that when very small she had been so badly frightened by the big gray spiders which lived in the outhouse that she had put off going into it as long as was physically possible, and then with much trepidation. When this memory had come back and had been subjected to a complete going over from the adult point of view, the old fear drive melted away, and, what was most important, a lifelong trouble with constipation vanished like magic and did not return.

Instances like this brought clearly to light the fact that there are many things which the low self will correct without outside aid, and quite apart from any action on the part of the middle self or the High Self, if the fixation causing trouble is removed. But it must also be recorded that in other cases no results at all were obtained after many hours of using the "writing down" method.

It must be remembered that the HRAs were working from a self-diagnosis as to the depths of their fixations. Few, comparatively, felt the need of analytical methods. Most were content to re-examine their habits of thought and revise them toward the "hurtlessness" pattern of Huna. Gradually this began to take effect as they checked themselves in intolerance toward others, in their own angers and jealousies. An overcoming each time made the course clearer and easier. There came about more peace of mind. Then, at last, they were praying with more sensation of contact with the High Self. Perhaps the blockings were not all removed, who knows? At any rate, the High Self began to take a hand.

The truth of the matter seems to be that, when a sufficient clearing of the aka cord to the High Self is accomplished by whatever means, the normal relation between the three selves is automatically reestablished and the High Self hastens to draw needed mana from the low self and cause the healing and corrections to take place, not only in body but also in mental attitudes and in conditions surrounding the individual. Many things have happened to the experimenters who have had success in getting the slight blockings removed, in which only the intervention and loving guidance of the High Self could account for the almost miraculous turn of events which brought happiness and success to replace unhappiness and failure.

CHAPTER XX

NEW LIGHT ON THE TEACHINGS
OF JESUS

In the foregoing chapters we have seen that the kahunas, including Jesus, the greatest of them all, divided
people roughly into two classes in so far as their normal
relationship with the High Self Father was concerned.

First, there was the class of persons who lived the
kindly life and who were naturally inclined to be helpful and constructive. What few complexes they might
have were of such a nature that they did not cause a
feeling of guilt in the low self which made it hide its
face from the High Self.

The second class covered those who lived the preda-
tory and hurtful-to-others life to a certain extent or, at
worst, were entirely bent on following evil ways of life.
These were the ones whose low selves were complexed
with hates and fears and guilts, and who would not try
to approach the High Self in prayer because of these
blockings of the aka cord path.

For the first class, the normally good and kindly
people, there was, in the teachings of Jesus, a simple set
of instructions to help them live the normal life in
which all three of the selves work freely and successfully together. These were the *outer* teachings. They
can be summed up in a few words. Jesus taught (1)
that one must love the Lord, or High Self Father, and

(2) one must love his neighbors. This last part of the commandment is inclusive of all kindliness and excludes all hates and deeds of hurtfulness.

But in his parable of the lost sheep, Jesus made it clear that his mission was, primarily, aimed at helping those who were cut off from the High Self, teaching them how to unblock their paths and restore contact. He said, (Matt. 18:11) "For the son of man has come to save that which was lost." Those "lost sheep" who suffered from the sins of evil deeds, or who were cut off from their High Selves by complexes or through the association with evil "eating companions," were his chief concern. As these individuals so seldom are able to help themselves to return to the fold of normal living, he placed the utmost stress on the need to carry the "good word" to them, to convert them, and to help them to live the good life.

It is to be supposed that the cult of secrecy which was all-powerful in the inner teachings through all ages, was necessary for reasons not clear to us today. In any case, the evidence that such a cult of secrecy was observed by the kahunas of the Old Testament as well as of New Testament days, is conclusive. We have seen how the knowledge was guarded by the kahunas of Polynesia, in modern times. Now that we have the key to the "secrets of the kingdom of heaven," mentioned by Jesus, we find that it unlocks the inner truths concealed in many passages in which the inner teachings were touched upon by those who wrote the accounts of the life of Jesus after his death.

In the Old Testament we find repeated passages (which could have been written only by men initiated

266

into the secret lore) which show through their use of symbols and code keys common to Huna, nothing more than that there are the several forms of "sin" which can cause the blocking of the aka cord to the High Self. There are repeated promises that these blockings can and will be removed provided proper steps are taken, but there is very little to tell what those steps were, or how they were to be understood and put to use.

On the other hand, Jesus instituted a sweeping reform movement intended to break down old and useless beliefs in the Jewish religion, and to make known the means of gaining release from hindering "stumbling blocks" which prevented men from contacting their High Selves. It is to be seen that the disciples were initiated into the Huna lore and were instructed by use of the "sacred language" of the kahunas. Because of this knowledge of the sacred language, with its symbols and codes, the disciples, after the crucifixion, set about preserving in writing the directions for removing fixations and becoming freed from the clutches of "eating companion" spirits. The Four Gospels all contain the veiled knowledge which we recognize as Huna.

Jesus, with his extraordinary intelligence and insight, was able to condense his main teachings into three such dramatic units of presentation that, for the sake of the dramas alone, they would survive with little change. Straight teachings, as we have seen, become dogmatized and misunderstood very rapidly; but in a drama, while there may be dogmas invented to explain their inner meaning, the story told suffers little change, and thus can carry down to following ages the means of understanding basic hidden truths.

Although there is a wealth of Huna hidden in other dramas in the New Testament, the three which will be discussed in the following chapters are:

1. The drama of the Baptism, in which was established the baptismal rite, followed by the Great Temptation.

2. The drama of the Last Supper, in which was established the foot-washing rite and the Communion rite.

3. The drama of the Crucifixion.

One of the significant things about the three dramas which have been selected for our discussion is the fact that each one was played out as an actual part of the life of Jesus and of his disciples. For this reason the word "drama" is none too good for our use. The real-life incidents and happenings had, it is true, all the elements of drama in the truest sense, but lacked all the make-believe which we have come in later centuries to associate with theatrical production. The "mystery plays" of early ages may have been patterned after the life incidents and put to use in initiatory rites, but never, so far as is now known, has there been a perfection of dramatization against a background of reality and history such as was attained by Jesus.

The greatest of the three dramas was embodied in the most startling dramatization on record, that of the crucifixion. In playing out his part in this, Jesus lost his life, but left an incident so dramatic and impressive and poignant that every detail of it has been remembered for almost two thousand years. It was recorded by his well-initiated disciples so carefully that at any future time, one understanding the ancient lore might find in the events the key to the oldest and most perfect philosophy ever evolved by mankind.

Looking back from our vantage point, as seekers of the ancient knowledge, we can see how necessary it was to make sure that the information embodied in the dramatic events should not be lost with the passage of time. It is apparent from the words of Jesus that he intended the disciples to initiate others into the secret lore, and that there should be continuous initiations from generation to generation. It is also evident that he hoped for a growth in numbers of the initiates and a spreading of the knowledge far and wide. But also, knowing human nature and the limitations of human intellect, he took the steps necessary to prevent the complete loss of the knowledge in case the disciples failed and the chain initiations were hindered or contaminated. Indeed, he no doubt foresaw the future in this case as in so many others.

Before his time, many of the kahunas in the Mediterranean Basin country had set off toward the islands of the Pacific, apparently to find a place where outside influences would be cut off, and their treasured secret knowledge could survive secure and uncontaminated. That it did so until the turn of the last century should enable men of this new age to use the recovered knowledge to learn again, through the use of symbols and code, the knowledge which Jesus built into the dramatic incidents surrounding the presentation of his most priceless teachings. And we are fortunate that the accounts given in the Four Gospels by the disciples were so simply written that even the translation into other languages and the accidents of much copying, failed to bring about basic changes. The "pearls of great price" were so carefully concealed that only the initiates knew they were there, and no outsider was able to find and destroy them.

In our discussion of the dramatic incidents, only the events in the life of Jesus and his immediate disciples can be trusted. The failure to find others who could and would accept the authentic initiations seems to have been surprisingly swift, while the growth of misunderstanding and of dogmatic and groundless assertions and teachings began almost immediately. Paul, who never knew Jesus, was one of the disruptive influences. The dogma superimposed by him upon the original teachings are still part and parcel of organized Christianity.

It is clear to the student that Paul was not an initiate kahuna. Not only was he unacquainted with Jesus, he hardly knew the disciples. After the crucifixion, and his conversion on the road to Damascus, he went to Arabia for a period of three years. Only after that did he go to Jerusalem where he stayed with Peter fifteen days. (Galatians I:17–18.) In Arabia he presumably invented his system of beliefs. These beliefs used Jesus as the cornerstone, but the main structure was Judaism pure and simple, brought up from the past. (Paul was a Jew, a Pharisee.)

Jesus had offered reforms in the rites and beliefs of the Jews. He had, from the time of baptism by John, rejected the use of sprinkled sacrificial blood as an instrument of actual forgiveness of sin—to say nothing of a symbol of such forgiveness.

But not so Paul. Lacking the initiation and the secrets that lay behind the three basic rites instituted by

Jesus, he went back to the early rites of the Jews to find justification for his dogmatic statements covering the real meaning of the life and teachings of Jesus. In his letter to the Romans, Paul elaborated his dogmas and doctrines in a most revealing manner. He declared that because Adam had sinned, his sins were shared by all his children—all mankind. The death of Jesus was necessary and right, he said, because it brought about forgiveness or "justification by his blood" for all who would perform the simple mental feat of accepting this dogma, and believing that in this manner Jesus had made atonement for all the sins of the world—had paid to the uttermost, and had "redeemed the world."

True, Paul taught that all should live the good and kindly life. That was the outer doctrine. But he was unable to see significance in the foot-washing rite or the rite of communion. He entirely misunderstood the inner significance of the death upon the cross, and could find in it nothing beyond a duplication of the savage blood sacrifice rites of purification which had been outgrown with the slow march of civilization, and which Jesus himself strove to reform. He made no effort to help institute a reform in the old rites, but stumbled about trying to make them fit into the new system which he was evolving.

Where Jesus had restated the meaning behind the covenant between God and the Jews, Paul declared (Hebrews, 9:12) that the old covenant obtained by Moses had "decayed" and was, for that reason, no longer in force. He went farther, changing the original concept of a *contract* between God and the Israelites, to the idea of a *will*, or a *last will and testament*—this being something left behind him by Jesus as his legacy to humanity. This legacy to save the world, it was represented, was earned by the shedding of his blood to appease a God of vengeance who held humanity in ransom for the sins of Adam—not the God described by Jesus as the "loving Father."

Paul argued that God never forgave sins except in return for a blood sacrifice: therefore, it was necessary that the actual blood of Jesus be shed in the same exact and literal sense as the blood of animals in the Mosaic times. In Hebrews, verse 22, we read this argument: "And almost all things are by law purged with blood; and without shedding of blood is no remission." Jesus is then described as a high priest, not entering the holy place once a year with the blood of animals as a sacrifice, but with his own blood, ". . . now once in the end of the world hath he appeared to put away sin by the sacrifice of himself." In verse 16 he explained: "For where a testament is, there must also of necessity be the death of the testator."

Paul was a great student of scriptural writings, using them constantly in trying to prove his doctrines. Therefore he must have been thoroughly familiar with Jeremiah's prophecy of a "new covenant" which was to come for the people. Jesus had the sacred writings at instant command in arguing with the temple hierarchy, and was well aware of the prophecy in question. Therefore when he said in the communion rite, "This is my blood of the new covenant," he means that which Jeremiah prophesied, as we shall see presently. (I am aware that the King James version has it, "This is my blood of the new testament," undoubtedly a confusion on the part of

272

the translators because they were working on the Pauline documents, too.) Jesus had never spoken of leaving a legacy. But Paul, in working up his doctrine, became so convinced of his "will and testament" idea that he ignored the use of the word "covenant," so all important in the earlier writings.

Let us now see what Jeremiah prophesied (Jeremiah 31:31 *et seq.*):

"Behold the days come, saith the Lord, that I will make a new covenant with the house of Israel, and with the house of Judah:

"Not according to the covenant that I made with their fathers in the day that I took them by the hand to bring them out of the land of Egypt: which my covenant they brake, although I was an husband to them, sayeth the Lord.

"But this shall be the covenant that I will make with the house of Israel; after those days, saith the Lord, I will put my law *in their inward parts*, and *write it in their hearts*, and will be their God, and they shall be my people."

These are the words of a kahuna. The words I have italicized show that God's law will be enshrined in man's consciousness, yes, even in his subconscious (heart). It will no longer be necessary, in that time to come, that men shall be led by the hand. This is God's part of the covenant. Now as to the people's part:

"And they shall teach no more every man his neighbor, saying, Know the Lord: for *they shall all know me, from the least of them unto the greatest of them*, saith the Lord: for I will forgive their iniquity, and I will remember their sin no more."

There we have the picture of each and every man having the knowledge and the power ultimately to make the contact with his High Self. Was not that the goal that Jesus in all his teaching was preparing man for? We note that the prophecy makes no mention of the shedding of blood to gain the salvation which Paul as-

273

serted could be gained in no other way, and which he further asserted demanded the blood of Jesus. This was a *"new covenant."*

Isaiah (53:3 *et seq.*) furnishes one of the most famous of the prophecies quoted to show that Jesus was the Redeemer. Here again, mention is made of a covenant (which is here in the making) and of the redemption from sin. But no word is said to support the Pauline doctrine of blood sacrifice which has superseded the true Huna teaching of the way and the means of redemption or escape from the stumbling blocks of "sin." Isaiah prophesied thus:

> "He is despised and rejected of men, a man of sorrows, and acquainted with grief: and we hid as it were our faces from him. . . .
>
> "Surely he hath borne our griefs, and carried our sorrows, yet we did esteem him stricken, smitten of God, and afflicted.
>
> "But he was wounded for our transgressions, he was bruised for our iniquities; the chastisement of our peace was upon him; and with his stripes we are healed. . . .
>
> "By his knowledge shall my righteous servant justify many; for he will bear their iniquities."
>
> (And 59:20) "And the Reedeemer shall come to Zion and unto them that turn from transgression in Jacob, saith the Lord.
>
> "As for me, this is my covenant with them. . . . My spirit that is upon thee, and my words which I have put in thy mouth, shall not depart out of thy mouth, nor out of the mouth of thy seed . . ."

The teachings of Jesus were such that at no time did he advocate the morning and evening blood sacrifices of the early Jews, or the sacrifice by priests for the remission of the sins of the tribe as a whole. He advocated no mass heaping of sins on a scapegoat. In his teachings the remission was a personal matter which every

274

man had to take care of for himself or with the aid of a friend, if necessary. There was no mass remission, no blood sacrifice at all.

The one occasion upon which he spoke approvingly of a blood sacrifice was that of the initiation of the Communion rite, and, as we shall see when we take up that rite for discussion, it was not actual shedding of his own blood that was meant, but behind his words and behind the Huna symbol of blood, lie something of an entirely different nature.

It is imperative, if we are to get a true insight into the teachings of Jesus, that the baseless dogmas of Paul be understood for what they are—meaningless things which have little or nothing to do with the inner teachings of Jesus. But it is not exactly fair to blame Paul too harshly for what he did. After all, he was not an initiate, he did not have the "eyes to see and the ears to hear." He was a zealot, like many others since his time, and not finding any dogma in the teachings of Jesus, he felt impelled to inject it into the new church being founded. He was a very complex character, suffering some kind of physical ailment of which he complained in his letters, and which he seemed unable to cure.

To Paul we owe some of the most beautiful of Biblical literature. He was intolerant and bigoted on some subjects (for example, the place of women in the church) and yet was capable of an inspired passage like the 13th Chapter of I Corinthians: "Though I speak with the tongues of men and of angels, and have not charity," etc. (That, of course, was one of the outer teachings of Jesus.) The pity of it all is that the early church, and men down through the centuries since, have

275

followed the Pauline dogmas, as if they were truly a part of what Jesus taught.

We need to see, as one example among many, that the crystallization of the Pauline errors was responsible for the crude concepts which later appeared in the Church as the Mass, in which the communicant is taught to believe in a transmutation of the wine and the wafer so that he actually drinks the blood and eats the flesh of a sacrificed third part of God. Dogmas, when not founded on fact, have a way of demanding the invention of other dogmas to support them. Christianity lost the true inner meanings of the teachings under a deep layer of misunderstanding, which I believe the rediscovery of Huna can clear away and replace with the original system of knowledge.

CHAPTER XXI

THE SECRET MEANING BEHIND THE BAPTISMAL RITE

It must be made very clear, as we take up the first of the basic rites, that of Baptism, that it marks the beginning of the revolt which Jesus led against the dogmas of the Jewish religion of his time. It marks the rejection of the old and ineffective rite of blood sacrifice, in which a sprinkling with blood was supposed to bring about forgiveness of sin.

The use of *water* in baptism marked the restoration of the understanding of Huna and of all the elements which it contains. Water, the Huna symbol of mana, came to the fore, and if there had been full and lasting understanding of the part played by mana in the intercourse between the three selves of man, the older idea of a cleansing through a washing with blood would have vanished forever. We should never have come into modern times prating of being "cleansed by the blood of the Lamb."

In Egypt, at the time when the kahunas were leaving for the Pacific, there appears to have been a prophecy of the return of the "true light," which was one of the names of Huna as well as one of the titles of the High Self. Those who knew the ancient lore had traditions of a return of the secret knowledge at the end of each period when it was threatened by extinction. Also, the return was always to be embodied in a great teacher who could revive the ancient wisdom and reestablish it.

In the Old Testament there was the "Messiah" or "Anointed One" who was to come and help men free themselves from sin so that the Kingdom of God might be established among men. In Polynesia, just as Huna was being lost, the arrival of Captain Cook was hailed hopefully as that of Lono, the "one who was to come" and who would restore the wisdom. A similar tradition and expectation was to be found in Central America in the days of the Mayans. The "Second Coming," foretold in the New Testament after the death of Jesus was, outwardly, his return to earth in the flesh. In the inner or Huna meaning, it is the next return of the true and inner knowledge—perhaps in actuality, the third, or even the tenth "coming."

Jesus, then, when he began his ministry after the rite of baptism had been performed, followed the tradition that was already as old as the secret knowledge itself, under the title of the "True Light." As the embodiment of it he taught in cryptic Huna symbols, saying, "I am the way, the truth and the life: no man cometh to the Father but by me."

This teaching was later warped to make the dogma that personal salvation depended entirely upon the acceptance of Jesus as a personal savior. This called for a following dogma which asserted that all men born before the birth of Jesus were beyond the pale of his salvation, and that all men after his advent, unless they came to God through Jesus as a personal savior would be lost.

From all the studies made of the words spoken by

Jesus, one thing emerges to stand out clearly. Jesus taught a way of bringing about the normal relationship between the three selves. Such a normal relationship is the sum total of "salvation." He did not teach that he, personally, was a direct means of salvation and that one might be forgiven his sins and be made whole physically, mentally or morally, by the simple act of believing that he, Jesus, was able to bring about such salvation.

Man must bring about his own salvation. Jesus offered instruction as to the methods to be used, and, to those near him, he offered help in putting those methods to use. He also taught his disciples to offer the same instructions and to give the same help to those who could not use the methods for themselves without at least some preliminary outside help. (This help, as we shall see, was particularly needed by those who were unable to free themselves of fixations or spirit influences so that they could open their paths to their own High Selves and get the real and lasting help from that source.)

Keeping in mind the fact that Jesus came to teach men how to work out their own salvation, not to offer it to them as some mystic gift to be won simply by "believing on his name," we are ready to examine the basic rites in which men were taught to save themselves—which, in the last analysis, turns out to be the only possible way in which they *can* be saved. We take up, then, the first rite—that of Baptism.

The rather startling appearance of John the Baptist, dressed in camel's hair with a girdle of skins about his loins, with his new and emphatic exhortations, had brought numbers of people to the Jordan River before

Jesus arrived there. John had instituted the new rite of baptism in water, telling the people that they must repent their sins and be cleansed of the effects of sin by baptism. He told of one to come, the latchet of whose shoes he was unworthy to unloose. Some people insisted on knowing who he himself was, and he answered:

"I am the voice of one crying in the wilderness. Make straight the way of the Lord."

Right there we know John was a Huna initiate. "Way" and "Lord" are the key words of this speech. Wherever the knowledge was carried by kahunas the aka cord was symbolized by (1) a way, (2) a path, (3) a highway and (4) a thread, a strand of spider's web, a cord, a lash, a whip, a rope. To straighten or stretch a cord symbolized the opening of the aka cord to the High Self. To clear stumbling blocks from the path or highway had the same meaning. The "Lord" was the High Self whom Jesus later distinguished from Jehovah by calling him "the Father." He was not Ultimate God. He was the *Haku* of the kahunas, "the Lord of the divided waters," or of the mana which must be shared or divided between the lower selves and the High Self if the latter is to play its all important part in the life of the man.

John's constant cry to the people was: "Repent ye! For the kingdom of heaven is at hand."

In the sacred language the word for "repent" is *mihi*. In addition to the outer meaning of feeling sorry that one has sinned there is the inner meaning of "to acknowledge an obligation." As an acknowledged obligation must be fulfilled, the act of repentance carries with it the making of amends for sins committed in so far as is humanly possible. The reader is aware, I am sure, from reading this far, that the rule held good among the kahunas of Hawaii. They refused to help open the paths and bring about healing through the help of the High Self until their patients had first made amends for hurts done others. The only vicarious atonement for such sins of hurts was not in having their amends made for them by another, but in their own good works to others in case amends could no longer be made directly to those formerly injured.

The wailing at the "mourners' bench" in modern revival meetings is not by any means the whole of the act of repentance. John the Baptist made it clear that deeds were a part of the process when he said, "Bring forth, therefore, fruits meet for repentance."

Repentance also included a remembering of past sins and the accomplishment of the task of making over any old attitude of mind which caused one to wish to hurt others. One had to go back and reconsider his usual attitudes and correct them to conform to the Huna standard of love and kindness. This recalling of past "sins" or hurtful acts was one that needed assistance so that the bad attitudes could be compared with the attitudes of reformed men and made to match them. This demanded "confession" of the sins and was a process that involved talking them over with someone who had his own life properly put in order and his own path opened.

It is recorded in Matthew that the people were "baptized of him (John) in Jordan, *confessing their sins.*"

To get to the hidden meaning of "confess" we have

to translate the word back into the sacred language, where it becomes *hai akaka*. This done, we make some very significant discoveries.

We find from *hai* that one not only tells his faults and mistakes—he *stops doing them*. In the telling, fixation memory tangles are "broken open."

Hai, used with the root *hoo*, the causitive, gives light on the qualifications of the one receiving confessions: "To make a sacrifice on an altar." The sacrifice is always the sending of the surcharge of mana to the High Self along the aka cord. "Altar" or "high place" is the symbol of the High Self. The implication is that during the confession period the one to whom the confession is made must have an open path and be able to send the mana to the High Self as the basically important act of making the prayer. There is another very important meaning, "To have very deep affection for another." This indicates the love of the High Self for the lower selves as a vital factor in the clearing of the path and the reuniting of the selves. It also points up the need of deep affection on the part of the two who work together.

The final meaning of "to tear, rend furiously, like a wild beast," gives us the unmistakable symbol of the fixations which damage men so greatly—the wolves and lions of memory tangles and obsessional influences.

The second word in *hai akaka* for "to confess," gives more details of the process. *Akaka*, when used with *hai*, had the meaning of "breaking open" to "make clear, transparent, fully understood"; to bring to light. The "breaking open" of a thing was one of the symbols of causing the low self to open up and divulge its hidden convictions of guilt or unworthiness, or its complexed and fixed beliefs.

According to Matthew, John the Baptist said, "I indeed baptize you with water unto repentance, but he that cometh after me is mightier than I, whose shoes I am not worthy to bear. He shall baptize you with the Holy Ghost and with fire."

Outwardly, John is predicting the arrival of Jesus, which was to take place shortly, and saying that he will offer a different form of baptism which will be more potent and effective. In terms of Huna, he is giving the inner meaning of the cleansing process, and is speaking of the High Self, not of Jesus, as the one who will, when the mana is supplied and it sets to work to clear the path of its man, provide the "baptism with fire," the all powerful high mana which is administered by the High Self or Holy Spirit (Holy Ghost).

The "baptism with fire" has puzzled men for centuries, but it is no puzzle to one who knows the Huna symbols. "Fire" makes light, and light is the symbol of the High Self, also of the low mana when taken by the High Self and its power stepped up in some way (perhaps to a high frequency of vibration) so that it may be used for the purpose of breaking up the fixations—or, a little later, when the path is clear, to bring about healing.

John goes on to say, in the same connection: "Whose fan is in his hand, and he will thoroughly purge his floor, and gather his wheat into the garner; but he will burn up the chaff with unquenchable fire."

The phrase, "Whose fan is in his hand . . . ," refers outwardly to one winnowing grain on the threshing floor, and the outward meaning is the only possible one if any language except the sacred one of Huna is used to contain the phrase. But in the Polynesian when the word for fan, *peahi*, is examined, we find a second and a third meaning, each of them telling us the secret of which the word "fan" is the key. These meanings are, "to anoint with fire," and "to break up."

The "anointing with fire" is the downpouring of the high mana, and this downpouring of force "breaks up" the stumbling blocks or fixations which have clogged the aka cord of contact. In Huna the symbol of "breaking up" is frequently used, and the thing broken is the thought-form cluster of which the fixation is composed. The "chaff" of the threshing floor, in the Huna sense, becomes the residue left from the broken down fixation thought-form clusters. This chaff is destroyed completely by being burned in a fire that is described as "unquenchable" because it is not ordinary fire, but is the high mana against which nothing can prevail.

Here, then, is the picture of John the Baptist, preaching a new way of achieving the Kingdom of Heaven, giving it importance to the low selves of the people by the physical stimulus of washing them with water in the river. The inner meanings of the things he told them was not understood by his listeners, but there must have been fire and fervor and conviction in the man himself, for they responded eagerly to the baptismal rite. Their need, their yearning, for more Light was undoubtedly great, or they would not have swarmed to the Jordan in such numbers as the accounts relate.

Into this scene on the bank of the river flowing through the desert country, with John the Baptist, in his attire of animals' skins, exhorting, hearing confessions, baptizing, Jesus came walking. He came quietly and alone. Where he had been in the years since the last account of his childhood, nobody knows. But certainly he had been undergoing a rigorous training from initiates somewhere. He was now thirty years old, and ready to begin his ministry.

Without fanfare, quite simply and humbly, he approached John. He asked to be baptized. John, who recognized him at once, protested:

"I have need to be baptized of thee—and comest thou to me?"

Jesus answered him. "Suffer it to be so now, for thus it becometh us to fulfill all righteousness."

He and John both knew that he had no sins of which to be cleansed, but it is plain that he wished to establish the rite universally by his own participation in it. John baptized him. When Jesus came out of the water, "Lo, the heavens were opened unto him, and he saw the Spirit of God descending like a dove, and lighting upon him. And lo, a voice from heaven saying, 'This is my beloved son, in whom I am well pleased.' "

In this last act of the drama, the recorders were careful to phrase it lest any mistake be made in the recovery of the inner meaning by initiates who might later read the account. In Huna, the symbol of a spirit of any kind is a bird. In this case it was the High Self or Holy Spirit or "Spirit of God," which was seen to descend. Outwardly, the Holy Spirit descended from heaven. Inwardly, it descended to establish contact with the lower two selves through the open aka cord. Such a descent and such a reestablishment of the full and normal contact is unmistakably the goal to be attained through the use of the rite.

The phrase, "This is my beloved son, in whom I am well pleased," applies to every one, and not only to Jesus. It is the expression of love and approval which all High Selves could well use when the path has been opened and contact has been restored. The High Selves are indeed well pleased with any "son" who takes the needed steps to get his blocked path opened—the needed steps of (1) repentance, with all which that entails, (2) confession, with the accompanying (3) baptism—with all the things which Huna reveals as involved in these three combined steps.

In and hidden behind these three steps, lies the great secret of the baptismal rite—the secret that the High Self, when supplied with sufficient mana can, providing the amends have first been made for sins of hurt, begin the work of removing the hidden and unknown fixations which are blocking the path.

While the words, "Ye must be born again," were not part of the baptismal rite, the idea has been associated with baptism down the years, due to the exhortations of the clergy. For that reason we may as well look into it at this point to find the Huna meaning. The phrase was actually used by Jesus when he was talking to Nicodemus, after his ministry was well started.

The secret meaning of "to be born" is found in the Maori dialect rather than the Hawaiian. (There are several Polynesian dialects, all of which must be considered.) The word is *whanau*. Its secondary or Huna meaning can best be translated into English as "to evolve," or "to progress in a mental-spiritual sense."

The basic concept of Huna was that men were born (or *separated* from the mother) and that they then grew and progressed in experience and knowledge. The goal of that growth was to learn that there was a High Self, that one must work with it freely, easily, in all ways. In order to work properly with the High Self, one must overcome the animal instincts of greed and fear and hate natural to the low self. One came to full and normal growth and stature only when he was UNITED with the High Self.

This *separation* followed by *uniting* was symbolized in many ways in the Bible. One separated from the old life of darkness and sin. One united with the High Self by coming to know it and by establishing contact through the aka cord. The union of the bride and groom symbolized this second step. The union of the Son with the Father symbolized it. The most favored symbol of all was that of becoming "ONE" with the Father.

In quoting excerpts of what Jesus said to Nicodemus (John 3:3–9) I am using the Ferrar Fenton translation for reasons of clarity. Jesus said: (and again the italics are mine):

". . . unless anyone is born *from above*, he cannot see the Kingdom of God. . . . If a man is not born from *water* and *Spirit*, he is unable to enter into the Kingdom of God. That which is born from the flesh is flesh; and that which is born from the Spirit is spirit. . . . You must be born *from above*. . . ."

The second stage of growth or birth, as we see in the above words of Jesus, was accomplished with the help of water or mana, and of the Spirit or High Self. The mana had to be set flowing along the aka cord to the High Self, and the HELP IN UNBLOCKING THE PATH CAME FROM ABOVE—that is, from the High Self as it used the mana to work downward, removing the blocks from the path until the union of the three selves was accomplished.

This gives us, I think, a rather complete accounting of what is meant by the exhortation "to be born again," when one is being urged to be baptized.

When the drama of the baptism of Jesus was completed, the very next thing that happened was the Great Temptation. There is no pause between the telling of the descent of the Holy Spirit, and the departure of Jesus, "led by the Spirit" into the wilderness, "to be tempted by the devil." The rite would have been incomplete, from the Huna point of view, had it not included the solving of the problem of the "eating companions." So these obsession spirits, symbolized by the "devil," were included in the cleansing process to be recorded, even if dealt with as a sequel to the baptism, and though we know that for most people the difficulty with obsessing spirits is not present.

We also know that Jesus was an initiate kahuna of the highest grade, and therefore had long since been freed of any fixations or eating companions which might have beset him at an earlier time. It was part of his training, however, to learn how to deal with such problems, and to teach others how to deal with them. For his purpose of presenting in lasting and dramatic form his own life experiences to embody and perpetuate the great lessons of Huna, he went into the wilderness forthwith, there to live the drama of "temptation."

288

The key to the hidden meaning lying behind the temptation by the devil, lies in the word "wilderness." The Huna word for this is *hihiu*. "Wilderness" is the symbol of the tangle of thoughts and emotions forced upon their hosts by evil "eating companions." They have their own fixations which they have carried over from life in the flesh, and these they force the living to accept as their own.

Hihiu has the secondary or Huna meanings of:

(1) "To be tangled," symbol of the tangles in the aka cord which keep it from being straight and open and clear.

(2) "To make a mistake." A mistake or an error in conduct, such as might be caused by the influence of a spirit, falls under the Huna classification of "sin."

(3) "To be wild, untamed, as a savage animal." Again we see the use of wild and savage animals in Huna to symbolize the "eating companions."

The devil offered Jesus various temptations and ended by offering him great power if he would fall down and worship him. But Jesus refused to worship him (*hoomana:* worship; literally, to make and give mana, as to the High Self, who alone can transform it to beneficient power and give it back.) Jesus replied, ". . . for it is written, Thou shalt worship the Lord thy God, and him only shalt thou serve."

And when the devil had ended these temptations, "he departed from him for a season." The key Huna word is "season," *maloo*, which means "to dry up" or dry the water out of anything. Water being the mana symbol, we find here that the devil, unable to get a supply of mana through being "worshipped," was powerless to continue his temptations and departed. Because he tried so hard to get mana, he can be classed as one of the eating companion spirits which feed on the mana of the living host.

The "drying up" of the mana supply of the evil spirit must be accomplished by a process of ceasing to "agree" with the evil spirits, by ceasing to respond to their evil urges, as Jesus did in the drama. This is something which the middle self must cause the low self to handle. It involves a complete conversion and change of the way of life from evil to good.

While an individual can turn over a new leaf and balance his accounts by making amends for past hurts with no outside assistance, there usually remain the fixations and sometimes obsessional influences of which he is unaware. These come under the general heading of sins, however, and must be removed. They are the things which the psalmist indicated when he said, "Who can understand his errors? Cleanse thou me from secret faults." It may also be noted that the psalmist looked to outside help in obtaining cleansing from the fixations and spirit influences.

In the drama of the temptation of Jesus, it is to be remembered that in this case he had already been placed in full and free contact with his High Self, as explained in the symbol of the Holy Spirit descending upon him as a dove. For this reason he needed no outside help from John or other men in dealing with the evil spirits. He had the help of the High Self, and that was enough. In later rites, we shall see what is to be done when the obsessing influences need to be removed before the path can be opened.

CHAPTER XXII

THE SECRET MEANING BEHIND THE FOOT-WASHING RITE

It is a difficult thing to pass over the three years of the ministry of Jesus. Huna principles are revealed in every parable, in every cryptic saying. It is fascinating to watch the great kahuna at work, healing the sick bodies and minds of the people, just as kahunas have done wherever the initiates of Huna have been at work.

We have said that Jesus healed many—perhaps thousands—by the laying on of hands. But it is in the detailed cases of his healing that we find corroboration of the methods used by the kahunas of Hawaii. He used suggestion. He broke down complexes, as in the case of the paralytic boy let down through the roof of the house where Jesus was staying with Peter. He drove out evil spirits, as in the case of the epileptic boy brought to him by the boy's father. He used physical stimulus in healing the man who was deaf and had an impediment in his speech.

Jesus had a highly developed psychic sense and used it in diagnosis. This may have been a natural gift, or his low self may well have been trained in telepathy during his years of work with initiates prior to his appearance as a kahuna. He diagnosed the troubles of patients by telepathic means, having thereby no need of questioning them. He used "absent treatment" in some cases, which we know is a telepathic process.

All this demonstration puts on a sound basis even our humble efforts in the HRA to develop the telepathic nature of the low self. It also corroborates and makes less strange the successful work of physicians today who are using the pendulum to get the low self telepathic knowledge of the patient's condition for diagnosis.

It would take an entire book to tell all that the teachings and healings of Jesus reveal as to Huna. Some day I hope that book may be written. There is space here only to indicate the importance of such a project. In the meantime, we are content to go on with the retelling of the three dramatic incidents in the life of Jesus, finding in them the deep and hidden Huna meanings.

So we come to the night of the Last Supper. Jesus knew, with that foreknowledge that comes only from the High Self, that he was to be betrayed and crucified. As a matter of fact, Caiaphas, the high priest, had already called a meeting of the chief priests, scribes and elders to plan to take Jesus by subtility and kill him. They had people on the watch for him, so that his whereabouts would be reported and they could arrest him.

It was one of Jesus' own disciples, Judas Iscariot, who went to the chief priests and offered to deliver Jesus to them—for a sum of money. They agreed upon thirty pieces of silver. After that, Judas was waiting for a good opportunity to fulfill his part of the bargain.

Jesus desired to observe the feast of the Passover in Jerusalem and sent Peter and John out to prepare it. He told them, with his foreknowledge from the High

Self, just where to find a suitable room, a furnished upper room in a house in the city. Peter and John found it as predicted by Jesus, and prepared the feast.

There we have the dramatic ingredients as the twelve disciples sat down with Jesus to eat in that upper room: the one who knew he was to be betrayed; the betrayer who had made the bargain; the eleven others unknowing of what was to happen, and all eating together as was their wont. Jesus, knowing that he was soon to leave them, wanted this last meeting because, as Luke says, "having loved his own which were in the world, he loved them unto the end."

They began the supper with the initiation of the rite of Communion, which will be discussed later. Then Jesus spoke, very sadly: "Verily, verily, I say unto you, that one of you shall betray me."

The disciples looked at each other, startled, wondering which one of them he meant. Judas must have masked his face successfully. The others began asking anxiously of Jesus, "Is it I?" Peter signaled to John, the beloved disciple, who was leaning on Jesus' breast, to ask Jesus to name the man, and John asked the question.

Jesus answered, "He it is to whom I shall give a sop when I have dipped it." He dipped a piece of bread into some kind of soup or sauce, and handed it to Judas Iscariot.

Judas tried to dissemble, asking, no doubt with the hope of appearing innocent, "Master, is it I?"

"Thou hast said," Jesus answered him shortly and bade him, "That thou doest, do quickly."

The other disciples did not know what this interchange meant, but since Judas had charge of their common purse, they took it for granted he had been sent on some errand when Judas left the room immediately.

Later that night, in a garden across the brook Cedron where Jesus and his disciples had adjourned after the Last Supper, Judas led unto him the chief priests and the scribes and the elders, together with a mob armed with swords and staves. Judas went up to Jesus and kissed him, a prearranged signal with his conspirators that this was the man they sought.

What was the matter with Judas? He had been associated for some time with Jesus, who could have cleared the terrible fixation of greed which possessed him. He had apparently gone along with the humble, almost poverty-stricken life of the followers, but had not expressed the depth of his greed until this time.

Jesus knew it, and said after the communion rite, "I speak not of you all. I know whom I have chosen. But that the scripture may be fulfilled, he that eateth bread with me hath lifted up his heel against me." Perhaps Judas was to be left as the great example of the depths to which greed in the low self can lead a human being.

It was Peter who really worried Jesus. Good, bluff, honest, loving Peter was to be saved to carry the new teachings, as he did later, to far pagan Rome where he gave up his life for it. But Peter's low self harbored a fear complex, and there was apparently no better way to resolve it than to let Peter express it in an act which would make him aware of it, be bitterly ashamed, and then remove it.

Jesus told Peter during the supper that he, Peter, would deny knowing his leader. Peter was astounded.

His middle self rejected such an idea as impossible, but he did not know the power of the fear complex in his low self. Jesus asked him, "Lovest thou me?" and Peter fervently assured him that he did. Then Jesus said, "Feed my lambs," looking forward to Peter's ministry for which he must be saved. Jesus asked the question three times, and three times Peter reaffirmed his love, and three times Jesus said "Feed my lambs." There is something of great significance in this from the Huna standpoint. The kahunas always repeated three times any important message or prayer, and always in the same words.

Peter did deny that he knew Jesus, and he denied it three times to different people. When Jesus was taken, a bound prisoner, to the palace of the high priest, love impelled Peter to follow Jesus there, and only one other disciple went that far. But fear gripped him, fear for his own safety, when these people recognized him as one of the followers of Jesus.

After the last denial, Jesus turned and looked at Peter. He said nothing, but what volumes must have been in that look. Peter, instantly remembering that Jesus had predicted that he would deny him thrice, went out and wept bitterly. In that moment the fear complex was utterly dissolved, and his whole subsequent history is that of a sublimely courageous man.

But let us go back to the supper table where the disciples, all but Judas, who had gone on his nefarious business, were sitting with Jesus. We have not yet told of the important foot-washing rite. It was mainly for Peter's sake, I think, that Jesus instituted the rite, though it taught all of them the necessary technique of removing complexes when they should begin their ministry.

The supper was finished. Jesus rose from his place and laid aside his garments. He took a towel and girded himself. Then he poured water in a basin and began to wash the feet of the disciples. He wiped them with the towel with which he was girded. This was a new and strange performance. The disciples did not understand it, and were abashed and uncomfortable to have their master doing a servant's work.

But when we look at this closely, we see that the things used and the things done are full of symbols and hidden meanings, once we translate them into the sacred language.

Jesus took a towel and girded himself. In other words, he made a loin cloth out of a towel. In the language of the kahunas that is a *malo*, and the same word means both loin cloth and towel. *Malo* has the secret meaning of "to dry out." Does not that have a familiar ring to the reader by now? Mana is to be dried out of the fixation memory clusters. Once the mana is taken out of such complexes, they are broken up. We know in the work of our modern psychologists that once the strength and energy of emotion tied up in fixations is released, the fixations die.

Jesus poured water into a basin. No one who has read this far can fail to recognize that water is the symbol of mana. Jesus was providing a supply of mana to his own High Self to be used for the benefit of those whose feet were to be washed.

Why were their *feet* to be washed? Feet are the Huna symbol for the low self. There was the blocking of fear in the low self of Peter, so that he could not send mana to his own High Self. As for the other disciples the record does not state—it concentrates on Peter. The Polynesian word for feet is *wawae*, made up of the roots *wa* and *wae*. *Wa* gives us for one meaning, "A space between two points of time." Such a space of time must be included in any memory when we recall a past event. In the method of an analyst working with a patient, the events causing fixations are recalled. Once such events are brought to the focus of consciousness, and are understood in their true perspective, they become rationalized and are no longer outlaw memories or fixations.

Another meaning of *wa* is "to think, reflect, ponder, turn over and over in the mind." This describes the rationalization process which takes place. A third meaning of *wa* is "to throw up, or vomit up, something." This is the symbol of getting rid of fixations lodged in the low self. The second root, *wae*, gives us "to break up and to sort the good from the bad," which describes the process of breaking down fixation memories and rationalizing them. Also, it means "to dwell upon in the mind in thinking of an event, to reflect, consider a case, to make a choice," all describing the process of weighing and rationalizing a fixation-causing event.

We see, then, the extremely significant fact that Jesus chose to wash the *feet* (the low self) of his disciples in demonstrating symbolically the method for the removal of complexes.

Even the word for the basin he used, *pa* in the sacred language, contains meanings which indicate the inability of those with blocked paths to send mana to their own High Selves ("to be dried out or parched"). The word *pa* also has the meaning of "to divide something be-tween parties." In the case of the rite as performed by Jesus, it is the dividing of the mana provided by him (as symbolized by the water in the basin) between his own High Self and the High Self of the one to be cleansed. A final meaning hidden in the word is "to touch," and this is the completion of the whole process: it is the symbol of reaching out along the aka cord to contact or "touch" the High Self. This must be done before the mana can be given to it.

Jesus, then, brought the basin full of Huna meanings, and used the towel, also full of meaning, to wash the feet of Peter.

Peter, uncomfortable and unhappy, objected. Jesus told him: "What I do thou knowest not now, but thou shalt know hereafter."

Indeed, Peter must have discovered very soon what was meant by the rite, after his denial of Jesus and after his complex dissolved out in tears. He must have pondered the matter deeply then, and used the technique in his service of healing others.

But at the time Jesus was washing his feet, Peter said impulsively, "Lord, not my feet only, but also my hands and my head."

Jesus told him that was not necessary—it was only his feet (low self) that needed washing. "Ye are clean, but not all." For he knew Peter's low self harbored the fear complex.

After he had finished washing their feet and resumed his garments and sat down, Jesus told them that he had given them an example, and that henceforth they should wash one another's feet.

The technique that emerges from the maze of symbols is substantially this: the person whose aka cord path to his own High Self is blocked by fixations, may seek the help of one whose path is not blocked. That man or woman can give the power of mana to his own High Self and ask that it be used to break up the fixations in the petitioner. This helper need not be a kahuna. The disciples were told that they could and should help each other in this way. It was evident that Jesus did not consider this aid possible only to one of his own great powers. It is sufficient that the helper be one who has demonstrated that he is in touch with his High Self—in other words, has had his prayers answered, and can accumulate a large surcharge of mana for the use of the two High Selves in breaking up the fixations in another's low self.

From the hidden meanings found in the Polynesian words for "feet" and "basin," I would also conclude that the foot-washing rite indicates a talking-out process between the complexed person and his helper, leading to a rationalization of the memory tangles. Because of the experience of amateurs today, attempting to do this for a friend and succeeding only in stirring up the hidden troubles, not knowing how to resolve them, it seems essential for any helper to have had some training along that line. A combination of a person who has his own path to the High Self in fine working order, plus a knowledge of how to use suggestion and physical stimulus and how to help rationalize the fixations when surfaced, would seem to be ideal.

If the knowledge uncovered in the Huna meanings of words used in this rite seems reminiscent of that gained in the rite of baptism, the fact is that it is the same. It was repeated by the initiate recorders of the events for reasons of emphasis, and to make sure the truth of the way to the salvation of mankind should be preserved. It was the method the Polynesians used, the hiding of the secret in commonly-used words. Would one expect to find a noble philosophy, and a technique for using it, in such words as way, confess, water, fan, basin and feet?

The very retelling of the foot-washing rite, which seems seldom to have been used in the Christian church as the baptism and communion rites have been, brings to light why it has been avoided. The clericals and scholars simply could not fathom its meaning. No wonder it has been passed over as merely a lesson in humility. But Jesus would never have acted it out as a rite, if it had not had a great and deep significance.

Another thing had to be guarded against for the future. Any of the rites might be discarded by those ignorant of Huna meanings, just as the foot-washing rite has been. But if even one remained to reveal the truth when the time came for it to be revealed, it would thus be preserved and available. The remaining initiates of the ancient lore disappeared from the Mediterranean region in the early centuries after the death of Jesus, so we have no further literature on the subject from that source.

CHAPTER XXIII

THE SECRET MEANING BEHIND
THE COMMUNION RITE

Historians and Bible scholars tell us that as the early church spread out from Jerusalem into Antioch and Greece, it had no scriptures for its use except a few scrolls of the ancient writings which were later incorporated in what is called the Old Testament. The elders of the Christian churches received letters from Paul and other evangelists, and periodic visits from them to help them direct their work. These letters were read to the congregations but in no wise were they considered sacred literature. It is really amazing that they were preserved. A long time afterwards, convocations of the organized Church incorporated them as sacred writings in what they called the New Testament, and Paul was canonized.

The four gospels of Matthew, Mark, Luke and John did not appear until long after the letters were written, some fifty to a hundred years after the death of Jesus. While I have spoken of the work of the initiates of Huna to be found in these accounts of the life and teachings of Jesus, it must be acknowledged that Paul's theology and the growing dogmas offered by lesser men, crept into the accounts. That has added to the confusion, always existing as the centuries carried on the Christian message, the confusion of contradictory statements in the gospels. Bible scholars tell us that these accounts were compilations of various writings by different authors. Nevertheless, Matthew, Mark, Luke and John were declared "saints" by the organized church. Our satisfaction is derived from the recordings of those portions remaining true to the original teachings.

My method of separating the priceless teaching of Jesus from the spurious dogma is, as I have explained before, to use the test of Huna. I should like to preface the examination of the Communion Rite by a few—a very few—examples, as space will not allow for more.

Jesus began his ministry by reading a passage from Isaiah. Now, Isaiah was a great Huna initiate, as proved by the translation of passage after passage of his writings into the sacred language. Let us recall to mind the moment Jesus announced his ministry as it is recorded in Luke (4:16–21).

"And he came to Nazareth, where he had been brought up: and he entered, as his custom was, into the synagogue on the sabbath day, and stood up to read.

"And there was delivered unto him the book of the prophet Isaiah. And he opened the book, and found the place where it was written,

" 'The Spirit of the Lord is upon me, Because he anointed me to preach the good tidings to the poor: He hath sent me to proclaim release to the captives, And recovering of sight to the blind, To set at Liberty them that are bruised, To proclaim the acceptable year of the Lord.'

"And he closed the book and gave it back to the attendants and sat down: and the eyes of all in the synagogue were fastened on him. And he began to say unto them, To-day hath this scripture been fulfilled in your ears."

There we see Jesus accepting the prediction that a new and greater prophet of the Huna order would arise, and he knew that in himself he embodied the fulfillment of the prophecies. In the prophecies he was described as the Son of God, and as one united to God (the High Self Father or *Aumakua* of Huna). Realizing his own union with his High Self, and being able to heal because of that union, he began at the start of his ministry to teach men that such a union was possible and that he had accomplished it.

It is necessary for our understanding of the position he took, to keep in mind the fact that he did not claim that no other person could attain to a similar union and oneness. On the contrary, he constantly urged others to strive toward this end. For one instance, there was the time that he was accused of blasphemy when he said, "I and my Father are one," and was about to be stoned for it. Jesus answered the accusers: "Is it not written in your law, I said, Ye are gods?" (He was quoting from one of the Psalms.) "If he called them gods, unto whom the word of God came, and the scripture cannot be broken, say ye of him whom the Father hath sanctified and sent into the world, thou blasphemeth because I said I am the son of God?"

Again, at the time of the Last Supper, when he was talking intimately to his disciples, he said:

"The words that I speak unto you, I speak not of myself, but the Father that dwelleth in me, he doeth the works.

303

"Believe me that I am in the Father and the Father is in me, or else believe me for the very works' sake.

"Verily, verily, I say unto you, he that believeth on me, the works that I do shall he do also; and greater works than these shall he do."

What else could he possibly have been saying, other than that he did his miracles through his High Self, and that the disciples (not afterwards uplifted to be part of ONE GOD, though they also performed miracles of healing) would be capable of even greater works through their own High Selves?

The words "God" and the High Self Father are interchangeable in his teachings at all points, just as are the Holy Spirit or Holy Ghost, and the High Self.

We must understand that he often stood before those he taught, as in a state of complete union with the High Self, and that he spoke as with the voice of the Father. This was customary in Huna circles where the highest order of kahunas were called "Those who speak for the god." In healing, the command, "Be ye healed," was spoken by the three selves in perfect union, not by the lower selves alone.

In the places in his teachings in which Jesus spoke as if he were God or the Father, and not a man, he was following the ancient Huna custom. Endless confusion has resulted from a lack of Huna insight into this matter. Men could not understand how Jesus could be a man and still a god. Lacking understanding, they developed dogmas in which they presented Jesus as a part of a three-fold Ultimate God who was composed of God the Father, Jesus the Son, and the Holy Ghost. This theology was not Huna, and not Judaism, and

Jesus himself taught nothing of the sort. He simply taught that it was possible for a man in the flesh to unite with his own High Self, whom he called "the Father" ("the Father that dwelleth in me"), and to become ONE in this union—NOT THREE IN ONE.

An instance of where the Pauline dogma crept into the gospels occurs in Matthew (28:19). This is the report that Jesus, as a spirit returning to his disciples after rising from the tomb, said: "Go ye therefore to all nations, baptising them in the name of the Father, and of the Son, and of the Holy Ghost."

Knowing Huna, we see that the High Self is given the title of the Holy Spirit as it descends on Jesus as a dove. Each self of man is a spirit to the kahuna, the Aumakua being the "holy" one. The word "ghost" is a word foreign to the Hebrew, Latin or Greek. It is nothing more than an alternate word taken from the Germanic *geist* meaning "Spirit" and borrowed to become our English "ghost."

It is a profitable thing to go down through the gospel accounts and see that when Jesus is expounding a truth and begins it "I am . . ." or ends it ". . . through me," etc., he is speaking as his High Self Father. Sometimes, of course, it is the usual personal reference to the middle self we all use, the context will tell that; but always in the exposition of fundamental truths, the "I" and "me" is the Father.

One HRA, trying this practice of reading old words anew, complained that, after a few pages, old habit beliefs of the low self, instilled in youth, began confusing it with the well-hammered-in dogma. It was suggested that she try reading one of the revised or modern English versions, which do not change the ideas expressed in the King James version, but help to cast off the spell of dogmatized interpretation.

I am using the Ferrar Fenton version in the next incident to be discussed. This is the teaching on the "bread of life," appearing in John 6:32 *et seq.*, which is a good preparation for understanding the Communion Rite.

Certain people sought out Jesus, impressed by his healing work, and asked for a sign that it really was the work of God. They reminded him that in Mosaic times their forefathers had received such a sign in the form of manna from heaven. Jesus answered them:

"I tell you assuredly, Moses did not himself give you that bread from heaven; but my Father will give you the real bread from heaven, for the bread of God is he who descends from heaven, and gives life to the world.

". . . I am the bread of life: the one who comes to me will never hunger; and the one who believes in me will never thirst."

Read this in Huna terms, Jesus speaking as for the Father, the High Self, and note that he mentions thirst, and thereby indicates the fact that water or mana was part of the "feeding" of which he taught. The figure of speech, "bread from heaven," points to the return flow of the High Mana, and is in line with the manna of the time of Moses, which "fell" from heaven to nourish spiritually the Children of Israel in the wilderness.

Another excerpt from the passage is, "I am the Living Bread, which descended out of heaven; if anyone should eat of this Bread, he will live forever; and the

Bread is also my body, which I will give for the life of the world."

This verse has been pointed to as a prophecy of his own death, and a proof that Jesus actually gave his own life on the cross to provide life for the world—to "save" it. Instead, he was teaching the lesson that the High Self provides the life of the world in the feeding back of the mana sent to it by the lower selves—otherwise there is sin, death, and disaster.

The report goes on to say, "The Judeans then discussed with one another, asking, 'How can this man give us his body to eat?'

"Jesus therefore said to them: 'I tell you most certainly that unless you eat the body of the Son of Man and drink his blood, you do not possess life in yourselves. . . . As the living Father sent me, I also live through the Father; so that the one who eats me, shall also live through me. . . . Whoever eats of this bread shall live forever.' "

The idea of "eating the god" in order to absorb his power and very substance, can be traced back to Egypt. In a degraded form it spread to several parts of the world and it was thought that a man might absorb his enemy's strength or courage or virility if, after the enemy had been slain, parts of him were eaten. Much cannibalism stemmed from this concept rather than from any hunger for human flesh.

In Huna the High Self, as a "god," is fed mana by the lower man, and, in its turn, the mana is changed to a more potent form and is fed back to the lower or physical part of man. The Polynesians had a saying to the

307

effect that if one did not feed the gods, they would die. And, if the gods died, men would die. The reciprocal feeding was something taught under the outer form as an actual eating of the body of the god and drinking of his blood.

No doubt Jesus expected that some of the people who had come to question him would be capable of understanding the inner meaning of the cryptic phrases he was using. He was always anxious to give to those who had "eyes to see and ears to hear." But none such was in this group:

"Many even among his disciples, however, on hearing this declaration remarked: 'This is an extraordinary declaration: Who can listen to it?'

(Jesus said:) "Does this make you stumble? Then what if you should see the Son of Man ascending to where he was at the first? The Spirit is the life-giver: the body is worth nothing. . . ."

"The body is worth nothing." Let us remember that statement as we come to examine the Communion Rite:

This rite was initiated during the dramatic action of the night of the Last Supper. After Jesus and the disciples were seated at the supper table, and before they began to partake of the feast spread before them, Jesus looked at them fondly and said, "With desire I have desired to eat this passover with you before I suffer." Then he "appointed them a kingdom" for their work, "that ye may eat and drink at my table in my kingdom."

I will select from Luke and Matthew to tell how the rite was established:

"And he took bread and gave thanks and brake it, and gave unto them, saying, 'This is my body which is given

308

for you: this do in remembrance of me. For I say unto you, I will not any more eat thereof, until it be fulfilled in the kingdom of God.'

"And he took the cup and gave thanks, and gave it to them, saying, 'Drink ye all of it, for this is my blood of the new testament (covenant) which is shed for many for the remission of sins.

" 'But I say unto you, I will not drink henceforth of this fruit of the vine until that day when I drink it new with you in my Father's kingdom.' "

This, then, was a ceremonial ritual of remembrance of Jesus' teaching. The breaking of the bread and the eating of it symbolized and called to mind the Huna truth that the High Self must be fed mana and that it then will, in turn, feed the worshipers with the High Mana. The same applies to drinking of the blood. It is part of the body, and symbolically it flows, like mana. Again, it represents the mana which must be fed to the High Self, and the High Self will feed it back to its man. The lesson is obvious to those who know the Huna meaning behind the rite.

It is not the most important lesson to be drawn from the Huna teachings in the Bible. All lessons are important and all are indispensable parts of the whole process of attaining the normal relationship between the three selves. The accident of chance that caused the breaking of bread and drinking of wine to assume the greatest importance in the rituals of the Church—the rite most often and solemnly observed—does not prove that it is more valuable than, for example, the removal of fixations or the putting to use of the aka cord in seeking union with the High Self.

As the "remission of sin" was given as the main purpose of the eating of the bread (as the body) and the drinking of the wine (as the blood) we see there the use of the mana, once it has been given to the High Self, to remove the fixations and open the aka cord path of contact and connection—to reestablish COMMUNION between the three selves.

The men who began constructing dogmas and doctrines after the death of Jesus, seized upon the Communion rite and this is what they made of it:

The bread and wine would be changed by God into the *actual substance of* the flesh and blood of Jesus so that it might be consumed by the worshipers. They must have overlooked his statement that the body (of flesh) was worth nothing. However, there was one advance to be grateful for. No sacrificial offering was made to God in the old way of the blood letting and blood sprinkling. There was no attempt to feed God with burned flesh of sacrificed animals, as Jehovah was fed by the followers of Moses.

What should have been understood, and understood as one of the great Huna foundation stones, was that mana was the one and only thing which could be used to feed the High Selves of the congregation and the priests.

We have already seen that the act of *worship*, which is basic and which is the primary act to be accomplished by the gathering of any congregation for any ritual observance, is not a matter of song, chanting, prayer and preaching. Worship is *hoo-mana*, and it means "to make mana" and then to give it to the High Selves through the aka cords of the worshipers.

310

The sacrifice of the Mass is, outwardly, the offering of the slain body of Jesus as an offering to God on an altar. After the offering, the members of the congregation participate in the "Communion" and eat the God. This is right in so far as the inner meaning goes, but it is savagery and ignorance if only the outer meaning is known.

As to the matter of the "new testament," it has been discussed in Chapter 20 in connection with the Pauline doctrines, and the conclusion reached that Jesus must have said "new covenant." Jeremiah's prophecy of the new covenant was quoted at that time. Since Jesus was fulfilling the prophecies to the letter in his own being and in his ministry, and had done so successfully, it is inconceivable that he would fail at this point when instituting the rite of the Communion. That he would forget the prophecies by which he lived and which had come from great kahunas of his same line and school of initiation, would have been forgetting the meaning of his mission. He was to institute a new covenant with new laws that were to be written in the hearts of those who could accept them.

I should like, at this point, to give the secret meanings of the Polynesian word for covenant, *kumu*. These are (1) "to begin an undertaking," signifying the beginning of the "feeding" process by sending mana to the High Self. (2) "A fountain of water." The rising of water in a fountain is one of the many picturesque symbols in Huna for the sending of the mana (water) up to the High Self along the aka cord. On the other hand, the word for testament gives no secret meanings of any kind, either in its complete form or in its roots.

John, in his version of the Last Supper drama does not give the Communion rite at all, but instead concentrates on the valuable last instructions of Jesus to his disciples. Among these, we find Jesus uttering a new commandment. In the covenants of old times there was nearly always a command to the people from God as part of the covenant. The Ten Commandments were part of a covenant. According to John, Jesus said: "A new commandment I give unto you, THAT YE LOVE ONE ANOTHER." Nothing could have summed up the new covenant better than that commandment, nor have been more revealing of Huna teachings.

Even the word for commandment in the Polynesian, *kana-wai*, gives us a significant secret meaning: "to cause water to appear," which, of course, is the symbol of accumulating a surcharge of mana.

Surely the mistake that Paul and others after him made about the death of Jesus being necessary in order to allow his blood to be shed as an actual blood sacrifice to redeem the world from the curse of the Adam and Eve sins, can now be corrected. The very cup filled with wine, and which was offered as a cup of blood "shed for the remission of sins" provides us with pregnant inner meanings when we recall the translation of "cup" into the sacred language, as mentioned in Chapter 8. (Cup: *ki-aha*. Root *ki*, "to squirt water, the companion of the "fountain of water," and giving the same symbolic meaning of sending mana upward to the High Self. Root *aha*, "a cord," the Huna symbol for the aka cord, and, when combined with the root *ki*, showing how the water or mana was sent to the High Self—along the aka cord.)

312

It may be well to explain that all the cups and basins the Polynesian kahunas possessed were made of gourds, and that cord nets were woven around the gourd containers so that they could be carried more easily by the ends of the cords. The word invented for "cup" or "basin" or "bowl" was built around the root word *aha*, meaning cord or cords. This significance also applies to the basin into which water was poured by Jesus before the foot-washing was begun.

So much for the symbolic cup. Now, as for the blood in the cup, we understand it as a symbol of mana, but the word for blood—*koko*—has interesting inner meanings:

(1) "The netting or net work of strings around a calabash." This is the same net mentioned above in relation to the gourd or cup. Again it is the symbol of the aka cord.

(2) "To fulfill; to fill up." The "blood of the new covenant," under this symbolic meaning, is the filling of the High Self with mana. It could also be the fulfillment of the prophecies by Jesus in issuing a new command and establishing a substitute rite in the Communion to take the place of the blood sacrifice in the older covenant. However, the inner meaning remains, essentially, that of sending the mana along the aka cord to the High Self so that it can then act to remove the fixation-obsession "sins" from the one to be cleansed—may "remit" or forgive.

(3) And lastly we have in the word for blood, "to rise up or extend" (with *hoo, the causative*.) This is the symbol of sending mana along the aka cord. It also symbolizes the fact that the aka cord rises up and extends to touch the High Self at the far end. It extends from the low self to the High Self.

Our final conclusion must be that Jesus did not shed his blood to repay the debt of original sin owed by mankind to a merciless God. In the symbolic presentation of truth in the Communion rite, he shed no blood at all,

313

and the wine in the cup which was offered to the disciples did NOT stand for the blood he later shed in his death on the cross.

The entire rite embodied a restatement of the great basic principles of Huna, the knowledge of which makes each man and woman able not only to obtain cleansing for "sin," but to make contact with the High Self—which is to "become one with the Father." And this is the goal aimed at by all the teachings of Jesus.

CHAPTER XXIV

THE SECRET MEANING BEHIND
THE CRUCIFIXION

And now we come to the great and awesome drama of the Crucifixion. Its mounting series of events, exemplifying man's inhumanity to man, and leading to the tragic climax, have held the minds and hearts of people down the ages. As such, its outer meanings alone have exerted an incalculable influence. But the recorders of the drama have couched it in such terms that we are able to discover the deeper, hidden meanings which reveal it as the final summing up of the things Jesus came into the world to teach.

The mission of Jesus was to make each individual aware of himself, know what he had to struggle with in himself and how to deal with it, and to give him a promise of the shining goal ahead when he had achieved the union with his own High Self Father—which he could and must do. He was not concerned with the tribe as a whole—mankind, the masses—as was Moses. Jesus knew that when each individual was a truly integrated person, the matter of society, composed of such individuals, would take care of itself.

According to Huna the consciousness of each individual (the middle self) is a spirit which lives as a guest in the body to help and control the low self and also to gain its own growth through life experience until permanent contact with the High Self is attained. Its major duty is to guide and teach the low self so that the latter may progress from the animal level of consciousness to that of the man or middle self level.

We must know that the animal or "instinctual" urges of the low self are very strong, and rightly so for the preservation of the race. But there are times when the middle self must control even such an urge. This is exemplified in the outward account of Jesus in Gethsemane, the garden to which he and his disciples repaired after the Last Supper.

The event occurred before Judas betrayed him. Jesus went apart to pray, telling the others that he felt exceedingly sorrowful. He fell on his face and prayed, "O my Father, if it be possible, let this cup pass from me. Nevertheless not as I will, but as thou wilt."

The low self in the body of a strong, healthy young man will put up a fight to save the body. It is making a plenitude of mana and it loves life. Jesus, if this was what troubled him, could not overcome it, the first time he prayed. He went back to his disciples and told them, "the spirit (his middle self) indeed is willing, but the flesh is weak." He urged them to pray, also, against such "temptation" in themselves.

He went away again and prayed, "O my Father, if this cup may not pass away from me, except I drink it, thy will be done." After an interval, he uttered the prayer again, in the same words. (We recall that the kahunas said an important prayer three times, in the same words.)

This time he conquered, with the help of the High Self, and came back to his disciples, again serene, and told them to sleep and rest.

We should be quite satisfied with this outer meaning, and there is certainly much to be learned thereby, were it not for that important word "cup" which Jesus asked to pass away from him. It has always been assumed to mean the "cup of bitterness," the "cup of poison" we meet throughout literature. And so it is in the Polynesian language, and there is a word for it: *pai*. It is not the cup (*ki-aha*) we have discussed more than once as symbolizing the sending of mana as a fountain to the High Self along the aka cord. *Pai*, the cup of bitterness, gives us entirely different meanings which broaden the scope of what the incident was supposed to exemplify.

We must remember that Jesus was cleansed of all fixation sins in the low self even before he was baptized. He proceeded in his ministry, completely in touch with his High Self Father. He lived a life of hurtlessness, and he taught it as the way for others. He taught the importance of the individual. He preached the inherent *dignity* of man.

It must also be kept in mind that he had foreknowledge from his High Self of exactly what was to happen to him, in detail no doubt. He was prepared always to fulfill the prophecies, but it can be believed that when the revolting details of what was to come appeared before his mind's eye, they were staggering.

Pai, then, the cup of bitterness, reveals three inner meanings. The first is "to scourge." One of the most degrading and humiliating things to be done to Jesus later was the scourging, first at the hands of Pilate, later by the soldiers who mocked him and spat upon him. The second secret meaning of *pai* is "to mingle blood and water in one mixture." After Jesus hung on the

317

cross, a spear was thrust into his side "and forthwith came there out blood and water." The third meaning is "to speak evil, to slander." If ever a man was slandered and unjustly accused, Jesus was, after he was arrested.

With these meanings to help, it can be seen clearly that what troubled Jesus so that he had to pray desperately for help, was not only the instinctual urge of the low self to survive, but a far greater fixation caused by the very work he did, fine and noble as it was. He so believed in the dignity of man that he could not bear to see it insulted. This seems to be the final "temptation" of all great spiritual workers, a sort of spiritual pride. It is significant that he warned his disciples against the temptation.

So, having dissolved this fixation through the powerful action of his prayer, repeated thrice, Jesus went through the next few days of almost incredible calumny, injustice and brutality visited on him, and maintained an extraordinary dignity through it all. He was to weaken only once, and that was when, half-unconscious on the cross, his low self sent out one last dying cry to his Father which was so touchingly human.

In his trial, Pilate could find no fault with Jesus under the law. But for reasons of political expediency he turned him over to the importunate chief priests and elders, to do with as they wished. They wished to be rid of him, for his presence and his teachings were drawing entirely too many people away from their established, dogmatic and profitable temple. So it has been with bigots always in any religion, in any place, not to speak of political bigots. Among the chief priests and

elders were rabble-rousers who incited the mob to demand that Jesus be destroyed. Even now, nearly two
thousand years later, people in "civilized" countries
have not learned the lesson this incident in the drama of
the life of Jesus portrays so graphically. Hitler could
still incite mobs of "educated" people to do violence
against the Jews he hated.

With the blood-thirsty cries of the mob to back them,
the chief priests and elders demanded that Jesus should
be crucified, and Pilate so ordained. It was a usual procedure in that time to execute criminals in this manner.
They were nailed to the cross and hung there until they
bled to death, which took long hours of agony to accomplish.

Jesus, then, after a series of insults at the hands of his
captors, was given his cross to bear, wearing a crown of
thorns they had put upon his brow. He was forced to
carry the cross a long way to Calvary, where the crucifixion was to take place. With him went two thieves,
bearing their own crosses, who were to be crucified at the
same time. The mob swarmed around Jesus on the
tortured way, reviling and scoffing and insulting him,
though his faithful followers, especially the women,
wept forlornly. Somewhere along the way, a young
man from the country was pressed into service to carry
the cross for Jesus for a distance, though Jesus resumed
the burden as they approached Calvary. (We are not
told by the writers of the drama just why this happened,
but we may be sure that there is a meaning to it.)

The *via dolorosa*, the Way of the Cross, has been part
of the procedure of worship in the Roman Catholic
church through the centuries, and is today. The scenes

are pictured in sometimes beautiful paintings, hung at intervals on the walls of the churches. These are called the stations of the cross, and the worshipers pause before each one to pray. The cross surmounts each building, from cathedral to small chapel. It is attached to the rosary handled by every individual during his prayers in the church and at home. The figure of the dying Jesus on the cross is everywhere, in pictures and sculpture, even in the humblest homes.

For most, I think, the symbol of the cross means little, except as a physical stimulus to act as a reminder of the dogmatic theology that Jesus died for the remission of their sins. The first Protestants, in their zeal to destroy anything "Romish," cast out the cross. But we see it coming back, little by little, to surmount the steeples of their churches. It is a symbol worth preserving, when one understands its wealth of real meaning.

The cross was a basic symbol among the Polynesians. As I have mentioned elsewhere, in the ancient days the Huna initiates placed a cross of wood before the entrance of their holy or taboo places as a form of "king's X" to warn the uncleansed not to approach. It was the symbol of the uncleansed who were afflicted by any of the several kinds of "sins." The Holy Place was the symbol of the High Self, and the entrance of the "path." The language contains two different words for "cross," each containing the hidden meanings which reveal the truths that the cross symbolized.

The first of these words for "cross" is *kea*. Its secondary or inner meaning is "to obstruct a path and prevent one from traveling it; to hinder one's progress in any way; to force or compel one to do something against his will; to get one into difficulty." This meaning gives a very complete description of what the "eating companions" force one to do. Also of the fixations as they block the path and prevent progress.

It is little short of amazing how the kahunas managed to perpetuate their knowledge of man's make-up, to show what caused the difficulties and how to surmount them. The language of the Polynesians is peculiar in that a variant of a word is often used (as *unihipili* and *unipihili*) which gives even further pertinent hidden meanings. Thus, the variant for *kea* is *pea* (which is a part of the word for "fan"—*peahi*, already discussed). From the roots of *pea* we get, first, "to anoint." This is the symbol of the one who has successfully carried his cross. In other words, it is one who has managed to gain control of his low self and to get his aka cord unblocked. "To anoint" was a form of cleansing—a ceremonial or ritual form. The Messiah was one who had attained the state of union with the High Self through cleansing. Jesus was certainly a Messiah in this sense. The Greek word for "anoint" gives us the title most used for Jesus, "The Christ," or "The Anointed," to use the English form. And second, we get from the basic root, *pe:* "to break," a symbol of the process of destroying the fixation thought-form clusters.

The carrying of the cross, then, is the Huna symbol for the successful accomplishment of the training of the low self, so that it is brought into line with the good and kindly life which must be lived before full contact with the High Self can consciously be made and kept. It is the promise that by so doing, the three selves will function as a single unit to the end that the normal and progressive form of life can be lived.

The symbology of the cross itself, the material object, includes the picture of the pitfalls included in the process. The upright post of the cross represents the aka cord rising to the High Self from the low self, and the bar which crosses the upright represents anything that causes the cord to be blocked and the flow of mana to fail to be sent upward to the High Self.

There is a special word in the Polynesian for the form of cross used in the crucifixion. This is *amana*. The reader will instantly note that familiar term mana, and will know what it means. So when we find that a secondary meaning of *amana*, a cross, is "to offer food or any sacrifice to the gods," we know that what was offered to the "gods" or High Selves was not actually food, but mana sent along the aka cord.

However, as I have just said, the cross-bar of this cross shows that the mana cannot be sent successfully when the aka cord is blocked. This fact may be seen in the other three meanings of *amana* which follow:

(1) "To drive one to do evil," pointing toward the "eating companions" and their obsessional powers and influences. (2) "To cause illness." This is one of the results of the contamination caused by blocking the path. (3) "A cluster of things." This is the symbol of the thought-forms of memories. In this case, because of the association of other bad meanings of the word in question, we see that the memories containing fixation-causing events are indicated.

That Jesus knew and used this Huna symbology of

the cross is apparent early in his teaching, when he said (Luke 9:23–24): "If any man will come after me, let him deny himself, and *take up his cross daily*, and follow me." Certainly he would not have urged others to suffer the crucifixion as he suffered it later—and daily, to make things more impossible. He was giving the teaching of what the cross symbolizes, and urging that the effort toward union be made daily.

While we are considering this passage for the sake of the word "cross" in it, we may as well pause to see what is meant by "deny himself."

The word "deny" is, in the sacred language, *hoo-le-mana*, with these meanings:

(1) "To deny, as to deny the authority of one over another." This is the outer meaning, but it is most illuminating, when we change the rather vague word "deny" into the Huna word. The low or animal self "will" or authority is what must be "denied" daily. It must be controlled.

(2) From the roots *le* and *mana* we get "to cause mana to fly upward." This is the inner meaning, and symbolizes the fact that the goal of training the low self is to get it under control, to make it join in living the good life, and to teach it to "make the mana fly upward" along the aka cord to the High Self when commanded to do so.

Now let us return to that scene on the way to Calvary. We have noted there the unexplained act of another man bearing the cross for Jesus part of the way. It undoubtedly happened, but the initiates who wrote the record knew the symbology in the act, and were careful to preserve it for that reason. We can certainly see it, knowing the meaning of the bearing of the cross, as a dramatization of the person who helps to remove fixations as in the foot-washing rite. Other significant symbols crowd the mind: Jesus wore a crown of thorns. We have already told that thorns are the symbol of fixations. He was accompanied by two thieves, who also were to be crucified.

The word for "thief" is *ai-hue*. The root *ai* means "food," and the root *hue*, "to steal." These two combined root meanings show that the thieves represented the "eating companions." The root *hue* also means "a calabash," and so refers us back to the "cup" symbol. Another meaning is "to flow out, as water," which is the symbol of the spilling or loss of mana caused by the evil spirits which live invisibly with men, feed on their life force, and drive them to evil deeds.

Arriving at Calvary, Jesus was nailed to the cross. It was raised upright so that he might hang there in agony until death set him free. In the sacred language "to hang on a cross" is *li-peka*. From the word *li* we get these inner meanings: "To hate, to abhor, to be filled with wrath, to be jealous. To be proud, haughty. To disregard the rights of others." These meanings describe the unregenerate low self and the attitudes toward others which are the very sum and substance of the fixations and obsessions which cause symbolic crucifixion with all the suffering it entails.

Jesus was crucified between the two thieves. In the account we are told that one of the thieves repented his evil ways and Jesus promised him help toward salvation. The other remained evil and unrepentant and nothing could be done for him. From this we see illustrated the Huna belief that those who die unrepentant and uncleansed and cut off by a blocked path, remain in the same state after death and haunt the living as "eating companions" when they find in the living those with like evil propensities. These will eventually progress and learn their lessons and will be able to receive help, but until they become ready, they must share the agonies of the cross which are brought on by their evil and by their blocked paths.

After his death, Jesus was taken from the cross and laid in a new tomb. The word for "tomb" is *i-lina*, in which the root *lina* gives the secret meaning, which is "to tighten or stretch, as a cord or rope," and here we have the indication that the death on the cross symbolizes the point in progress at which the suffering caused by evil comes to an end and the progress into the god life begins, with the aka cord being freed of knots and tangles, and opened. The word for "new," in the phrase, "a new tomb," is *hou*, which has for one of its meanings that of "to extend." This is the symbol for reaching out along the aka cord to make the contact with the High Self.

"Death," *make* in Huna, means a transition from one kind of life to another. It also means "to be made right, fitting and proper." This is the inner meaning of the death on the cross or the end of the period when the low self is out of control and is evil and savage enough to attract and harbor evil spirits. In death the evil spirits have no more mana to feed upon, so they leave. If the individual has reached the turning point into the good ways, the fixations can more easily be broken down, and progress begun in earnest.

The great stone which closed the tomb—the symbol of the stumbling block—was rolled away by unseen hands even while the women who had come to the tomb were saying, "Who shall roll us away the stone from the door of the sepulchre?" In this again we have evidence that the High Selves can remove even the most powerful of the obsessing entities, even the "Lord of Darkness."

Jesus had risen from the dead. The outer meaning of the resurrection is that he rose and appeared to his disciples to prove that one does survive death. In Huna "resurrection" is *ala hou ana,* which gives the secret meaning in its literal translation of "to open the path anew." The inner meaning of the resurrection, then, is its promise of ultimate victory over the symbolized evil and death on the cross and the restoration of normalcy and progress through the opened path and full contact with the High Self.

The fact that Jesus actually did return and talk with his disciples after the death of his body has been ignored and disbelieved in our world of materialistic thinking. No doubt the theology that, as an aspect of Ultimate God, anything was possible for Jesus—and only Jesus— to perform sufficed in the Christian churches. But when one inspects the work of the kahunas with spirits, casting out the evil ones, and securing the help of the good spirits, one becomes more and more aware of the progression of life beyond the short span of which one is conscious in the body. The common people among the Polynesians sense the presence of spirits, and to them it is an accepted and ordinary part of life. They have no fear of the so-called supernatural—it is natural in their experience—and they treat these visitations casually. "My grandmother just passed the banyan tree over there—have some more *poi,* will you?"

In the Western world, Spiritualists and researchers into psychic science have proved quite conclusively the continuance of life after death, even after a large amount of fakery has been drained from their experiments. It is a compelling and vital climax to the life and teaching of Jesus that he should return for a brief period before going on in the greater life of the spirit.

In Jesus we see a man who had learned the lessons of life and who had attained perfect union with his own High Self Father. We see in him one ready, upon death, to progress a step higher in the scale of life and being. If we accept the ancient Huna beliefs on this point as on many others, we may believe that after his "ascension" Jesus passed through the graduation or transitional stage, and the middle self Jesus rose a grade to become a High Self. His low self, at last taught the ways of man and the necessity of ceasing to react as an animal, rose to become a middle self, undoubtedly experiencing rebirth into a new physical body with a new low self for a companion.

The "Father" so loved by Jesus, and who was one with the Great and Shining Company of *Aumakuas*, would, according to Huna, also rise a grade and become one with the *Akua-Aumakuas*, who stand one grade higher in that great outpouring of life that comes from the Vastness of the Ultimate, and which moves slowly upward, we can only suppose, to the Source from which all come.

One of the last things that Jesus said, when he returned in spirit to his disciples was, "Lo, I am with you alway, even unto the end of the world." This promise, and the love, and the warm and selfless personality of

Jesus, has endeared him to men and women down the ages. By revealing the Huna meanings in his life and teachings, and by setting forth the common-sense belief (as attested by everything the Huna initiates wrote about him) that he was one of the greatest human beings who ever lived, I would not wish for a moment to destroy that loving sense of companionship with him.

For me, brought up in a fundamentalist type of orthodox church against whose doctrines I early rebelled, this study has returned Jesus all the more as a man to be loved, to be revered, and above all, to be *followed*.

"Lo, I am with you alway, even unto the end of the world." He is still with us, as close as our own High Selves because he is one with them in the Great Company. We may still pray in his name, for that is at the same time in the name of our own High Self Father. And, as the ruling passion of Jesus, while living on earth, was to serve and teach and help and guide the lost sheep of the world, we may be very sure that any slightest aid or comfort or guidance we offer to "the least of these" in his name, will draw us closer to him and the Shining Company with whom he now labors and continues his ministry on a different and wider level.

We are living in one of the periodic times of world upheaval, which means drastic change and progress. To many of us, it appears that the world is being crucified. But there is no reason to fear and despair, for there are signs, too, of a new and golden age ahead. The time that was prophesied so long ago appears to be at hand, the time that man can begin to understand himself, and so, individually to work out his salvation.

No matter where we stand in our evolutionary progress, there can be joy and health and success for each according to his needs and capacities in Service. The promise of salvation still stands, just as certain, just as bright and just as clear, as it stood twenty—yes, even twenty-five centuries ago—when Isaiah spoke in the veiled words of the ancient secret, crying out in the exultation of his vision:

"Then the eyes of the blind shall be opened, and the ears of the deaf shall be unstopped.

"Then shall the lame man leap as an hart, and the tongues of the dumb sing: for in the wilderness shall waters break out, and the stream flow in the desert.

"The parched ground shall become a pool, and the thirsty land springs of water; in the habitation of dragons, where each lay, shall be grass with reeds and rushes.

"And an highway shall be there, and a way, and it shall be called the way of holiness; the unclean shall not pass over it; but it shall be for those: the wayfaring men, though fools, shall not err therein.

"No lion shall be there, nor any ravenous beast shall go thereon, it shall not be found there; but the redeemed shall walk there.

"And the ransomed of the Lord shall return, and come to Zion with songs and everlasting joy upon their heads: they shall obtain joy and gladness, and sorrow and sighing shall flee away."

CHAPTER XXV

CONCLUSION

The prospect ahead is very bright, now that we have in sight the completion of the long investigation of Huna. The HRA, by the splendid work of its members over a period of nearly five years, has proved that those who have their paths sufficiently open to contact their High Selves, can put Huna to use after a short period of training, and after revising some of their old ideas on religion and psychology.

The earnest persons who read this report and who find, after a proper effort, that they cannot make Huna work, and who decide that this may be because they have unknown blockings in their paths, will need help of the foot-washing kind. Fortunately such help is easy to give, and there are a great many who should be able to assist.

I am thinking particularly of the good men and women who belong to the many progressive religious organizations in the world today. I do not know how many dedicated healers there are in New Thought circles or in other circles in which mental-spiritual healing has been taught, but the number must be very large. These people are professional healers for the most part, and it has been my experience that they often welcome the information furnished by Huna and put it to use despite the fact that it is not officially recognized in the groups to which they belong.

If I were convinced that my path was blocked, and that I needed help in getting my High Self supplied with mana so it could begin working from the top downward to clear the path for me, I would look up one of the newer and more open and liberal churches and inquire what one of its healers was familiar with Huna and was ready to assist in opening my path. If none knew of Huna, I would introduce the subject and see that the proper people became acquainted with the literature on Huna. That done, I would continue to urge that one of the members take me in hand.

Most of the old and established religious organizations, of course, will be content to go on with the old dogmatic views and beliefs which have replaced the doctrines of love and service. They will go on preaching hate programs in their pulpits, and attacking blindly all churches and dogmas which they feel to be in competition with their own. The rediscovery of the inner teachings of Jesus will mean nothing to the older men in authority in most Christian churches. They will be so frozen in their dogmas, and so fearful of the frozen state of belief of their older parishioners, that they will refuse to give even slight consideration to anything which attacks their dogmas.

On the other hand, many eager and serious young men make the decision to become ministers. They go to special schools for their training, and their minds remain comparatively open for a time. It is barely possible that these men may be approachable and may be more inclined to understand Huna and even to use it if such use is not prohibited entirely by those over them.

Groups outside regular organizations may also be

formed. A small group is always best because there can be work between friends. Two people who understand each other, trust each other and are motivated by love, form a "church" all by themselves. "Where two or three are gathered in my name . . ." embodies this idea. Confession is a helpful thing, but it should be done in the greatest privacy, not as it has recently been done in some of the great religious movements where public confession degenerates into a contest between enthusiasts to see who can confess the most wicked deeds.

The vow of inviolate secrecy which gripped Huna for so many thousands of years has become unnecessary, now that the darkness of mass ignorance and savagery has lightened and literacy and enlightenment is to be found the world around. However, there is one vow of inviolate secrecy which we cannot yet do without. This is the vow that every man and woman of good will must take and keep, if agreeing to act as one to receive the confessions of another. In addition to the vow of utter and enduring secrecy as to the confession, there must be the greatest effort to remain entirely impersonal and to refrain from passing the slightest mental or inward judgment. "Judge not that ye be not judged" is the teaching here. One becomes, in accepting the obligation of hearing a confesssion, a substitute for the High Self. One prays to the High Self of the one who is about to bare his heart, and one sends a goodly supply of mana with the prayer which is made, asking that the misdeeds which are confessed be shaken free at any point in which they form fixations or have attracted "eating companions."

The sending of the mana must never be forgotten,

nor must one ever allow himself to forget that this is a sacred obligation and not a "superstition of savages" as one dogmatic minister once called it in a letter to me. May I say again that faith, which Jesus showed to be something absolutely essential, is not simply an act of perfect belief. It is, primarily, an act of reaching out to contact the High Self, and then sending the mana and the thought-forms of the prayer so that they may be made REAL—made into something veritable on the High Self level first, and later on the earth level as the answer to the prayer. (See the presentation of the word for "faith," *mana-o-io*, in Chapter 8.)

Groups are also valuable in the training process. Telepathic practice and the box and pendulum work can often be carried on to advantage in groups, especially to help the less experienced understand what to do and how to go about it. The low self learns from other low selves in a surprising way, and one who cannot use the pendulum may suddenly find himself doing it after watching another demonstrate the use of this simple instrument.

A word of warning, however, needs to be said concerning the work in larger groups. There is usually a tendency to fall to arguing about things quite foreign to the purpose in hand. Often there is some person in the group who has a love of talking and who will insist on holding the floor. Then there are always those who wish only to be entertained, and who will not or cannot take part in the serious work of learning to understand and to use Huna. No group should allow new members to come into it after a course has been set and training begun. Let others form their own groups or wait until a new training session is begun—a session in which all will begin work on equal footing. I once formed a group and left it open to new members and visitors. At each meeting my friends happily brought with them people who had never heard of Huna, and at each meeting I had to begin from the beginning and tell the new arrivals what Huna was and what we planned to do. Needless to say, we accomplished nothing to speak of, because the older members soon were bored and stayed away.

Now that we have completed the full circle of investigation and have come back from the wisdom of the grass huts of Polynesia to that of Jesus who trudged homeless with his disciples through Palestine, healing and instructing his chosen group, I believe that the knowledge of these ancient basic truths and symbols will gradually filter into organized Christianity from the bottom, if not from the top. It will spread more rapidly amongst the thousands who have become unwilling to accept the dogmas and sterility of the orthodox Churches, and so have turned to other sources of light and inspiration. The sheer workability of Huna, as attested by thousands of letters which I have received in the past several years, will guarantee that spread. It will not be too long before those who set out to use Huna in their own lives and to help others, will find companionship and mutual interest and understanding in an increasing number of those around them.

I can envision a time, not too many years ahead, when men will have learned that the hurtless and kindly life is always best, and that those who are truly blessed are the ones who have learned to love others as well as to be kind and hurtless. There will appear among us men and women who will begin to bear the mark of the New Age in their minds and hearts. They will be known by a certain characteristic which will at first seem very strange, very new, and very incredible: they will be UTTERLY TRUSTWORTHY to the limit of their human ability in every word and thought and deed. They will be the men and women who have caught the gleam and who are moving quietly and strongly ahead toward graduation at the end of this life into the level of being occupied by the *Aumakuas*, the "Utterly Trustworthy Parental Spirits."

As these words are being written, late in the year 1952, the long period of research and investigation seems to be coming to a close. There remains a little more testing to be finished, and then the HRA will have completed the work for which it was organized, and can disband.

My work with the HRAs has been one of the bright spots in my life, and I wish in closing to thank again my many clear-seeing, selfless and loyal friends of the organization, most of whom I know only through their letters and the telepathic contact of the prayer hours. Without their help, the restoration of Huna could not have reached this point.

INDEX

Aaron, 5
Adam, 205
After life, The, 112
Aka aura, 179, 180
Aka body, 10, 15, 17, 19, 34, 35, 38,
    46, 50, 51, 56, 57, 58, 59, 62,
    65, 69, 70, 72, 75, 79, 82, 84,
    120, 180, 185, 226
Aka cord, 10, 11, 16, 35, 36, 37, 39,
    40, 61, 62, 65, 68, 70, 71, 84,
    87, 89, 91, 93, 95, 97, 98, 99,
    113, 114, 115, 117, 120, 121,
    122, 125, 127, 135, 137, 138,
    151, 163, 170, 180, 186, 187,
    189, 190, 191, 193, 198, 199,
    202, 205, 206, 209, 235, 236,
    241, 252, 259, 263, 265, 267,
    280, 282, 284, 285, 287, 288,
    289, 298, 299, 309, 310, 311,
    312, 313, 321, 322, 323, 325
Aka finger, 34, 35, 36, 37, 38, 39, 40,
    43, 46, 48, 61, 68, 75, 90, 146,
    187
Aka mana, 79, 80, 146, 147, 187
Aka molds, 85, 143
Aka projection, 41, 79
Aka substance, 16, 17, 35, 38, 54, 62,
    75, 85, 90, 102, 122, 146, 180,
    187
Aka thread, 33, 34, 36, 37, 38, 39,
    61, 62, 63, 64, 67, 68, 69, 70,
    71, 91, 151, 152, 153, 154, 155,
    158, 161, 169, 177, 179, 180,
    187, 191, 192, 201, 202, 205,
    206, 210
Altar, 282
Ancient Secret, 93
Animals, 18, 19, 38
Animal magnetism, 139, 141

Animal self, 19
Amends for hurts, 92, 114, 117, 120,
    127, 128, 208, 257, 281, 286,
    290
Astral body, 77
Astral projection, 34
Astral shell, 49
Astral travel, 38
Atlas Mountains, 3, 5
Aura, human, 56, 58
Aura of signatures, 181
Aura of water, 55, 56
Aurameter, 51, 52, 53, 54, 55, 56,
    57, 58, 59, 71, 170, 180, 190,
    191

Babylonians, 187
Babylonian bowl, 187, 188, 189
Baptism, 268, 270, 277, 278, 279,
    280, 283, 284, 285, 286, 288,
    300
Behaviorism, 14
Berbers, 3, 4
Bible, The, 36, 87, 88, 93, 94, 112,
    116, 119, 137, 196, 205, 214,
    215, 221, 229, 242, 255, 275,
    287, 302, 309
Biometer, 172, 173, 174, 175, 177,
    178, 179, 180, 181, 186, 190,
    191, 192
Black magic, 49
Books, reference to:
    Borderland Science Research Asso-
        ciates, 51
    Co-operative Healing, 184, 206
    Dianetics, 216
    E-Therapy, 218
    Freud: Dictionary of Psychoanaly-
        sis, 209

Books, reference to: (*Continued*)
Perceptive Healing, 224
Projection of the Astral Body, 38
Psychoanalyse Yourself, 260
Recovering the Ancient Magic, ix
Scientology, 223
The Secret Science Behind Miracles, ix, xi, 14, 55, 76, 92, 124, 147, 148, 167, 189, 255
Thirty Years Among the Dead, 229
Thoughts Through Space, 39
Words: The New Dictionary, 209
Bovis, M., 171, 172, 173, 174
Box experiments, 39, 40, 41, 42
Breathing, 77, 79
Brigham, Dr. 6, 7
Brunler, Dr. O., 77, 78, 169, 170, 174, 176, 179, 186

Calvary, 319, 323
Cameron, V. L., 51, 52, 54, 55, 56, 57, 58, 59, 179, 180, 190
Catholic Rites, 237, 319
Catholic Mass, 276, 311
Christianity, 88, 90, 112, 138, 139, 197, 256, 270, 276, 300, 301, 326, 331, 334
Clairvoyance, 43
Colors, 156, 159, 160, 161, 174
Communion, The, 293, 302, 308, 309, 310, 311, 312, 313
Complexes, 8, 10, 18, 20, 92, 99, 120, 138, 141, 179, 188, 195, 207, 209, 210, 211, 212, 213, 214, 215, 216, 218, 220, 230, 235, 238, 263, 294, 296, 297
Confession, 281, 282, 286, 332
Connell, Dr., 223, 225
Conscious mind, 8, 12, 43, 130, 133, 248, 261
Consciousness, 14, 18, 19, 51, 68, 85, 86, 160, 174, 177, 185, 189, 242, 260, 273, 297, 315, 316
Cook, Capt., 1, 278
Coué, 146
Creation, The, 231, 232
Creative ability, 37
Cross, The, 206, 319, 320, 321, 322, 323, 324, 325, 326

Crucifixion, The, 268, 270, 271, 314, 315, 319, 322, 324, 328
Cummins, Geraldine, 223, 224
Cup, The, 97, 98, 99, 312, 313, 324
Cup of bitterness, 317
Cup of Man, The, 259

D'Angelo, 47
Death, 17, 19, 34, 69, 177, 185, 237, 238, 326, 327
Death from mana loss, 83
Dianetics, 216, 217, 218, 220
Disease, 183
Dowsers, 26, 44, 45, 51, 54, 55, 70, 170
Dreams, 103, 211, 212, 222

Ectoplasm, 33, 46
Eeman, L. E., 182, 183, 184, 185, 186, 215, 216
Egypt, 3, 5, 94, 98, 277, 317
Embryo, effect on, 226
Emotions, 15, 16, 19, 20, 31, 158, 202, 203, 204, 213, 220, 227, 228, 240, 241, 245, 248, 249, 287, 296
Engrams, 216, 218
Etheric body, 185
Etheric double, 10
Evolution, 85, 175
Examination chart, 243
Extra Sensory Perception, 43, 44, 45
Eye disease healed, 149

Faith, 106, 107, 108, 163, 333
Farrow, E. P., 260
Fasting, 138
Fenton, F., 94, 287, 306
Fersen, Baron, 76, 78, 79
Fire-walking, 6
Foot-washing rite, 295, 296, 297, 298, 299, 300, 323, 330
Free will, 199
Freud, 14, 209, 210, 211, 212, 213, 214, 221, 222, 228
Future, The, 31, 44, 89, 100, 102, 107, 108, 109, 110, 111, 128, 135, 154, 163

Garden of Eden, 1, 5, 99, 205, 232, 233, 234, 235, 236

George, 20, 21, 22, 23, 24, 25, 26, 27, 29, 30, 31, 32, 39, 40, 41, 42, 43, 63, 64, 65, 66, 67, 68, 69, 70, 73, 74, 75, 76, 77, 78, 80, 81, 103, 104, 105, 110, 121, 146, 156, 171

Ghost, 305

God, 37, 85, 86, 87, 88, 89, 92, 193, 197, 198, 199, 205, 214, 218, 251, 252, 253, 254, 271, 273, 276, 278, 303, 304, 306, 310, 311, 313, 326

God, Hebrew, 85, 86, 272

Guilt, 138, 141, 142, 144, 199, 201, 205, 207, 208, 213, 241, 253, 257, 263, 283

Hawaii, ix, xi, 1, 2, 5, 7, 12, 210, 258, 281, 291

Hawaiians, 3, 7, 10

Healers, magnetic, 139, 141

Healing, 12, 13, 85, 137, 138, 139, 140, 141, 142, 144, 145, 146, 147, 151, 157, 159, 160, 162, 165, 167, 168, 219, 220, 304

Healing pictures, 190, 191, 192

Health, 106

High Self, 10, 11, 12, 15, 16, 17, 18, 19, 36, 37, 40, 43, 44, 48, 70, 71, 72, 73, 83, 84, 85, 87, 88, 89, 90, 91, 92, 93, 94, 95, 96, 97, 98, 99, 100, 101, 104, 107, 108, 109, 111, 112, 113, 114, 115, 116, 117, 118, 119, 120, 121, 122, 123, 124, 125, 126, 128, 129, 130, 131, 132, 133, 134, 138, 142, 145, 147, 151, 152, 154, 155, 157, 158, 159, 161, 162, 164, 166, 167, 179, 191, 194, 196, 198, 199, 200, 202, 205, 206, 207, 209, 210, 214, 221, 230, 232, 235, 236, 237, 240, 247, 248, 250, 251, 252, 253, 254, 263, 264, 265, 266, 267, 273, 277, 279, 280, 281, 282, 283, 285, 286, 287, 288, 289, 290, 292, 293, 296,

High Self (Continued) 297, 298, 299, 303, 304, 305, 306, 307, 309, 310, 311, 312, 313, 314, 315, 316, 317, 320, 321, 322, 323, 325, 326, 327, 328, 330, 331, 332, 333

Higher Beings, 73, 167, 221, 243

Holy Ghost, The, 138, 283, 304

Holy Spirit, 285, 288, 290, 304, 305

Hubbard, L. R., 216, 217, 218, 219, 223

Human survival, 69, 221, 227, 238, 326, 327

Huna, x, xi, xii, 4, 5, 13, 18, 33, 36, 43, 46, 49, 50, 51, 53, 58, 79, 82, 85, 87, 89, 90, 93, 94, 98, 106, 113, 114, 116, 117, 118, 120, 121, 144, 145, 148, 150, 152, 156, 165, 169, 177, 181, 182, 185, 186, 192, 193, 194, 195, 198, 199, 206, 209, 210, 219, 226, 231, 233, 234, 235, 236, 237, 242, 247, 255, 256, 259, 263, 267, 268, 274, 275, 276, 277, 278, 280, 281, 283, 285, 286, 287, 288, 289, 291, 292, 295, 296, 298, 299, 300, 301, 302, 303, 304, 306, 307, 309, 310, 311, 312, 314, 315, 321, 322, 323, 324, 325, 327, 328, 330, 331, 332, 333, 334, 335

Huna, Ancient Wisdom, xii

Huna symbols, 5, 11, 17, 98, 151, 152, 160, 231, 267, 278

Huna Research Associates, 4, 10, 12, 13, 14, 20, 24, 27, 30, 37, 39, 41, 42, 43, 45, 51, 55, 56, 67, 69, 70, 74, 75, 77, 80, 81, 82, 90, 101, 107, 108, 113, 115, 118, 121, 122, 125, 133, 142, 144, 146, 147, 148, 150, 153, 156, 157, 160, 165, 169, 170, 173, 182, 187, 189, 190, 191, 192, 193, 194, 209, 217, 219, 220, 242, 243, 249, 250, 253, 254, 255, 259, 260, 261, 262, 263, 292, 305, 330, 335

Hypnotism, 17, 195, 211, 227

Ikon, 189, 190
Ills, emotional, 144
India, 1, 49, 76, 98, 112, 196, 262
Initiates, 5, 87, 106, 269, 275, 280,
    285, 300, 302, 311, 323, 328
Insanity, 72, 82, 215, 228, 238
Inspiration, 126
Isaiah, 5, 89, 140, 233, 274, 302, 329

Japan, 152, 190
Jehovah, 87, 88, 280
Jeremiah, 272, 273, 311
Jesus, xiii, 2, 5, 37, 72, 88, 89, 90,
    91, 92, 93, 94, 95, 100, 116,
    118, 138, 176, 189, 230, 231,
    251, 255, 257, 258, 265, 266,
    267, 268, 269, 270, 271, 272,
    273, 274, 275, 276, 277, 278,
    279, 280, 283, 285, 286, 287,
    288, 289, 290, 291, 292, 293,
    294, 295, 296, 297, 298, 299,
    300–328, 331, 333, 334
John, 292, 293, 301, 302, 306, 312
John the Baptist, 113, 279, 281, 283,
    284, 285, 290
Joshua, 137
Judas, 292, 293, 294, 316
Jung, 18, 19, 212, 214, 223

Kahunas, ix, x, xiii, 1, 2, 3, 5, 6, 7,
    8, 10, 11, 12, 13, 14, 17, 18, 36,
    44, 46, 49, 58, 73, 74, 76, 79,
    84, 86, 89, 94, 98, 99, 100, 112,
    113, 116, 119, 121, 122, 123,
    125, 131, 132, 135, 140, 141,
    142, 145, 147, 151, 165, 185,
    192, 194, 195, 201, 205, 207,
    210, 221, 226, 229, 230, 231,
    232, 235, 237, 248, 257, 258,
    266, 269, 270, 273, 277, 280,
    281, 288, 291, 295, 296, 299,
    304, 305, 311, 316, 321, 326
Karma, 112, 196, 200
Kilner, Dr., 56
Kingdom of Heaven, The, 5, 284,
    287
Kitselman, A. L., 218
Knowledge, intuitional, 92
Kubie, Dr. L. S., 239, 240

Language:
    Berber, 4
    Hawaiian, 88, 90, 116, 117, 119,
        286
    Maori, 286
    Polynesian, 8, 233, 284, 286
Last Supper, The, 268, 275, 292, 294,
    303, 308, 312, 316
Laying on of Hands, 13, 137–145
Legends, Hawaiian, 86
Levites, 137
Light, 93, 163, 231, 232, 283, 284
Light, The True, xiii, 277, 278
Lord's Prayer, The, 118, 119, 120,
    247
Lost Sheep parable, 266
Lotus, The, 98, 99
Low Self, 10, 11, 12, 14–32, 46,
    48, 50, 53, 54, 57, 59, 60, 61,
    62, 63, 66, 67, 68, 70, 71, 72,
    73, 74, 75, 79, 82, 83, 84, 85,
    89, 90, 91, 93, 95, 96, 97, 98,
    99, 100, 102, 103, 104, 105,
    106, 108, 110, 113, 114, 115,
    118, 119, 120, 121, 122, 123,
    124, 125, 126, 127, 128, 130,
    131, 132, 133, 137, 138, 140,
    141, 142, 143, 145, 146, 147,
    150, 151, 152, 153, 158, 159,
    162, 165, 170, 171, 172, 173,
    177, 178, 179, 180, 186, 187,
    189, 192, 194, 195, 198, 199,
    200, 201, 202, 204, 205, 206,
    207, 210, 211, 213, 226, 230,
    241, 242, 246, 247, 248, 249,
    250, 251, 253, 254, 255, 256,
    257, 258, 259, 261, 263, 282,
    284, 285, 287, 290, 292, 294,
    295, 297, 298, 299, 305, 313,
    315, 316, 317, 318, 321, 322,
    323, 324, 325, 327, 333
Low Self control, 15
Low Self, definition of, 15, 16

Mana, 10, 11, 12, 16, 17, 54, 61, 62,
    70, 71, 72, 73, 74, 75, 76, 77,
    78, 79, 80, 82, 83, 85, 89, 90,
    91, 93, 94, 97, 98, 99, 105, 107,
    113, 115, 116, 117, 119, 120,

Mana (*Continued*)
121, 122, 123, 124, 127, 128,
129, 130, 131, 132, 133, 134,
136, 137, 139, 140, 141, 142,
143, 144, 145, 146, 147, 148,
151, 152, 154, 155, 157, 158,
159, 163, 164, 165, 180, 182,
183, 184, 185, 186, 187, 189,
193, 194, 195, 203, 204, 205,
207, 210, 219, 228, 229, 230,
233, 234, 235, 236, 237, 242,
246, 252, 263, 277, 280, 283,
284, 286, 288, 289, 290, 296,
297, 298, 299, 306, 307, 309,
310, 311, 312, 313, 316, 322,
324, 325, 331, 332, 333
Mana, accumulation of, 77, 78
Mana, a living force, 62
Mana, origin of, 74
Mana, surcharge of, 78, 79, 82, 83
Matthew, 94, 116, 281, 283, 301,
302, 305
Mayans, 278
Measuring stick, 171, 172, 173, 174
Memories, 17, 18, 19, 21, 22, 23, 24,
31, 35, 50, 58, 59, 60, 62, 63,
64, 65, 66, 67, 69, 200, 201,
202, 203, 204, 205, 206, 207,
210, 211, 224, 226, 227, 245,
254, 257, 260, 261, 262, 297,
322
Memorising, 132, 146
Mental creation, 49
Mental pictures, 35, 67, 76, 100, 101,
102, 103, 125, 134, 143, 144,
157, 163
Mesmerism, 17, 75, 80, 139, 230
Middle Self, 10, 11, 12, 14, 15, 16,
17, 18, 19, 20, 21, 25, 28, 29,
33, 35, 36, 39, 40, 42, 44, 48,
54, 57, 59, 62, 63, 64, 65, 66,
68, 72, 73, 74, 78, 82, 83, 84,
85, 87, 89, 95, 96, 97, 99, 104,
106, 108, 110, 115, 122, 123,
127, 128, 133, 140, 145, 146,
152, 170, 171, 201, 202, 204,
205, 207, 210, 213, 226, 246,
248, 250, 254, 256, 259, 263,
290, 295, 305, 315, 316, 327

Miracles, 2, 5, 7, 8
Missionaries, 1, 210
Moses, 5, 137, 306, 310, 315

Near East, 1, 4
New Age, The, 335
New Testament, 5, 88, 93, 94, 198,
205, 230, 231, 255, 266, 268,
278
New Thought, 330
Nicodemus, 286, 287

Obsession, 227, 228, 229, 230, 238,
243, 282, 288, 290, 326

Pauline dogmas, 270, 271, 272, 273,
274, 275, 276, 301, 305, 311,
312
Pendulum, The, 25, 26, 27, 28, 29,
30, 31, 42, 44, 53, 69, 70, 75,
80, 81, 104, 105, 170, 171, 172,
178, 190, 191, 192, 250, 251,
292, 333
Peter, 270, 291, 292, 293, 294, 295,
296, 297, 298
Pilate, 317, 318, 319
Polynesians, ix, 1, 2, 5, 94, 112, 152,
229, 300, 307, 320, 326, 334
Prayer, 12, 13, 16, 33, 36, 37, 38,
40, 48, 71, 74, 84, 85, 87, 91,
92, 97, 98, 99, 103, 104, 106,
107, 108, 109, 110, 111, 112,
113, 115, 116, 117, 118, 120,
121, 123, 124, 127, 128, 129,
130, 131, 132, 133, 134, 135,
137, 138, 139, 142, 152, 153,
196, 197, 198, 199, 200, 204,
206, 207, 215, 220, 243, 247,
248, 250, 252, 253, 254, 259,
299, 316, 318, 332
Prayer, Huna, xii, 7, 32, 100, 101,
112, 116, 134, 150, 151, 152,
163, 165, 187, 192, 194, 248,
250
Probert, Mark, 57
Prodigal Son, The, 122, 123
Projection, 47, 48
Psychical Research Societies, 223
Psychic science, 6, 50, 182, 327

341

Psychoanalysis, 18, 19, 103, 214, 215, 219, 222, 226, 239, 242, 260
Psychometry, 68, 69, 153
Psychology, 6, 8, 14, 18, 182, 205, 210, 214, 221, 227, 296, 330
Psychology, Huna, 4, 8

Radiations, 33, 44, 45, 46, 166, 167, 170, 172, 174, 177, 184, 186, 188, 189, 190, 191
Reasoning Self, 16
Recording Self, 16
Reincarnation, 112, 177, 223, 224, 227
Relaxation circuit, 183
Religions, xii, 6, 182, 196, 197, 198, 214, 215, 218, 256, 312, 328, 330, 331
Religion, Jewish, 267, 270, 271, 274, 277, 278
Rhine, Dr., 43, 46

Sacred language, 3, 4, 87, 94, 106, 140, 267, 280, 302, 323
Sacroiliac case, 145, 146
Salvation, 278, 279, 300, 329
Satan, 231, 233
Second Coming, The, 278
Seed, 99, 100, 101, 118, 121, 126, 132, 134, 136, 207
Secrecy cult, 266
Secret code, 5
Secret knowledge, 2, 277, 278
Secret lore, 11, 98, 101, 267, 269
Shadowy bodies, 10, 16, 17, 33, 185, 226
Sherman, Harold, 39
Shock treatment, 229
Signatures, 169, 170, 175, 176, 177, 178, 179, 180, 181
Sin, 8, 91, 92, 114, 120, 138, 196, 197, 200, 205, 206, 230, 232, 234, 235, 241, 267, 274, 278, 280, 281, 285, 289, 290, 320
Solar plexus, 34, 70, 122
Spirits, 31, 36, 50, 57, 58, 75, 79, 84, 86, 112, 189, 190, 195, 215, 220, 221, 226, 227, 228, 229,

Spirits (Continued)
230, 231, 233, 234, 235, 236, 238, 242, 247, 267, 279, 288, 289, 290, 291, 305, 315, 324, 325, 326
Spirit revenge, 195
Stewart, W. R., 3, 4
Subconscious self, 8, 9, 12, 13, 14, 18, 43, 210, 213, 214, 218, 260, 273
Suggestion, 141, 143, 184, 186, 187, 195, 211, 299
Superconscious self, 8, 9, 12, 13, 212, 216, 218

Tarot cards, 98
Telekinesis, 46
Telepathy, 35, 36, 37, 38, 39, 40, 43, 48, 60, 61, 62, 63, 64, 65, 66, 67, 68, 70, 90, 97, 100, 102, 104, 105, 118, 127, 132, 150, 151, 154, 156, 157, 158, 159, 161, 165, 166, 167, 169, 184, 220, 291, 292, 333, 335
Telepathic Mutual Healing Group, 150, 152, 153, 154, 155, 161, 162, 164, 165, 169, 191, 194
Temptation, The, 288, 289, 290, 318
Theosophy, 49, 102
Thought forms, 17, 35, 36, 48, 49, 50, 51, 58, 59, 60, 61, 62, 64, 65, 66, 71, 83, 91, 97, 99, 100, 103, 105, 116, 117, 118, 119, 121, 127, 132, 133, 134, 151, 152, 154, 155, 200, 201, 202, 206, 207, 210, 235, 236, 241, 284, 322
Thought photography, 51
Ti leaves, 6, 142
Tibet, 49, 237, 238
Totem pole, 72, 73
Toynbee, 1, 2

Unconscious, The, 14, 209

Vital force, 8, 9, 10, 11, 16, 17, 61, 70, 74, 75, 82, 89, 141, 182, 186, 203

342

Vital force, accumulation of, 76, 77, 82

Vital force, creation of, 10, 11, 16

Waite, 98

Water, 11, 44, 99, 165, 171, 277, 284, 287, 289, 296, 298, 306, 311, 312, 313, 324

Wickland, Dr. C., 229

Wilkins, Sir H., 39

Will, The, 73

Willow Twig, 51, 53, 170

Word of God, The, 86

Zen Buddhism, 92, 158

Zischang, John, 47

Polynesian words

aha, a cord, 158, 313

ai-hue, thief, 324

aka, shadowy body, 10

akaka, to bring to light, 282

akua-aumakuas, higher grade of au-makuas, 327

ala hou ana, resurrection, 326

amana, crucifixion cross, 322

aumakua, High Self, 210, 303, 305, 327, 335

hai, to sacrifice, 282

hai akaka, to confess, 282

haku, lord, 280

hala, to miss the path, 205

hewa, to make a mistake, 205

hihiu, wilderness, 289

hoo-le-mana, deny, 323

hoomana, worship, 289, 310

hou, new, 325

i-lina, tomb, 325

ino, to hurt others, 205

kana-wai, commandment, 312

kea, cross, 320, 321

ki-aha, cup, 312

kihapai, garden, 235

koko, blood, 313

kuma, covenant, 311

lomi-lomi, manipulation, 13

li-peka, to hang on a cross, 324

make, death, 325

malo, towel, 296

maloo, season, 289

ohia, a tropical tree, 234

pa, basin, 297, 298

pahi, sword, 236,

pai, cup of bitterness, 317

pea, cross, 321

pe, to break, 321

ti, a plant with long, slender leaves, 6, 142

uhane, the spirit that talks (middle self), 10, 210

ulu, breadfruit, 234

unihipili, low self, 9, 15, 210, 321

wahine, woman, 3

wai, water, 11

walewale, tempt, 233

whanau, to evolve, 286

wawae, feet, 297

343

For information about the author, write to:

The Max Freedom Long Library
Dolly Ware, F.H.F. Curator
1501 Thomas Place
Fort Worth, Texas 76107